DRYDEN
THE PUBLIC WRITER

DRYDEN

THE PUBLIC WRITER
1660–1685

GEORGE McFADDEN

PRINCETON UNIVERSITY PRESS
PRINCETON, NEW JERSEY

Library of Congress Cataloging in Publication Data
will be found on the last printed page of this book

Publication of this book has been aided by a
grant from The Andrew W. Mellon Foundation

Printed in the United States of America
by Princeton University Press, Princeton, New Jersey

CONTENTS

PREFACE

THE purpose of this investigation is to open up the process of Dryden's writing and to show how it involved an exchange between his experience and his art. The outcome is presented as a supplement to Charles E. Ward's indispensable biography, in the hope that it will lead to a more sympathetic understanding of the achievement of a great poet. Dryden was also a great critic, and perhaps our first public critic. He was the first poet to become, as a poet, a notorious public figure. My thesis is that he worked with the poet's gifts of language and fictive power to put the life of his time before the imagination of his contemporaries; that with the critic's sense of what is and what ought to be he enabled them to judge their life. It is natural that my emphasis should be placed on Dryden's work for the theatre. I have concentrated, however, on hitherto neglected approaches to his writing by following leads to be found in the dedications. These link Dryden closely to the political life of Charles II's reign and enable one to see the plays in a new light: their creative relation to the great political satires.

I happily acknowledge the value to me of the California Edition of Dryden's works. The editors' breadth of knowledge of the Restoration period, as well as their feeling for the problems and concerns of present day criticism, have enriched and clarified the writing of Dryden for us all. In particular, I am obligated to Samuel Holt Monk and H. T. Swedenberg, Jr. for helping to make earlier stages of my research possible. Alan Roper's criticism was very valuable at a later point. I owe the greatest debt to Earl Miner, who was able to see before I did the kind of contribution my work might make. If the book lacks much that distinguishes what these scholars have written, it marks their generosity and willingness to look at Dryden from yet one more point of view. I have also benefited from a Folger Library Fellowship and from several grants by the Temple University Faculty Research Committee; I am particularly grateful to my colleagues William Rossky, C. William Miller, Peter Tasch, Jacob Gruber, and Dean George W. Johnson, for help at various times. At Princeton University Press, Joanna Hitchcock has guided my work throughout with the gifts of editor, coach, and helmswoman. Virginia Morgan's intelligent care bolstered an author's sense of the importance of his text. They are worthy of their Press; I hope the same may be said of my book.

GEORGE McFADDEN

Southold, New York
March 8, 1977

BOOKS AND PERIODICALS
FREQUENTLY CITED

Bryant: Arthur Bryant, *King Charles II*, 1931

Carte: Thomas Carte, *History of the Life of James, Duke of Ormonde*, 1736

Clarke: *The Life of James the Second*, ed. J. S. Clarke, 1816

Foxcroft: H. C. Foxcroft, *The Life and Letters of . . . Halifax*, 1898

Foxcroft, *Trimmer*: H. C. Foxcroft, *A Character of the Trimmer*, 1946

Haley: K.H.D. Haley, *The First Earl of Shaftesbury*, Oxford, 1968

HLQ: *Huntington Library Quarterly*

LS: *The London Stage, 1660–1880, Part I: 1600–1700*, ed. William Van Lennep, Emmett L. Avery, and Arthur H. Scouten, Carbondale, Ill., 1965

Macdonald: Hugh Macdonald, *John Dryden: A Bibliography of Early Editions and of Drydeniana*, Oxford, 1939

Oliver: H. J. Oliver, *Sir Robert Howard*, Durham, N.C., 1963

POAS: *Poems on Affairs of State*, New Haven, 1963–

Scott: *The Works of Dryden*, ed. Sir Walter Scott, 1808

Spingarn: *Critical Essays of the Seventeenth Century*, ed. J. E. Spingarn, Oxford, 1908

S-S: *The Works of John Dryden*, ed. Sir Walter Scott and George Saintsbury, Edinburgh, 1882–1893

Ward: Charles E. Ward, *The Life of John Dryden*, Chapel Hill, N.C., 1961

Ward, *Letters*: *The Letters of John Dryden*, ed. Charles E. Ward, Durham, N.C., 1942

Watson: *John Dryden: Of Dramatic Poesy and Other Critical Essays*, ed. George Watson, 1962

Wilson: *The Rochester-Savile Letters*, ed. J. H. Wilson, Columbus, 1941

Works: *The Works of John Dryden*, ed. Edward N. Hooker, H. T. Swendenberg, Jr. et al., Berkeley, 1956–

DRYDEN
THE PUBLIC WRITER

INTRODUCTION

D RYDEN'S critical attitude toward success and failure
prevented him from being merely immersed in the life
of his time; a sense of pressing need to begin afresh, because
he was cut off from his inheritance, could be cited as his
central impulse. It would help to account for many things
in his career and work—from his attachment to James Stuart,
the threatened heir, to his strange manipulations of the
Jacob and Esau image. It is not my wish, though, to give a
psychological concentration to the present study, but rather
to inquire into the extraordinarily integrated range of writing
that, in Dryden's work, was the outcome of merely contin-
gent events and circumstances. I hope I can show that, amid
all the give-and-take, there was a continuity in the poet's
response based on his critical understanding of his art and
its demands, as well as a day-by-day matching of himself and
his gifts against the exigencies of an often chaotic reign.[1]
What I have seen emerging from this study is the picture of
a man with an intensely social outlook and a startling in-
timacy of public address, who wrote for the pleasure and the
enlightenment of a national audience. In prose especially he
was a very "open" writer practically from the start; the prefa-
tory letter before *Annus Mirabilis* is unusually candid in
telling the writer's secrets of style and designs upon his audi-
ence. A year and a half later, confessional passages in the
"Defence of an Essay" left him personally vulnerable to all
sorts of enemies for the rest of his life.

However much Dryden suffered because of his notorious-
ness, he continued to invite as well as endure it by his way
of presenting himself to the public in a well-defined char-

[1] Earl Miner has stressed Dryden's sense of the epoch in "Renais-
sance Contexts of Dryden's Criticism," *Michigan Quarterly Review*, 12
(1973), 97–115, 104.

acter. It may be outlined as follows. Essentially, he figured as "Dryden the poet." This is the phrase Samuel Pepys used in 1664, recording his first visit to Will's Coffee House.[2] At Will's Dryden appeared as the complete, professional poet. His ready familiarity with the classics, for example, was at the service of all comers.[3] Before 1672 he had acquired a following of young men,[4] wits or admirers of wit, to whom he acted as literary arbiter and verse-doctor. Meanwhile, he maintained a superiority in the three classic forms of epic, drama (both tragic and comic), and lyric, with the highest competence, and upheld his claim to the laureateship without a rival. This achievement gave him a certain status. It might have conveyed a fuller measure of security, if Dryden had not chosen to be so consistently self-critical. He spoke as the judge of his own success or failure, as if he could guide public opinion in this as in other literary matters. During the long period (1667–1681) when writing for the theatre was his only product, he many times acknowledged specific flaws in his plays, despite the pleasure they gave to the audience. In other words, he was the complete poet-critic, controlling his own success through his skill in his art and his knowledge of his audience. Buckingham skillfully attacked this self-characterization on the score of vanity and arrogance, not directly, but as a side-blow of his satire on Arlington. His Bayes was a great comic success. Yet in the long run Dryden was able to retaliate with his Zimri, and what is really much more important, he showed that he could critically reconsider the whole question of the heroic and learn from his enemy.

I have devoted much attention to the alliances and enmities in which Dryden was engaged, in part because of the importance of one's "professional complex," one's métier and source of livelihood. The fact that almost every one of

[2] *Diary,* 3 Feb. 1663/64.
[3] See Letter 7, "To an Unidentified Person," in Charles E. Ward, *Letters of John Dryden* (Durham, N.C., 1942), pp. 14–16.
[4] Dryden's "Cabal of wits" was the pretended source of *The Friendly Vindication* in 1673.

4

Dryden's poems, plays, and essays is an address, immediately related to its historical moment and to a patron or dedicatee, has appeared to detract from their integrity as individual works of art. However, from a collective point of view, their overall impact is thereby much stronger. From the Lord Hastings's death by smallpox in 1649 to the ringing in of the next century with *The Secular Masque*, the poet consistently addressed real people, tried to please and to influence actual audiences, chastised or cajoled active enemies, praised or consoled real friends. This means he was always in a rhetorical situation, struggling with the constraints that role implies for free poetic creation. When he died in 1700, there was a dialogue between Dryden and his age of many years' standing. He always tried (obviously he did not always succeed) to redefine imaginatively each addressee, each audience, even each target of satire, into the ideally appropriate recipient for what he, the poet, wanted to say; and he tried to recast the norms of each literary form he used so that the work might be an enduring poetic realization while still meeting the rhetorical needs of the moment. That these were usually moments in the history of the English nation need not destroy their immediacy for us, since in Dryden's work we find an imaginative reorientation of feeling in the face of the needs of his time, and the molding of poetic forms so as to generate new feelings.

In patterning the behavior of his characters, their motives and ideals, Dryden also worked out dramatic devices to reflect the struggle of political forces, during perhaps the most formative period of parliamentary politics. Thus he succeeded in interpreting to his age some of its deepest and still inchoate social and political attitudes. His originality lay in a secular vision, not without its nostalgia for the supernal, presented to his contemporaries opportunely enough and boldly enough to signify a new humanitarian ethos.[5] It of-

[5] This "secular" emphasis distinguishes him from his predecessors, but does not mean that Dryden lacked their sense of what Maynard Mack

fered a possible mode of feeling in an era when behavior was ceasing to be tied to old sanctions in religion and a clearly organized society and beginning to depend upon individual self-interest and voluntary association. For the old motives of religious zeal, personal glory, and institutionalized homage to one's master (what J. H. Plumb has called "Patriarchalism")[6] Dryden provided new ones: humanity, personal integrity, and an almost romantic sense of unselfish dedication. In the transit, Dryden's art helped to initiate one of the great changes in human awareness and to introduce the sentiment of common humanity not as a concept or a dogma, but rather as a well-defined sense of dedication to a common interest in rational good will, one that was felt and acted upon rather than commanded and attested to.

It might be more apparent to us that Dryden belongs near Ibsen as a source of new, exciting ideas had he been less attuned than he was to the latest tendencies of his own lifetime, less skillful in bringing them to the light artistically, and less successful in gaining acceptance for them among the critical part of his audience. His success closed the gap between later generations and himself—and in the process his original achievement has been dwarfed.

One way to restore the perspective is to make sure that Dryden's writing is presented to the general reader today so that he can see it for what it is. This is especially the case with his plays, until very recently the most neglected of his works. We cannot see a Dryden play phenomenally by way of historic recreation, as it was acted in the Theatre Royal by Mohun and Hart and Gwyn and Kynaston, before an audience including the King and Queen, the Duke and Duchess of York, Ormond, Buckingham, Newcastle, the Town poets, undergraduates from Oxford and Cambridge,

has called "the supernal," which did indeed set him apart from his contemporaries and successors. His faith in a transcendantly mysterious Providence is an example.

[6] *New York Review of Books,* 16 Feb. 1970, p. 16.

and all their ladies; even scholars can only hope to approximate this experience imaginatively. The only practical substitute is to reproduce the reading experience of the poet's contemporaries, the work that he gave them in printed form. This experience would include the play, with its prologue and epilogue, and also the dedication, preface, and other material that accompanied editions printed during Dryden's lifetime. I should like at least to open the argument that all these elements together constitute "the whole work" in reading Dryden's plays, in the conviction that what is good isn't the play alone, but the whole combination of dedication, preface, prologue, play, epilogue; the sense of the writer choosing a target, poising the dart, aiming it, throwing it, and judging the accuracy of the cast—with a strong awareness of the response of two audiences, one supremely qualified, the other turbulent, muddle-headed, very human.

Dryden obviously wrote these auxiliary pieces as well as he did because he enjoyed doing them and reveled in the opportunity they provided to share with others his interest in the theory and craft of poetry. Even the dedications, despite what one might expect, seem to be anything but mere bread-and-butter work. Some are flattering, but others are personally confessional or else truculent, as he deals with friend or enemy. It is a serious mistake to treat the dedications lightly, for they are as much a part of Dryden's "self," as we are seeking it, and of the influence he exerted upon other poets, as anything he wrote. They constitute a set of guidelines for the interpretation of his plays by critics, and, I believe, for the intelligent appreciation of them by the general reader as well.[7]

For example, Dryden's words to Anne Scott before *The Indian Emperor* tell us a good deal. First, about the heroic play. It owes its favor to the Court, where persons of wit and honor in the royal circle have approved its verse as an appropriate form "to entertain a Noble Audience, or to express a noble passion." Here begins a pretty metaphor: it isn't the

[7] For Alan Roper's defense of Dryden's dedications versus Dr. Johnson, see *Works*, XVIII, 510.

high rank of Court people that draws the gaze of such as himself, any more than would the intimidating crags of a mountain top. It's because the Court also offers the "shades and greens" of a beauty such as Anne's. Beauty can reconcile one to the most austere demands, as the poet well understands. If only the beauty and honor of Anne could mingle, like the mother liquor in a wine, with the beauty of her husband ("no part of *Europe* can afford a parallel to your Noble Lord, in masculine Beauty, and in goodliness of shape"), then, says Dryden, "your Graces would be immortal." There is some skillful mountaineering here on the dedicator's part. He has carefully refrained from saying that the Duke of Monmouth was virtuous; that he was handsome is true. Dryden, however, is hypothesizing an infusion of Anne's virtue sufficient to offset the weak nature of her nineteen-year-old husband. On this fragile support he ventures a bold ascent: "You are a pair of Angels sent below to make Virtue amiable in your persons, or to sit to Poets when they would pleasantly instruct the Age, by drawing goodness in the most perfect and alluring shape of Nature."[8]

This is flattery indeed. We know what Dr. Johnson thought of it—and we agree with him. Yet it is also literary criticism. Dryden is illustrating the nature of the heroic genre by selecting two of the most beautiful and one of the most virtuous young people of princely rank, and he is making the virtue more accessible by stressing the link with beauty, for beauty in nature is the most pleasing of things. Thus the heroic play presents a beauty that is natural but also lofty, at a considerable distance above ordinary mortals. It is also a dizzying kind of beauty in a court—sweet and benign to have, but a dreadful trial to the young persons who lack it: they "seem to be there to no other purpose than to wait on the triumphs of the fair . . . or at best to be the refuge of those hearts which others have despis'd; and, by the unworthiness of both, to give and take a miserable comfort." Beauty has, therefore, a terrible side, and there is

[8] *Ibid.*, IX, 23–24.

need for compassion from its high level. Dryden is expounding the ethos of the courtly heroic, with its baroque heightening, its privilege, its self-conscious pleasures, and its heartbreak. He is also trying to insinuate an appropriate kind of virtue to qualify the life style of this select class and to bring it closer to the rest of society: "Goodness and humanity, which shine in you, are Virtues which concern mankind, and by a certain kind of interest all people agree in their commendation, because the profit of them may extend to many." Here is a paradox, for the word "*interest*" normally meant a selfish interest. The suggestion is that there is something compelling about "goodness and humanity" just as there is in beauty. It "concerns mankind" and this "concernment," as Dryden called it in many future evocations, is a powerful bond between high and low.

It has been assumed, very naturally, that Dryden wrote dedications to obtain favors or money, yet there is no evidence that supports such an assumption. Most of them were written out of gratitude for past favors—a rather different motive, it seems to me.[9] Then one learns that Restoration grandees such as Clifford, Danby, Rochester (either John Wilmot or his successor Lawrence Hyde) did not normally give presents to people at all. If their good will was very strong, they put a man on the payroll by getting him a place in government; more usually, they won sincere thanks by merely taking care that a client got his just due, minus the normal fees and tips, from the Treasury. Dryden, a placeholder because of his laureateship, was an exceptionally modest beggar in that he tended to avoid Whitehall and

[9] Nietzsche on gratitude fits Dryden well: "What, then, is praise? A sort of restoration of balance in respect of benefits received, a giving in return, a demonstration of *our* power—for those who praise, affirm, judge, evaluate, pass sentence: they claim the right of being *able* to affirm, of being *able* to dispense honors. A heightened feeling of happiness and life is also a heightened feeling of power: it is from this that a man praises. . . . Gratitude as virtuous revenge: most strenuously demanded and practiced where equality and pride must both be upheld, where revenge is practiced best." *The Will to Power*, trans. Walter Kaufmann and R. J. Hollingdale (London, 1967), pp. 406–407.

the levees of influential courtiers and attempted to pay his court with his pen. The remarkable fact about this habit is that Dryden's courting was done in public and has remained in print for the world to read ever since. I am not familiar with any body of writing like Dryden's dedications in this public aspect. He made a practice of characterizing his patrons rather definitely and memorably, and also placed them upon the national scene in reference to their political attitudes, allegiances, and enmities. In this process, he made it quite clear to contemporary readers where he stood himself.

In contrast to what has often been said about Dryden, the dedications show, not opportunism, but a constant regard for his own integrity and for a certain type of public man whom he genuinely admired: one who was a careful administrator, not too much a timeserver or a self-seeker, and above all a preserver of continuity in government.[10] If in addition he was an approachable and cultivated person, he would then qualify for one of those panegyrical portraits which mingle politics, literature, and details of personal life and attitude according to a heightened, but carefully proportioned scale of values that Dryden repeatedly compared to those of portrait painting. In these portraits genuine good qualities are made resplendent, not merely to give praise for performance in the past, but to keep the subject up to this mark in the future. Weaknesses are left in shadow; their failure to register is part of the artist's conception, and it is his critical judgment that calls for their absence. The composition of a gallery of these portraits over the years helped Dryden to frame the images of public men that do so much for *Absalom and Achitophel*. It also has the effect, once we grasp the substance of his judgments, of allowing us to become much better acquainted with the poet himself, for the more we know about his subjects, the more we can learn about Dryden. The writer who was making these judg-

[10] The dedication of *Amboyna* to Sir Thomas Clifford is a significant example; it was followed, more than thirty years later, by one to Clifford's son.

ments in the course of twenty years came to speak with insight into political as well as literary matters.

In Restoration politics, it is now understood that personal connections or class sympathies were much more significant, especially during the earlier decades, than "Whig" or "Tory" affiliations.[11] The study of Dryden's friends in politics, and of their friends and enemies also, is a necessary supplement to our analysis of contemporary ideas or attitudes, literary, political, or religious. Just as the refusal of the Duke of York and Lord Treasurer Clifford to submit to the religious Test Act of 1673 evidently made a lasting impression upon the poet (it may have become the strongest personal motive for his own conversion to Roman Catholicism), so five years earlier his disgust at the hounding into exile and continued persecution of the old Earl of Clarendon (the work of Buckingham and Sir Robert Howard) foretold his lifetime political allegiances. The currents of feeling aroused by these complex and momentous events flowed into Dryden's poetry and his plays, channeled (to use one of his favorite images) so as to create simple, powerful emotions: loyalty as a form of inner personal commitment that gives one the capacity for renunciation of all lesser interests; and compassion for the vulnerability and pain of mankind, especially when it springs from conflict between the public and the private self.

My view is the reciprocal of one stated by Eric Rothstein: "The primary function of the politics in Restoration tragedy is to foster that pathos which the theoretical critics demanded."[12] Often, I think, the pathos was there to civilize the politics. First there was the Rebellion, whose beginnings were described in these words by Clarendon himself: "The court was as full of murmuring, ingratitude, and treachery, and as willing and ready to rebel against the best and most bountiful master in the world, as the country and the city. A barbarous and bloody fierceness and savageness had ex-

---

[11] Confirmation will be found in (e.g.) the works by J. P. Kenyon and J. H. Plumb cited in this study.
[12] *Restoration Tragedy* (Princeton, 1967), p. 109.

tinguished all relations, hardened the hearts and bowels of all men; and an universal malice and animosity had even covered the most innocent and best-natured people and nation upon the earth."[13] Then there was the Interregnum, when Cambridge and especially Trinity College (Dryden's) were subjected to Puritan interference.[14] After the Restoration, there were renewed defeats and humiliations for the nation that had seemed for a brief while providentially restored: the King's negligence, the Plague and the Fire, the Dutch in the Medway, dependence upon Louis XIV, the Treasury Moratorium of 1672–73, and the repeated failure of Toleration, met each time with a new outbreak of the "barbarism" Clarendon deplored in 1642. Also, there was disgrace or ruin for men Dryden strongly admired, Clarendon, Ormond, James Stuart, Clifford, as well as prolonged financial dependency for himself after 1672.[15] These were the years when he could get nothing but promises of support for his projected epic and when all the poets were being shamefully neglected, in contrast to Louis XIV's magnanimous treatment of their counterparts. France also had passed through her interval of barbarism during the Fronde and had recovered more completely; but Dryden was never willing to accept the French price of autocracy.

In part, no doubt, because of this experience of barbarism, shared by all of Europe during the horrible wars and local uprisings of the earlier seventeenth century, critics had developed a post-Renaissance formulation of Aristotle's catharsis of pity and terror. For J. C. Scaliger's catalogue of atrocities suitable for tragedy they substituted, in Boileau's words,

[13] *Life* (Oxford, 1827), I, 464.
[14] On Trinity College during 1649–1653, see Vivian H. H. Green, *Religion at Oxford and Cambridge* (London, 1964), pp. 150–151: "The drab cloak of religious rigidity enshrouded" both universities; Green cites at length the rules of a tutor at Trinity during Dryden's time there.
[15] As Charles E. Ward has shown, Dryden's inheritance of property in Northamptonshire was enough to make him a member of the landed gentry; but it was hardly adequate to support him and his family in London. See *The Life of John Dryden* (Chapel Hill, N.C., 1961), p. 20.

douce terreur and *pitié charmante*. These agreeable affects were evoked and aimed at mankind's two most prevalent vices: pride and hardness of heart. Thus Rapin affirmed, and Dryden quoted him in complete agreement.[16] However, Dryden made much greater use of politics in achieving these feelings than Racine did, for example. He had an important political purpose, feeling as he did that barbarism, unless skillfully opposed, would again come to power in England. If instead the English became notoriously the most humanitarian people in Europe during the next three centuries, we have to give Dryden credit for some success in reclaiming them to the good nature Clarendon reported they had lost at the time of their Civil War.

What happened historically, then, was that in 1674 or 1675 Dryden found formulae in Boileau and Bossu for uses of feeling he had already been experimenting with dramatically. The *Indian Emperor* scene where Montezuma (a venerable figure, no longer young) is racked by Pizarro and an Inquisitor, is the most famous example.[17] Pride and hardness of heart are there presented in what Dryden saw as their two most threatening forms: the rapacity of agents of governmental power who act as if they were above the level of common humanity, and the inveterate bigotry of the clergy, based upon the conviction that they have a heavenly right to the obedience of mankind. (The young Voltaire copied this scene extensively into his notebooks.)[18] Dryden had seen men he knew and otherwise had reason to admire, the Earl of Shaftesbury and the Duke of Buckingham among them, slipping into these vices, and letting loose upon the nation once again the flood of barbarism.

Fear of a return of barbarism was justified, for political events in Restoration England, beginning with the failure of the Savoy Conference to effect a religious *modus vivendi*, repeated events of the 1640s with ominous fidelity. Perhaps this is why Dryden's plays often seem to be models of events,

---

16 Watson, I, 245. 17 v. ii. *Works*, IX, 98–101.
18 For Voltaire's later use of the play, see *Works*, IX, 315.

foretelling things to come. His basic dramatic situation (which varies little) could be fitted in with the political one of Charles I in 1640: an aging or otherwise vulnerable ruler is under attack in his capital city. He is also threatened by disloyal citizens, secretly led by a power-hungry courtier. He is aided by a younger man, the hero, who acts out of love for a woman who in turn is an emblem of legitimate rule, politically, and of virtuous self-rule, personally. Often friendship, both male and female, becomes an important bond of support to the young hero. He usually makes good his claim to the lady by force, directed however by friendly love, which has replaced an original erotic desire.

This model is close to the classical notions of Plato and Aristotle, who stressed the importance of friendship among good men as the explicit city-building eros. They also extolled the value of common fellow feeling, philia, and of the greater happiness of loving than being loved. Herein is the germ of Dryden's humanitarianism and of his urbanity too. The model also fits the actual situation of Charles II. Charles was not an old monarch, but he was vulnerable because of his careless ways and the lack of an heir. Also, his government was subjected to attack at every session of Parliament after 1661 and was never strong enough to extract an adequate supply of money from the House of Commons. Each summoning of Parliament, therefore, became the signal for a sort of invasion of London by its members from the country at large, some of them inveterate in their hostility to the Court, and most of them intent mainly upon forcing their own interest upon the King. The London populace, meanwhile, remained consistently anti-Court, and as early as 1662 Buckingham was seeking to manipulate it against the ministry of Clarendon, as Shaftesbury did a decade later against Danby's. The young hero of the model corresponds fairly well with James Stuart, who was viewed as the legitimate heir as soon as the politicians realized Catherine of Braganza could bear no children. The insistence in the model upon classical philia fits the attitude incumbent upon James, whose

14

role was to serve his brother the King loyally and self-effac-
ingly, though with little love in return. James, unfortunately,
was not a likable person, but he tried hard and managed to
work very effectively with others toward common adminis-
trative goals, in complete contrast to his arch rival, Buck-
ingham. Thus James's motive could reasonably be seen as the
community-building philia, typified in the plays by the sex
figures Almahide or Indamora; Buckingham's was the self-
interested eros, desire for the sake of pleasure, power for the
charm of superiority, typified by Lyndaraxa or Nourmahal.

The great anomaly of this model lies in its equation of the
Commons in session with an external hostile force. Perhaps
the anomaly is more apparent than real, for a reasonably sat-
isfactory rationale can be offered: Charles's subjects, influ-
enced all over England by an intolerant, intransigent clergy,
and represented in the Commons by too many quarrelsome,
self-seeking members, really needed to be kept in awe by
visible strength, before they would submit to be won by the
King's natural (all too natural!) clemency and bountifulness.
This view, however, suggests that Dryden failed to grasp
the nature of parliamentary development during his lifetime.
He may have begun by agreeing with Clarendon that parties
were to be avoided in government. An indication of this
attitude is the use of terms such as *"the party"* and *"the
faction"* in the singular, to denote a malcontent minority
opposing its own interest to the nation's, i.e., to the King's.
As late as 1683, in the *Vindication* of *The Duke of Guise*,
he deplores the use of party names and the polarization of
men, who formerly met affably, along party lines, into groups
of hostile strangers. However, since historians now seem dis-
inclined to place the actuality of two-party politics quite so
early, it is probably safe to conclude that in Dryden's mind
the true nature of Parliament was to be a collegial rather
than a bipartisan body. In that case, its corruption during
Charles's reign, amounting in the majority of influential
members to what we should consider treason if it occurred
today, and the savage hostilities among men driving to over-

reach rivals rather than to serve the nation, would justify the poet in seeing the assembly of Parliament as the muster of a threatening, even a barbarian force. The beleaguered king of so many Dryden plays is, then, an emblem arising out of the poet's vision of a potentially happy nation continually threatened by the barbarism of its own worst instincts. The dramatic structure of the serious plays arises, therefore, out of a double opposition: a psychomachia developed from the classical distinction between a self-seeking and a generous love; and a conflict for power emblematic of actual politics during Charles's reign.

Aside from dramatic and poetic structures, we of course cannot forget the circumstances of theatre-going in the Restoration. Pepys gives us ample evidence that the politicians, from King Charles on down, frequented the playhouses, that they used plays to attack their enemies, and that they defended themselves by having plays banned and actors beaten. *The London Stage* has at last made it easy to determine the chronology of performances and to relate them to contemporary events and controversies. We can now see that hardly one political crisis, after the ouster of the Rump Parliament, failed to have some reflection on the stages of the King's Theatre and the Duke's Theatre.

Finally, I state the claim that, as Dryden was the first public man of letters in England, he was also her first public critic. James Sutherland has admirably appraised his status in his own time: "Dryden is by far the most important, not only for the range and flexibility of his critical writing, but for the example he gave to his contemporaries. He fertilized the whole field of polite letters in his own day by constantly turning over the soil, and he established a habit of urbane and unpedantic writing about books and authors which, with certain notorious exceptions, has continued to be the main English tradition."[19]

Our definition of the public critic includes several addi-

[19] *English Literature of the Late Seventeenth Century* (Oxford, 1969), pp. 411–412.

tional elements. Most of all, he must be engaged, out front, attacking and being attacked. Not, of course, on side-issues and campaigns without genuine literary interest—for example, defenses and illustrations of his own personality—but, when he writes exactly as a man of letters, for and to his fellow writers. He will be appealing to a national public (potentially, perhaps, to an international one) that, in all likelihood, has not merely been delivered to him by membership in an ecclesiastical or an educational institution, but rather one that he has constituted for himself by his writing. Even though he does not only speak for himself, he will have a personal tone in stating points of view that normally belong to some new movement, some not merely utopian locus of thought and feeling in the contemporary community. Over the years, such a critic will have something identifiable to say on his art, on public taste, attitudes, behavior; his comments on current or past writing will not only lead to the focus on a literary canon, they will bring out a set of principles whereby it is selected, judged, and found of value. He will in his own work exhibit this process of judging, reflecting, and focusing, giving shape to a body of practical criticism wherein a particular outlook can be seen, and which will often be adopted without their knowing it by those, even, whose stand on public issues is quite opposite. Such a critic must, of course, achieve success for himself—at least to the extent of having his audience—but he will be eager to confer a share of this success upon other writers he admires, living or dead. Here is a pitfall, for many a great writer's judgment of his contemporaries shows him limited indeed. Some fine critics have been modest enough to avoid all open judgment of their own contemporaries, but their caution is incompatible with the public critic's role. His comment on writers and texts, even those remote in time or place, will always have some implicit bearing on the life of his own community and will imply some kind of judgment on the work of living authors.

Such a description fits Dryden, I think, as well as it does

Johnson, Coleridge, Emerson, Ruskin, Arnold, Eliot, Pound, or anyone now writing. Its original basis, that the critic be "out in front," had in Dryden the form of risk taking, both in his stylistic and formal innovations and in the remarkable ingenuousness of his personal tone, especially in the dedications, where much of his public criticism appears.

One could say, of course, that Dryden was institutionalized as Poet Laureate and Historiographer, reigning officially over both provinces, the ideal and the actual, and that he had a ready-made national audience. Oddly, his tone of address seems to belie this assumption. He never seems to think of representing himself to the nation as a spokesman for the Court. His function is rather that of analyst and guide than of public relations officer. He is very aware that his office requires him to entertain King and Court, and that he holds it only so long as he does give pleasure. His place was no sinecure. As Dryden saw it, in fact, his office also required him to instruct the mighty. He fulfilled this obligation with a resoluteness that kept him on the brink of offense throughout Charles's reign. Had it not been for an equally bold resourcefulness, especially a kind of comic insouciance that matched his peculiar ingenuousness,[20] Dryden's career would probably have ended in disaster.

At Court, Dryden was anything but an insider—he was a layman there as much as in the Church. His real base was Will's Coffee House. There he was high priest; but his cult was an intensely secular one, comprehensive, tolerant, even indulgent. As a center of literary formation there has probably never been anything like Dryden's forty years at Will's —not Mallarmé's twenty years of Tuesdays nor even Pound's factoring for a whole generation of American and English writers. The style of the age, as Sutherland very accurately describes it, emerged at Will's. Its first principle was refine-

[20] Alan Roper understandably convicts Dryden of "disingenuousness" for concealing his appropriation, throughout a passage of a half-dozen pages, of a compilation by Dugdale. Yet since the material consists of "garbidge" in Dryden's word, the crime is high-handed rather than sly. See *Works*, xviii, 532.

ment, both linguistic and social. Long after the coming of Malherbe in France, English vocabulary and literary usage continued to proliferate *ad libitum,* for a while gorgeously, but at length in a merely unkempt growth that only a genius could cope with. Dryden fought this battle in his epilogue to *The Conquest of Granada* and in its "Defence," and except for a few lapses into the "voice of Mr. Bayes" he offered a consistently good example of the principles there established, despite undergoing unprecedented personal abuse on every level, from the Duke of Buckingham and the Master of Charterhouse down to the ineffable Richard Flecknoe.

At first, Dryden associated the ill-bred, emptily exploitative uses of language with "dullness," and he gave it a local habitation and a name in *MacFlecknoe.* At the same time he impregnated its barrenness with the heroic, making dullness productive of great satire for fifty years to come. He learned the satiric trick in part perhaps from Dorset, but certainly from Boileau.[21] As for the heroic, his commitment to Virgil, Tasso, Milton, Longinus—and Bossu—was spread on the record of his prefaces and dedications. He drew his current of fresh ideas from sources old and new in Greek, Latin, Italian, Spanish, French, and even German. Not long after, he drew upon all this "humanity" in order to pass judgment on the condensed dullness of the sectarian faction when they took social and political form as an anticommunity. Both in his prose (the *Vindication*) as well as in unheroic verse (*The Medal*), he extended the satiric tone in the direction of the comic rather than the demonic. His satire, unfortunately, brought no profit to its principal butt, the first Earl of Shaftesbury. Yet in a different age the latter's grandson was a brilliant convert (though unacknowledging) to the urbane, witty mode and its social utility. The difference between the civility of 1681 and that of 1711 is one that Dryden did more than anyone else to create.

[21] See the writer's "Dryden, Boileau, and Longinian Imitation," *Proceedings* of the Fourth Congress of the International Comparative Literature Assn. (Paris, 1966), 751–755.

For several reasons, it is justifiable to bring this book to a close with the death of Charles II. The most pervasive reason is that Dryden ceased to work for the stage during the next reign, and the present study is nourished most by his theatrical activity. Under James, his service was considerably changed. Charles was very willing to be pleased and would tolerate instruction, but he was sparing of commands. His Treasury was, also, a most unpleasant ordeal for Dryden, which he hardly approached unless he had recent services for which to claim payment. James, on the other hand, seemed to care little for poetry, but he paid salaries promptly and in full. The pressure of contingencies (which has been my subject) lapsed as financial pressure relaxed. There was a deeper change, too. Dryden had never been a Court spokesman; it was much more normal for him to address King or Court as a representative of the Muses, humanity, posterity, or his fellow Englishmen, than to speak from an official rostrum. This stance resulted from his allegiance to a succession of underdogs or victims, as I have shown. Over the years he had been closely identified with James, and as soon as James became top dog it would seem that Dryden, like many others (the old Catholics most significantly), became uneasy at his hard and hasty movement in the opposite direction to what he had promised those who trusted his vaunted word. Dryden carried out his few assignments as Historiographer, but showed no initiative on the public scene until *The Hind and the Panther*, and then he found his artful fable roughly forestalled by the King's Declaration. After the Revolution of 1688, things became interesting all over again, but so transformed as to require another study.

PART ONE

DRYDEN THE POET

CHAPTER ONE

DRYDEN'S EARLY ATTITUDES TOWARD POLITICS AND THE HEROIC

I. THE EARLY VERSE

BECAUSE some members of Dryden's family had anti-royalist or Puritan associations, his early political sentiments have often been guessed at, with results in direct conflict with the evidence of his own writing. The boy John left his Northamptonshire home very early in his teens, on a King's Scholarship to Westminster School in London. There he lived for several highly formative years under the influence of the staunchly royalist master, Dr. Richard Busby. When King Charles I was executed in 1649, John Dryden was in his last year at Westminster; and as the King mounted the scaffold, Dryden and the other Westminster boys were assembled in prayer for him only a short distance away.[1]

Shortly after, in his earliest printed poem, Dryden expressed warm royalist feeling coupled with a sense of the heroic. "Upon the Death of the Lord Hastings" appeared during the year of regicide in a memorial volume that drew contributions from a number of Westminster boys. In Dryden's poem Hastings (he was nineteen, the poet's age, at his death) is "this hero." The Civil War is "the nation's sin"—only so loathsome a crime could cause Heaven to remove the promising youth by so horrid an agency as the blisters of smallpox:

[1] C. V. Wedgwood, A Coffin For King Charles (New York, 1965), p. 229.

23

> Who, Rebel-like, with their own Lord at strife,
> Thus made an Insurrection 'gainst his life.
>
> (61–62)[2]

The anti–Civil War sentiment is as typical as the figure of speech—an early example of the poet's weakness for all-too-concrete comparisons between the physical and the psychic. The royalism is obvious in the metaphorical allusion, which makes monarchy part of the healthy order of nature.

The same theme of opposition to the Civil War and its promoters runs through the *Heroic Stanzas* for Cromwell's funeral (1658), which uses the stanza form introduced eight years before in Sir William Davenant's heroic poem, *Gondibert*. War is "our consumption"; Cromwell "fought to end our fighting." "Peace was the prize of all his toils and care." He deposed Mars (not Charles!), and "arms to gowns made yield." Further, he compelled the turbulent House of Commons to a sullen compliance, which persists still: "No civil broils have since his death arose." Cromwell too is "heroic" —an example

> . . . to show
> How strangely high endeavours may be blest,
> Where *Piety* and *valour* joyntly goe.
>
> (147–148)

This poem is an early instance, the most unlucky one so far as the poet was concerned, of Dryden's encomiastic manner. This praise of Cromwell became a reproach often thrown at him after the Restoration. Yet, as with Dryden's praise in general, this panegyric is both critically selective and strongly tendentious. Cromwell, he says, was old when power came to him unsought, too old to make the rash mistakes of youth, and too sincere to drag out the war for his own glory. So much for internal English affairs; the poet quickly moves

---

[2] Quotations from Dryden's earlier verse are from *The Works of John Dryden*, ed. Edward Niles Hooker and H. T. Swedenberg, Jr. (Berkeley, 1961–) 1. This, the "California" edition, will be cited as *Works*.

abroad. Oliver Cromwell exacted tribute from greedy Holland (an early indication of Dryden's lifelong dislike of the Dutch) and kept all Europe in awe: "He made us freemen of the continent" (113). Finally, he extended English commerce, a theme already dear to the poet's heart as these fine lines give witness:

> By his command we boldly crost the Line
> And bravely fought where *Southern Starrs* arise,
> We trac'd the farre-fetchd Gold unto the mine
> And that which brib'd our fathers made our prize.
>
> (121–124)

Also important in its own way is the poet's theoretical basis for making a hero out of Cromwell. His heroic virtue was to understand and handle men as an artist does in a history painting, by creative intuition:

> When absent, yet we conquer'd in his right;
> For though some meaner Artist's skill were shown
> In mingling colours, or in placing light,
> Yet still the faire Designment was his own.
>
> For from all tempers he could service draw;
> The worth of each with its alloy he knew;
> And as the *Confident* of *Nature* saw
> How she Complexions did divide and brew.
>
> Or he their single vertues did survay
> By *intuition* in his own large brest,
> Where all the rich *Idea's* of them lay,
> That were the rule and measure to the rest.
>
> (93–104)

This vision of the hero's intuitive sense of design is quite the same as Dryden's more famous praise of Shakespeare: "he was the man who of all modern, and perhaps ancient poets, had the largest and most comprehensive soul. All the images of nature were still present to him, and he drew them not laboriously, but luckily. . . ."[3] He already draws the contrast between the "lucky" inward look of genius and the calculating observation of art that he was to apply to the disadvantage of Jonson. Dryden, it is clear from the start, was one of those grateful souls who feel admiration keenly, as an intense pleasure. Yet the admiration he expresses seldom lacks control. His favorable comments on Cromwell refer to abilities and successes admitted (grudgingly, and along with some vicious innuendo) even by Clarendon in his hostile character of the Protector in the *History of the Rebellion.*

There seems no reason to doubt that in these early years Dryden regarded the exemplary hero not as a mere literary concept but as a valid basis for practical English politics. If the nation's leader were to be, instead of a vigorous usurper, an hereditary monarch, then, lest his virtue be "poison'd soon as born / With the too early thoughts of being King," it would be the poet's function to hold before his prince the heroic ideal and stimulate him to rise to it. This is what Dryden does in *Astræa Redux,* his poem of welcome to Charles II, written immediately after the Restoration (May 1660). Recounting the exile's deprivations, he projects as a logical conclusion from them the wise future conduct of the King:

> Inur'd to suffer ere he came to raigne
> No rash procedure will his actions stain.
>
> (87–88)

Dryden, in fact, sees Charles as a Prince Hal on the threshold of self-vindication and regal greatness. He is one who, in his exile,

> . . . viewing Monarchs secret Arts of sway
> A Royal Factor for their Kingdomes lay.
>
> (77–78)

---

[3] For the reader's convenience, Dryden's prose will be cited where possible from *Of Dramatic Poesy and Other Critical Essays,* ed. George Watson (Everyman), 2 vols. See 1, 67.

The suggestion is that Louis XIV will play the Hotspur to Charles's Hal, a most sanguine one indeed, but useful to save face, for England was already aware of "the long-grown wounds of . . . intemperance" in Charles while he lived as a pensioner of Louis. A pleasing hope, to "exchange / His glorious deeds for my indignities," as Prince Hal tells his father, arguing, through the image Dryden picked up, that

> Percy is but my factor, good my lord,
> To engross up glorious deeds on my behalf.
> (*I Hen. IV*, iii. ii. 145–148)

Nevertheless it was an image that had some historical meaning. Dryden's program for Charles is that of the ideal Shakespearean king who preserves peace at home by fighting abroad. Like Henry V Charles will bind up the wounds of hateful Civil War through foreign conquest:

> Some lazy Ages lost in sleep and ease
> No action leave to busie Chronicles;
> Such whose supine felicity but makes
> In story *Chasmes*, in *Epoche's* mistakes;
> O're whom *Time* gently shakes his wings of Down
> Till with his silent sickle they are mown:
> Such is not *Charles* his too too active age,
> Which govern'd by the wild distemper'd rage
> Of some black Star infecting all the Skies,
> Made him at his own cost like *Adam* wise.
> (105–114)

Already, one of Dryden's favorite images, the Fall in the Garden, suggests Charles's awareness of hard reality by its reference to Adam and his tasting the fruit of the Tree of the Knowledge of Good and Evil, at the same time as it acknowledges the lost innocence of the King.

His disapproval of the Rump Parliament agrees with what he wrote in the *Heroic Stanzas* to Cromwell, but here, not surprisingly, his words are much stronger. He commends the General, "whom Providence design'd to loose / Those real bonds false freedom did impose," for concealing his intentions from the Rump:

> To scape their eyes whom guilt had taught to fear,
> And guard with caution that polluted nest
> Whence Legion twice before was dispossest,
> Once sacred house which when they enter'd in
> They thought the place could sanctifie a sin. . . .
> Suffer'd to live, they are like *Helots* set
> A vertuous shame within us to beget.
>
> (180–184; 205–206)

The same idea of a national sin had appeared in the Hastings *Ode* of 1649. In the later poem we have the additional suggestion of a double profanation—the murder of an anointed king and the abuse of the institution of Parliament, honored through the centuries at Westminster. The poet looks for a cleansing of the "sacred house" as the Helots of the Rump are ousted; Parliament itself, however, figures in its full ancient dignity as a part of his vision of the restored nation. Continuity with the past, rather than a break with it, is Dryden's ideal in politics, as he will soon profess it to be in poetry.

Still concerned for the spread of English trade, and still hostile to the Dutch competitors, Dryden marvels that Charles should have embarked for England at the beach of Scheveline, and that "*Batavia* made / So rich amends for our impoverish'd Trade." In a mixture of irony and hyperbole he comments, "True Sorrow, Holland to regret a King." The entire peroration, beginning "And welcome now (*Great Monarch*) to your own," and ending in the cry of prophetic joy, "Oh Happy Age!" with which the poet acclaims the end of barbarism in a "joint growth of Armes and Arts" under a new Augustus, presents a highly idealized version of what in fact did come into being as the British Empire:

> Our Nation with united Int'rest blest
> Not now content to poize, shall sway the rest.

Abroad your Empire shall no Limits know,
But like the Sea in boundless Circles flow.
Your much lov'd Fleet shall with a wide Command
Besiege the petty Monarchs of the land.

(296–301)

Lest Dryden's vision of empire make him out a jingo be-
fore the fact, it must be said that the rest of *Astræa Redux*
presents the picture of a king who is much too mild to play
the role of conqueror. Clarendon's *History of the Rebellion*
makes it clear that Charles I's unwillingness to deal severely
with his opponents had cost him his crown and his life, and
cost England twenty years of anarchy, war, and autocratic
oppression. Dryden accepts this uneasy parallel, but hopes
for the best in lines that have a remarkable significance and
foreshadow a major development of his own sensibility:

But you, whose goodness your discent doth show,
Your Heav'nly Parentage and earthly too;
By that same mildness which your Fathers Crown
Before did ravish, shall secure your own.
Not ty'd to rules of Policy, you find
Revenge less sweet then a forgiving mind. . . .
Your Pow'r to Justice doth submit your Cause,
Your goodness only is above the Laws;

(256–261; 275–276)

The beginning of this passage shows the extent to which
Dryden was a believer in divine right, and the extent to
which he was not. Charles is God's anointed, as such his
parentage is in heaven; yet the King's personal link with
God is not in his royal power—which is subject to earthly
law—but in his mercy or goodness, which alone is above the
"rigid letter" of the law. The poet sees clearly that Charles's
mercy, like his father's, is impolitic ("not tied to rules of
policy" is his tactful way of putting it). He nevertheless puts
his faith in the grateful response of a happy and united na-
tion and hopes that the charm of Charles II's "life and blest

example" of mercy (317) will win the hearts of all the people for the King. He counts on their loyalty and grateful affection—in a word, he counts on sentiment as a political force.

As everyone knows, Good King Charles continued to be kind, but his people were far from being united in gratitude to him—or in anything else. The honeymoon of May, 1660, that brought with it Charles Stuart and the flowers, expired rather soon. By coronation day, April 23, 1661, it was no longer true that

> At home the hateful names of Parties cease
> And factious Souls are weary'd into peace.
>
> (312–313)

The deserving Old Cavaliers were not being rewarded for their loyalty, and the new servants of the Crown, such as Pepys, were experiencing the first qualms of what soon became a complete disillusionment with the King's capacity to get the business of the nation done. Awareness of their misgivings did not, of course, prevent Dryden and the rest of the poets from celebrating the anointing. Yet it is evident in *To His Sacred Majesty, A Panegyrick on His Coronation* that the best is being made of a rather disappointing case. Looking over Charles's first year of power, Dryden could point to very little accomplishment. Sedition, and the zealots who warmed it, he says, are not being subjected to the laws, but to the goodness, calmness, and patience of the King, and above all, to his short memory:

> Among our crimes oblivion may be set,
> But 'tis our Kings perfection to forget.
>
> (87–88)

Charles has already indicated that the iron of a Caesar is alloyed in his nature by a paternal softness. He ventures his life like Julius; not in conquest, however, but on his private yacht; he builds like Augustus, but so far only a canal for his ducks. The poet avoids such mean terms and the punctured expectations they would bring to mind, and doggedly insists still that Charles is "born to command the mistress of the seas," and that his "pleasures serve for our defense," but these are slender gleanings; as he would need to do for thirty-five years, Dryden is using the panegyrist's chiaroscuro to set things in a good light.

What must be recognized (how seldom it has been!) is the selective and projective nature of Dryden's praise, in the *Coronation Ode* as elsewhere. We have lost the taste for praise, which is the outgrowth of generosity, preferring the forthright acknowledgment of merit, which is a vindication of justice and of rights we all share in and hope to rise by. An age that understood praise knew that there has to be something supererogatory in it, especially for kings and great persons. These, accustomed to the odor of incense in the air they breathed every day, required a supercharged draught before they could take a special pleasure in it. Informal as he was, Charles, like all the great, desired his favors to be received with extraordinary signs of gratitude—and not actual favors only, but possible ones as well. Such praise could go to almost any length without being overdone, provided it had some reference to reality and did not run so counter to it as to suggest irony, conscious or unconscious. Dryden's practice is to give full credit, and overflowing, for genuine good qualities (or good intentions) that the person exhibits, and further to imply the possession of qualities the person ought to have, according to the poet's hopeful idea of his role. Evelyn spoke to this point in defending a dedication he wrote to Clarendon: "greate persons, & such as are in place to doe greate & noble things, whatever their other defects may be, are to be panegyrized into the culture of those vertues, without which 'tis to be suppos'd they had neuer arriv'd to a power of being able to encourage them. . . . nor is it properly adulation, but a civilitie due to their characters."[4] Where Dryden has reason to be dissatisfied, he resorts to charitable imputation:

[4] J. E. Spingarn, ed., *Critical Essays of the Seventeenth Century* (Oxford, 1908), II, 321–322.

A noble Emulation heats your breast,
And your own fame now robbs you of your rest;
Good actions still must be maintain'd with good. . . .

(75–77)

The truth here is that Charles passes little time in sleep; the imputation, that he is nobly concerned for his good name. A very proper suggestion—it is not Dryden's fault that Charles was up most nights drinking and gambling, or making love in the Whitehall apartments of Barbara Palmer, newly made Lady Castlemaine. A king with a tender conscience would read these lines as a reproof. What they truly were was a gentle reminder of how nobility is defined, in case the subject of the poem might deign to be taught the lesson.

In the *Life of Pope,* Dr. Johnson applauds Pope's wisdom or good fortune in avoiding merely occasional or commendatory verses. The privilege to select his own topics and publish in his own good time was never enjoyed by Dryden. He could and did, however, choose among occasions and especially among dedicatees for his poems, and if we look over his work as a whole we discover, not only a recurrent pattern of themes, but a remarkably consistent series of addresses to the same kinds of people for the same purposes, from 1649 to 1700. Today these addresses are notorious for extravagant flattery—because, of all the dedications written in the latter half of the seventeenth century, only Dryden's are read today; the dedications of others (Thomas Shadwell for example) are more flattering, not less. Almost none of Dryden's *encomia* lacks its own special mission, either literary or political—usually both. The normal function of one of his dedications, in fact, is to give exact direction to the play or poem that follows, and to zero it in, so to speak, on the target at which he aimed.

The rules he accepts for a dedication or a commendatory poem are the same ones a portrait painter would observe. The purpose is to make the most of the sitter's good points, and to subordinate his less attractive features, while still preserving a likeness and furnishing a pleasing example of the painter's art. The poet is at an advantage over the painter in some respects; he can be more selective, and he can praise a trait so emphatically as to suggest the absence of its complement. In the general "heightening" of a patron's portrait, some qualities will receive but passing mention, and others will be ignored; to the discriminating reader such neglect is a plain act of judgment, at times a severely critical one. The panegyrist will also show his art by avoiding praise where it only brings to mind a shortcoming known to the well-informed. If, however, he can keep an unfavorable quality in perspective—foreshorten it as a subordinate part of the character as a whole—the candid panegyrist will include it. Dryden obliquely directed the attention of the greatest in the land to their weaknesses and "blind sides." The self indulgence of Charles II, the obstinacy of his brother James, the slowness of the Earl of Clarendon, the intriguing of Castlemaine, the arbitrary egotism of the Earl of Rochester: these characteristics, so prominent in the judgment of posterity, are strongly suggested in the midst of Dryden's compliments. As for compliments, where they were bestowed they were merited: the Duke and Duchess of Monmouth really were a beautiful couple, he physically brave and she generous and good; the Duke of Newcastle and the Earl of Dorset knew and loved verse and were magnanimous patrons of poets; Sir Thomas Clifford was an honest treasurer and an upright man; the Early of Danby was a politician capable of executing the wise national policy Dryden sketched out to him. Even Princess Mary Beatrice d'Este, James Stuart's bride, when Dryden addressed the dedication to her that Johnson found so scandalous, was beautiful, innocent, and disarmingly young. The success of these dedications, it must be remembered, enabled Dryden to forgo attendance at Court, for which he felt himself totally unfitted. In addition, they enabled him to make points, in this public way, of importance to the republic of letters and the government of England.

For these reasons, a rather careful reading of Dryden's dedications to public figures furnishes an important share of the evidence that can still be drawn upon to give definite shape to our idea of his character, political attitudes, and feelings. This is particularly true because his prose takes a different tone according to the person he addresses, and here careful rhetorical analysis is called for.

While it is evident, for example, that Dryden did not adopt the tone and voice of a prophet in Israel to King Charles, it is equally true that he refrained from praising him lavishly in any particular during the rest of his life, except for one good quality that no one has denied: his "easiness," his peaceable disposition, which took the form of affability, readiness to forgive most injuries, and reluctance to deny a request. Charles's good behavior during the Great Fire of 1666, a noteworthy exception in his career, is allowed by the poet to speak for itself in *Annus Mirabilis* (stanzas 260–289). The prayer that the King is made to utter (263–270) is honestly written though in the vein of idealized heroic sentiment:

Thou, who has taught me to forgive the ill,
    And recompense, as friends, the good misled;
If mercy be a Precept of thy will,
    Return that mercy on thy Servant's head.

Or, if my heedless Youth has stept astray,
    Too soon forgetful of thy gracious hand:
On me alone thy just displeasure lay,
    But take thy judgments from this mourning Land.

                          (1053–1060)

In contrast, an earlier line, in which Charles regrets his inactivity abroad during the first five years of his reign, is shrewdly critical in its comparison with Cromwell: "He grieved the Land he freed should be oppress'd, / And he less for it then Usurpers do" (39–40).

Dryden's fundamental political attitude, as we have seen,

was the one that emerges from Shakespeare's English histories, the idea that domestic quiet needs to be balanced with action abroad if the nation is not to fall victim to internal dissension. He too saw France as the natural, inveterate opponent. The present danger, it was true, came from the Dutch, because they were directly contesting for the empire of the seas that was the English nation's claim by a kind of natural insular right. The Dutch, however, could be overrun at any time by the powerful armies of France—so Dryden thought—and therefore Louis XIV fostered Dutch gains at sea and welcomed English losses:

> See how he feeds th' *Iberian* with delays,
>   To render us his timely friendship vain;
> And, while his secret Soul on *Flanders* preys,
>   He rocks the Cradle of the Babe of *Spain.*
>
> Such deep designs of Empire does he lay
>   O're them whose cause he seems to take in hand:
> And, prudently, would make them Lords at Sea,
>   To whom with ease he can give Laws by Land.
>
> (29–36)

At the end of the *Coronation Ode*, Dryden had referred to the negotiations for Charles's betrothal, involving the Spanish Infanta and the Portuguese princess Catherine of Braganza, the latter of whom Charles eventually married. In conjunction with these negotiations, the fleet was put in readiness shortly before the coronation, and speculation arose as to its objective: either the Dutch East Indies or the Turks at Algiers were to be struck. The secret was disclosed to Pepys and the others on April 20, 1661—the fleet would sail for Algiers. Instead of a direct blow for empire, there would be a rather tame diversion to protect the bit of dynastic property at Tangier that Catherine's dowry would bring to the King. This inglorious and unheroic decision obviously had much to do with what Pepys recorded on April 3, that "the Dutch have sent the King a great present of money."

35

To see how disappointingly unheroic Charles's kingly
style was, especially to one who, like Dryden, hoped for a
change of character resembling that of scapegrace Prince
Hal into heroic Henry V, we need only run through
Pepys's entries from May 1660 to April 1661. On the one
hand, Charles is settled and loved by all; but, when he
freely talks of his misadventures after the Battle of Worces-
ter, he represents himself as less a hero than a picaro. In his
fondness for his dogs and for Barbara Palmer he shows
himself all too human and unheroic. His concern for sea
policy appears only as a dislike for the need of paying sailors
off with tickets, because he lacked current money; other-
wise, he is occupied with progress in building his yacht, the
Jenny (or *Jemmy*), which was in actual fact his only attempt
to outdo the Dutch.[5] He shows a great respect for the Bible
and touches with gravity for the King's Evil; but his efforts
to make peace between the Episcopalians and the Dissenters
are unpromising. He is known to wish for the pardon of all
the regicides; but the hangings, drawings, and quarterings
still occur, and new rebels are caught and butchered on the
scaffold after the failure of Venner's "great plot." It is al-
ready evident that Charles, with his forgiving nature, will
not lack for culprits to forgive. Factions are alive in Parlia-
ment and the Church, just as in Charles I's time, and in the
fleet, too, the officers are full of mutual jealousies. Above all
Charles's delight in spending money is plain. Pepys records
his joy at the gold coins sent to him by Parliament early in
1660, and the lavishness of the coronation parade in 1661,
so great that it tired the eyes and satiated the imagination.
Ominously, Parliament was already balking at further sup-

[5] On 13 Aug. 62 Pepys saw at Lambeth "The little pleasure boat in
building by the King, my Lord Brunkard, and the virtuosoes of the
town, according to new lines, which Mr. Pett cries up mightily, but
how it will prove we shall soon see." On September 5, Pepys records
with satisfaction, the little Dutch yacht *Bezan* beat the virtuosoes' craft
by "above three miles." This was perhaps the first attempt at building
a yacht by the rules instead of "by guess and by gosh." See *Mariner's
Mirror*, 5 (1919), 108–123.

plies of money. Although neither Pepys nor anyone else realized it, the financial ineptitude of the King's old ministers had launched his reign with a built-in deficit of over £200,000 a year, which he never did make up except by foreign subsidies.[6]

Thus, in matters of war as well as peace, foreign as well as domestic, a pattern is established that will hold good for the twenty-five years of Charles's reign: At home, indulgence and good will to all, hampered and sometimes frustrated by faction and the demands of the gentry and the established Church; abroad, peace or war, for present money and not to advance a consistent policy of national expansion and enterprise. This latter was what Dryden feared was in danger when he wrote the final lines of the *Coronation Ode*, wherein Charles weighs his choice of a Spanish or a Portuguese alliance:

Choose only, (Sir), that so they [the English] may possesse
With their own peace their Childrens happinesse.

Charles chose neither the incense of the Indies nor the gold of Spanish America, to use Dryden's terms, but cash in hand; of heroic actions that would lay the foundation for the prosperity of future generations he gave no sign.

The preceding analysis of Dryden's poetic response to the political events of 1649, 1658, and 1660–1661 indicates that his feelings were strong, though somewhat mixed. The behavior of the regicides and the Rump Parliament repelled him to a degree that seems far to exceed the satisfaction he took in the "heroic virtue" Cromwell displayed while ruling the nation. There is ample evidence to show that what tipped the balance definitely against the Commonwealth in his mind was the grim inhumanity of its life style. He felt that what we call the Interregnum had robbed him of his youth—he was twelve when the Civil War began and thirty

[6] D. T. Witcombe, *Charles II and the Cavalier House of Commons* (Manchester, Eng., 1966), p. 2.

at the Restoration. His acquaintance with the men who set the public tone in London and Cambridge during those years, especially the clerics, seems to have filled him with a lifelong disgust. It appears much later in his repudiation of his own university, Cambridge, but it is present, clearly stated, in the opening lines of the poem of welcome to Charles, *Astræa Redux*:

> For his long absence Church and State did groan;
> Madness the Pulpit, Faction seiz'd the Throne:
> Experienc'd Age in deep despair was lost
> To see the Rebel thrive, the Loyal crost:
> Youth that with Joys had unacquainted been
> Envy'd gray hairs that once good days had seen:
> We thought our Sires, not with their own content,
> Had ere we came to age our Portion spent.
>
> (21–28)

A little reflection makes one realize that these lines, seemingly so abstract and general, describe the almost total loss of the most important part, by far, of a poet's lifetime. Dryden is unique among poets in that there is almost nothing that counts of his, which was written before he passed the age of thirty. His youth was unacquainted with joy. It is a pity, on our side, that we are so unacquainted with Dryden's youth. The only expression we have of it, his valentine letter to his cousin Honor, is cheerful, witty, and already very self-possessed, indicating a temperament not only unsympathetic to the Puritan mood but capable of severe frustration by it. The "contumacy" for which he was punished at Trinity is one of only three bits of information about his four years at that most distinguished college, toward which, in *The Life of Plutarch*, he was so late and so chary in the expression of grateful feelings—he who was usually so voluble in thanks. The sense of frustration and waste brings with it the first appearance of one of Dryden's obsessive images:

We thought our Sires, not with their own content,
Had ere we came to age our Portion spent.

Later, in *Of Dramatic Poesy*, he applied this image to the exhaustion of the resources of dramatic poetry in the course of the great "Last Age" of Shakespeare, Jonson, and Beaumont and Fletcher. In poetry and politics he saw himself and his generation as the heirs to a bankrupt estate, coming of age not to be emancipated but rather to be faced with the hard fate of bringing under cultivation ground either exhausted or grown wild. The image, nevertheless, is one that expresses a feeling for continuity; along with the sense of being cut off and thrown resourceless into a new age, there is the clear acknowledgment of a lineage extending back into the past. In *Of Dramatic Poesy*, also, he expressed his strong feeling of waste during the Commonwealth years; Neander speaks of "the fury of a civil war, and power for twenty years together abandoned to a barbarous race of men, enemies of all good learning," which "had buried the Muses under the ruins of monarchy," and he terms the return of Charles, simply, "the restoration of our happiness."[7]

It was Dryden's habit, then, to view his productivity as a poet, and indeed his own sense of fulfillment and happiness, in conjunction with the political fortunes of his country, and in particular with the mode of life of the men who wielded power over it. In keeping with the spirit of the time in the arts (if not in politics), he wished to see these men as heroes. For one thing, he saw the hero and the poet as reciprocal figures, one with a mutual interest in the other. The hero needed the poet to inspire him to deeds of virtue, and to celebrate them when performed; and the poet needed the hero as a living counterpart of the epic figure he would project—a lens in which there could come to focus, life-size, those rays by which his myth would be cast on the screen of the past in grander proportions. Above all, the hero would be

[7] Watson, I, 76.

distinguished by a kind of natural affinity to the poet and affection for his song: *Carmen amat, qui carmine digna gerebit*—"That man is a lover of poetry, whose deeds are worthy of its song."

Unlike the grim and mean Commonwealth men, the hero would openly favor the poet and give him the means, as well as the subject matter, to celebrate worthy deeds in verse. This hope, above all, was what the Restoration brought to Dryden.

II. THE ADDRESSES TO COURT FIGURES

When a poet without sufficient means of support addressed the great in the latter seventeenth century, he may have been hoping for money, but hardly as a direct gift; his aim would be to gain or to preserve a lucrative "place" somewhere in the apparatus of government. Of Dryden's forty-odd works that carry addresses to living persons, all but a half-dozen are related to his needs as a breadwinner. This fact is well known, even notorious, and the adjective that springs automatically to the pens of commentators when they refer to these dedications is "fulsome," if not something even more condemnatory. Now fulsomeness is a quality that Dryden's style and entire manner of composition positively excludes, along with the more commended qualities of ambiguity and multiplicity of reference. The dedications might be venal, meretricious, or mendacious, but they are never fulsome. If we study the whole list of dedicatees it becomes obvious, to begin with, that they were a picked lot. The poet exercised a clear line of choice in applying for patronage; he considered not only the power of the patron to reward him, but also the things the patron stood for in the public view. Sometimes the written dedication was an exploration of the possible ways in which the patron's public image might be developed, as in the exhortation to a heroic career in arms with which he conveyed

Tyrannic Love to the young Duke of Monmouth. All the dedications, though, being panegyric in nature, tended to project, into the realm of the ideal, qualities that the persons truly needed for their station in life, whether or not they possessed them adequately in fact. Repetition on this point is a simple necessity if justice is to be done. It is truly remarkable, once one is tuned in to Dryden's dedicatory manner, to note the wide range and sharp discrimination of his praise, and especially to recognize the ways in which he can suggest not only need for improvement, but even positive blame. Operating in the single dimension of praise, he nevertheless sets up an axis of more and less praise (and, of course, significant omission) that gives to his praise a surprising weight of critical evaluation.

This axis of discriminating praise is discernible in the very first of Dryden's addresses to a man chosen from the ranks of the great. He offered Edward Hyde, Earl of Clarendon, as a New Year's gift in 1662, the fairly long poem *To My Lord Chancellor*. Clarendon was the principal minister of Charles's regime, as he had been chief adviser to the young King in exile. He was, of course, in an excellent position to secure preferment for anyone he favored, and from this point of view it would have been only natural for an ambitious and now not so very young poet to seek his notice. There were, however, other and equally important reasons why Dryden should choose him. For one, Clarendon had foregathered with the poets of Ben Jonson's circle as a young man and still retained an interest in letters. His own *History*, partly written by that time, is one of the two or three best in English. Dryden was fond of history from childhood, as he himself tells us, and as is evident from the wealth of reference to historical figures in his early poems. Whether or not this mutual interest was known to one another at the time, Dryden would certainly have been aware of Clarendon's reverence for the English past and its traditions. From a strictly political point of view, the Chancellor had always stood out against the Francophiles in Charles's Court (the Louvrians, they were called while the King was in exile).[8] They wanted to use the military aid of Louis in reconquering England. Dryden's lifelong anti-French attitude, asserted already more than once, agreed with Clarendon's.

In *To My Lord Chancellor*, the poet rather confidently brushes aside the crowd of other New Year's suitors to present the case for all the Muses, who had gone (he says) into exile with Charles. This is the first time Dryden assumed the right to speak for the rest of the poets; the stance seemed to come naturally to him. After this, the Chancellor's present service to Charles II and the nation is imaged in a way that shows the King's willingness to have someone else do the hard work of government:

> In you his sleep still wakes; his pleasures find
> Their share of bus'nesse in your lab'ring mind.
>
> (45–46)

As evidence, perhaps, of his rather startling statement (37) that the virtues of Charles and Clarendon agree, Dryden praises the Chancellor for sharing the quality of mercy with the Stuarts, father and son. He seems (in the unusually allusive and sometimes recondite language of this poem) to be suggesting a distinction between the processes of law in public and in private cases:

> Justice that sits and frowns where publick Laws
> Exclude soft mercy from a private cause,
> In your Tribunal most her self does please;
> There only smiles because she lives at ease. . . .
>
> (49–52)

The suggestion is that Clarendon manages his Court of Chancery with an easy directness that mitigates its notorious

---

[8] The "Anglican Constitutionalists," led by Hyde and Ormond, "who looked to a national uprising," were abandoned when Charles II embarked on his Scottish adventure in 1650. J. P. Kenyon, *The Stuarts* (London, 1958), p. 112.

formalities. What Dryden probably alludes to in these lines is the domestic nature of Chancery business, where the parties are frequently related to each other and are better off for the interposition of a fair-minded, even if somewhat willful, authority. In particular, he may well be referring to Clarendon's good offices in a case that very materially concerned himself.

On the evidence of a poem Dryden wrote in 1660 we know that he was friendly with Sir Robert Howard, the sixth son of the Earl of Berkshire; there is other evidence to show that he and Sir Robert shared lodgings in London during the first years of the Restoration. At the end of 1663, Dryden married Sir Robert's sister, the Lady Elizabeth Howard. The marriage has always puzzled scholars to a certain extent, for the poet (though of good gentry stock) was quite poor to be marrying the eldest daughter of an earl. Indeed, the Earl himself was quite poor, having been forced to compound for his estates because of his loyalty to the King during the Interregnum; also, he was old and financially erratic. The suggestion has been made that Lady Elizabeth, who was about twenty-five when she married, was a somewhat tarnished prize, because of her age and some shreds of gossip connecting her with the Earl of Chesterfield in 1658.

Amid this speculation there is one indubitable fact that has never been presented until now, although it is of the highest authority. There is a famous series of papers exchanged between Charles II and his Chancellor at meetings of the Privy Council, consisting mainly of brief suggestions and reminders from Clarendon, along with the King's responses, written in the rather cramped and aging hand of the one and the clear, running style of the other. During January, 1662 (that is, in the month after receiving Dryden's New Year's poem, since January 1 rather than March 25 was the day for such gifts), Clarendon passed this note to Charles: "Indeede you are to blame, that you have not yett giuen your warrant to my Ld. Barkeshyre. I pray do not defere it." Underneath is the King's reply: "Is it not to make his

warrant of one thousand a yeare to continue for 11 yeares."
The reminder was effective; on 27 February 1662 warrants
were issued for payment of £8,000 to the Earl of Berkshire, by
£1,000 a year, and of £3,000 to his daughter Dame Elizabeth
"in the same way." The hardships of suitors at King Charles's
Court are tellingly illustrated, however, by the further fact
that Dame Elizabeth's £3,000 did not begin to be paid until
1666. The Earl mortgaged his own £8,000 in 1662. The sig-
nificance of the King's note is that it gives the manner of
payment in yearly installments, and also the total of £11,000.
Lady Elizabeth presumably was entitled to her £3,000, proba-
bly as a marriage portion, for some time before the 1663 mar-
riage, so that it is unnecessary to speculate that the Earl of
Berkshire assigned her the sum as a dowry after being unable
to get her off his hands.[9]

The *Notes* further illustrate the irony and bitternesses of
a courtier's life, especially under Charles II. Sometime in
July, 1662, Clarendon passed to Charles the following sug-
gestion: "take my Ld Berkeshyre aside, and perswade him,
in reguarde of his Age and infirmity, to be contented to be
left out" in the commission of the Middlesex Militia. The
King adroitly replied: "you are my Ladyes greate fauorite
and will be the fittest person to perswade my Ld Barkesheere
to so reasonable a thing, it would looke from me as a com-
mande."[10]

It was in such commissionerships, of course, that the Earl
might have hoped to make up some of the losses his loyalty
had brought upon him. We see him here being rather gulled,
intentionally or not, by his wife's friend Clarendon. His good
will secured by a promise of restitution long delayed and
perhaps never carried out, the Earl is to be cajoled into giving
up a post that might have brought him ready money. Of

[9] See W. D. Macray, ed., *Notes . . . Between Charles II and the
Earl of Clarendon* (London: Roxburghe Club, 1896), p. 54 and note;
Charles E. Ward, *The Life of John Dryden* (Chapel Hill, N.C., 1961),
pp. 35, 41–42, and 341. The latter will be cited as "Ward."
[10] Macray, p. 70.

course, the national security gained, for the Earl was old and incompetent.

It tells us something about Dryden and his attitude to the Court that, having married an heiress with £3,000 of her own money in 1663, he should have to wait until 1669 to collect the sum (minus £500) from the Royal Treasury. He spent the intervening years ungrudgingly, enjoying a long period of study at his father-in-law's country estate of Charlton in Wiltshire, and earning his own way the rest of the time by his writing for the theatre. It is informative, also, to reflect upon the Earl's "ladye," whose "greate fauorite" Charles perceived Clarendon to be, and who was Dryden's mother-in-law. As we shall soon see, Dryden never lacked for success among women of a certain type—which may be classified for present purposes simply by mentioning a few of its members: Anne Hyde, Clarendon's daughter; Anne Scott, Duchess of Monmouth; Mrs. John Evelyn. (The first two were dedicatees, the last warm in her praise of *The Conquest of Granada*.) These women were lovers of literature; they knew the world; their personal lives were irreproachable; of a somewhat devout cast despite their proximity to a scandalous Court, they were sincerely religious. I am not sure about the Countess of Berkshire's literary tastes, but otherwise she fits very well into the group that Dryden knew how to please. In this largely feminine circle Clarendon moved with ease and authority, as the King saw. So, apparently, did Dryden. Dryden's audience, therefore, contained some members who really cared about such heroic virtues as chastity and honor; but it was decidedly ambivalent as to the heroic virtue of loyalty to one's lord, for to many of them that lord was a self-indulgent ingrate.

It is ironical that the Old Cavaliers should have blamed the Chancellor for their continued ill treatment, for (as Witcomb has shown) he understood them and shared their most deep-seated convictions, not to say prejudices. Yet he was incapable of understanding all-important phases of government in the new age, especially finance. The Old Cavaliers now wanted

45

money and places in government where money was to be made. Clarendon had no ideas as to how they might be satisfied, in practice, any more than did his best friend, the old Earl of Southampton, who was Lord Treasurer. That he could move the King to approve a warrant, but could not manage to have a penny of it paid, is a good measure of the limitations of Clarendon's power. In *To My Lord Chancellor*, Dryden seems to have misunderstood or misrepresented the then state of affairs. He seems to have his eye on two things only: the end of faction at home and continued expansion abroad. Once again he applauds a policy of indulgence but couples it with a warning:

> Heav'n would your Royal Master should exceed
> Most in that Vertue which we most did need,
> And his mild Father (who too late did find
> All mercy vain but what with pow'r was joyn'd,)
> His fatal goodnesse left to fitter times,
> Not to increase but to absolve our crimes. . . .
>
> (55–60)

To say that England needed to earn the forgiveness of Charles II was to utter an anachronism, even in early 1662. Dryden, however, wanted to make the perhaps overhopeful point that in the present, less barbarous times, indulgence will compose faction and thus put an undivided nation behind the King. However, to preserve his people's loyalty, the poet says once again, the Crown must enhance its own glory: and that is the Chancellor's principal responsibility:

> By you our Monarch does that fame assure
> Which Kings must have or cannot live secure:
> For prosp'rous Princes gain their Subjects heart,
> Who love that praise in which themselves have part. . . .
>
> (79–82)

A prosperous prince, one might add, would be able to share more than mere praise with his people. Dryden suggests that peace can be a time of labor and pains no less than war: that, therefore, it might prosper a people. Yet he can go no further with this suggestion than to present a series of cosmological and Arcadian images, all tending to show that Clarendon is most active when he seems most at rest. Addressed to an elder statesman who tended to fall asleep during meetings of the King's Council, this might have been discreet correction. It might have been, again, the truthful effort of a poet who was unwilling to desert reality, although he still hoped for the best.

Looking back with hindsight and the knowledge of Clarendon's fall six years later, we can read two warnings in this praise: that the Lord Chancellor was allowing too much credit to himself instead of imputing it to the King, and taking too much into his own hands:

> While emp'ric politicians use deceit,
> Hide what they give, and cure but by a cheat;
> You boldly show that skill which they pretend,
> And work by means as noble as your end;
> Which should you veil, we might unwind the clue,
> As men do nature, till we came to you.
>
> (67–72)

A very alert chief minister would conclude from these lines that, if men were going to give him credit anyhow, perhaps he should imitate nature and do things the quiet, indirect way.

When the poet later says that fortune's wheel has stopped turning for the Chancellor, who has accumulated over the years so much merit by his faithful service to Charles and his royal father that his place is secure beyond the reach of envy, he states what anyone knows to be incredible. Yet this was exactly what Clarendon seemed to believe, to his own destruction. Again the poet may be presenting a warning to Clarendon, in hyperbolical lines that form an excellent definition of hubris; perhaps he felt other, less farfetched admonitions would be doomed from the start with the extraordinarily self-righteous old minister, who could never forget he had been a fatherly presence, guide, and mentor to youthful royalty.

Dryden's first prose address came in 1664, with the printing of his more-or-less heroic play *The Rival Ladies*. In it his praise of the Earl of Orrery must appear reasonable, for Orrery's play *The General*, circulated in MS as a stimulus to the production of rhymed verse drama, was one of the originals during the formative stage of the new genre, along with Davenant's *Siege of Rhodes*, Tuke's *Adventures of Five Hours*, and the Dryden-Howard *Indian Queen*. Here, for the first time in prose, we can see Dryden accounting for his interest in the literary heroic. His attitude is fundamentally that of the great critical tradition of sixteenth-century Italy as it appears in J. C. Scaliger and Tasso. The poet is a second creator, after the Almighty Poet. In his poetic cosmos, Orrery has fortune at his command, "with which wisdom does often unsuccessfully struggle in the world" (Watson, I, 4). That is, in the world of politics—the actual world. The Earl of Orrery as poet could creatively fashion his heroes and control their behavior at his leisure. Though skillful as a practicing politician, he must find his Irish subjects less manageable than his poetic creatures. Poetry, then, offers a world freed from the bondage of chance and human vagary and is capable of presenting examples of the ideal and the heroic. Yet Dryden in his reference to the theatre, makes it clear that he personally does not regard drama as an ideally appropriate medium for such poetry. Not only is *The Rival Ladies* disgusting to him because it is not close to the ideal, but "I am apt," he says, "to conclude our best plays are scarcely so. For the stage being the representation of the world, and the actions in it, how can it be imagined that the picture of human life can be more exact than life itself is?" It is interesting to see that here, and in several other characteristic statements, Dryden quite belies the generalization about neoclassical critics that Ronald S. Crane applied to him, that they regarded the genres of their plays as autonomous fabrications determined only by the rules of the stage.[11] From other comments by Dryden we know that his first choice of medium was not the drama but the epic or heroic poem. His statement to Orrery shows him struggling against, but not refusing, the demand for a necessary minimum of reality—specifically, political reality—even in the most ideal of heroic plays. This again is in accord with the Renaissance critical tradition, which set aside a special function of importance for the dramatic poet: the instruction of princes.

For Dryden's fullest presentation of a king as ideal hero, we can turn to his first serious play, *The Indian Queen* (January 1664).[12] Its hero, Montezuma, is a combination of Sir Percival in medieval romance, Achilles in Greek epic, and the Platonic lover of *précieux* court novels. He does not begin as an ideal hero; he must learn perfection from his rival and friend Acacis and his beloved mistress, Orazia. Yet he does learn the lessons of obedience, pity, and self-sacrifice, and thereby merits an eternity of happiness and love. The death of Acacis, however, indicates that the most perfect merit does not guarantee a this-worldly reward; as Dryden had complained, ill fortune plays too big a role in life to be omitted from its reflection in the theatre. It is no accident that the ideal sides of his portraits of living political figures all find their counterparts in Montezuma. Like King Charles's, the Indian king's youth was spent in harsh and insecure exile

---

[11] "When neoclassical critics like Dryden talked about comedy and the comic or tragedy and the tragic, they had in mind forms and qualities which owed their existence to the contrivances of poets rather than to the nature of things or of the human mind. . . ." R. S. Crane, "The Varieties of Dramatic Criticism," *Carleton Drama Review*, 1 (1956), repr. *Context and Craft of Drama*, ed. Robert W. Corrigan and James L. Rosenberg (San Francisco, 1966), p. 204.

[12] My theory is that Dryden "wrote" practically all of *The Indian Queen*, making some use of a prose plot outline contributed by Sir Robert Howard, as will be explained. For my argument here, it would suffice that he merely assented to the ethos, which, even though it is highly idealized, is applicable to political reality. A character such as Acacis (cf. Acacia, or "Innocence" in *Albion and Albanius*) is idealized by opposition to the greater "reality" of the European ones, especially the more sinister figures.

—first in a cave, where his foster father taught him "the noble thirst of fame," and then at the Peruvian court. In the recognition scene the hero first learns he is "the issue of our murthered King" (v. i. 281). It is as if Dryden used the poet's prerogative to make fictionally real what he could only suggest in his *Astræa Redux*, the advantages of a royal education deprived of its usual security, luxury, and flattery. "Father" Garrucca plays the role of Chiron to the young Achilles of Montezuma; he initiates him into the honorable life of action that is the hero's destiny. At first, Montezuma, like Achilles, is too concerned for his kudos (note that he even makes use of the heroic stanza!):

> The Gods that in my fortunes were unkinde,
> Gave me not Scepters, nor such gilded things;
> But whilst I wanted Crowns, inlarg'd my minde
> To despise Scepters, and dispose of Kings.
>
> (II. i. 25–28)

The play goes on, however, to show the young hero learning a higher form of courage from Orazia and Acacis (a manly friend conscious of personal honor but even more considerate of the good of others). This is an early instance of the movement in the hero from individualism to social responsibility, to which attention has been called by Arthur C. Kirsch in the later heroic plays.

The virtues of the hero-king are stated more unambiguously in *The Indian Queen* than they were ever to be stated again. Montezuma is energetic, unyielding in defeat and generous in victory, faithful to his friends, and devoted to his cause. He hates cruelty and loves to forgive. Yet, most ideal trait of all (and one never to reappear), he is unselfish; he learns to be content with expecting a reward in another existence, where eternity

> Has room enough for both, there's no desire,
> Where to enjoy is only to admire:
> There we'll meet friends, when this short storm is past.
>
> (v. i. 164–167)

These are the words of the perfect friend, Acacis. They mingle the Platonic and the Christian heaven in a poetic one where desire is appeased and, hungry no more, becomes unselfish love—a region Dryden's heroic vision never touched again. It was too ideal, too lacking in the kind of actual reference to life that Dryden felt the theatre demanded. He knew that to exist in the real world of Stuart politics, even heroes had to mind their "interest."

Otherwise, political realities are adverted to in ways that Dryden was to use throughout his career. In the prologue, there is a remonstrance that the poet was to make to his countrymen more than once:

> Why should men quarrel here, where all possess
> As much as they can hope for by success?

$$(7\text{--}8)$$

The idea of rebellion, though the most terrible political possibility of all, is prominently dealt with. (Rebellion and civil war constitute the "archetypal" extreme of evil all through the Restoration, even in *Paradise Lost*. Probably that is why plays—including heroic plays—that dealt with this theme could be taken seriously, even tragically, by contemporaries. Living in much greater *political* security, we find the subject rather thin today.) Montezuma rebels against the Peruvian king—it is his hamartia—and immediately tries to undo his crime. The suggestion seems to be that a feeling of rivalry with kings is a natural enough disposition in a hero, though tragically wrong, and that (almost as if it were original sin) it requires universal acknowledgment, expiation, and forgiveness: all of which in turn requires sensitivity of feeling and good will.

There is an un-Calvinist predominance of mercy over justice in Dryden's ethos, as if he recognized the unconverted as a large majority, of whom the hero was typical, who might better be won over by royal lovingkindness than by force. For this reason, at all times he favored Toleration, in opposition to the dominant attitude in Parliament that defeated Charles in five separate struggles during 1660, 1662, 1664, 1668, and 1673. The repentant Montezuma offers to die as a surrogate for all rebels:

> 'Tis I, that wrought these mischiefs, ought to fall
> A just and willing sacrifice for all.
>
> (v. i. 37–38)

His guiltless friend Acacis actually does immolate himself to redeem the guilt of the hero. If the ethos of the play stresses mercy, its pathos centers in the sacrifice of self for love and loyalty.

The paradigm of heroism was still visible, if somewhat blurred, in the sequel, *The Indian Emperor* (c. April, 1665). Although Montezuma had become an old emperor, more pathetic than heroic, Cortez is active, noble, and unselfish enough. Yet there is such an irruption of the secular world as to indicate a different, far less naive approach by the poet to his, and its, problems. Dryden had become more familiar with the Court and its ways, and evidently felt impelled to represent "the world, and the actions in it" by showing self-interest in its true dimensions, and by setting other-worldly religious assurances satirically against a background of this-worldly clerical chicanery and intolerance.

One of the poet's earliest opportunities to become acquainted at first hand with the Court came, no doubt, when the Countess of Castlemaine persuaded her lover King Charles to order a Whitehall performance of Dryden's first play, *The Wild Gallant*. He thanked "the Lady" in a poem of fifty-six lines that alludes directly to her position of power and the restrained use she was then making of it in Court intrigues:

> Your pow'r you never use but for defence,
> To guard your own, or others Innocence.
> Your Foes are such as they, not you, have made;
> And Virtue may repel, though not invade.
>
> (29–32)

Lest this seem a damning instance of falsehood and flattery, compare the character of Castlemaine as it was given by her old enemy Clarendon: "The lady, who had never declined in favour, was now greater in power than ever: she was with child again. . . . She did not yet presume to interpose in any other business, than in giving all the imaginable countenance she could to those who desired to depend upon her, and, in their right as well as her own, in depressing the credit of those who she knew wished hers much less than it was; but in this last argument she was hitherto wary, and took only such opportunities as were offered, without going out of her way to find them."[13] Dryden's four lines would have been even more unexceptionable when he wrote them, in 1663 (Clarendon referred to 1666). They have, clearly, the projective purpose of singling out a good quality and amplifying it so as to suggest to the Lady the opportunity and advantage of living up to an attractive image of herself. The important point, however, is that Dryden could easily have stayed away from dynamic moral issues and confined himself to the safe topics of Castlemaine's ancestry and beauty. That he took the risk shows his inveterate will to teach, even in this case where Horace himself might have lacked the aplomb to try.

He probably wished to cement the favor of the Hydes with his next public poem, *Verses to Her Highness the Duchess*, addressed to Anne Hyde. Her spouse, James Stuart, Duke of York, was already (in 1665) the acknowledged Successor to the throne, and what was then particularly important to Dryden was that James seemed to be the possible hero he had not found in Charles or Clarendon. This poem is the first hint of an allegiance to James Stuart that lasted until Dryden's death and was continued by his three sons. In this rather simple copy of verses the poet tells the Princess how honorable she has been to send her beloved hero off to the Dutch War; as for the Duke,

---

[13] Edward Hyde, Earl of Clarendon, *Life* (Oxford, 1827), III, 61.

'twas for him much easier to subdue
Those foes he fought with, then to part from you.
That glorious day, which two such Navies saw,
As each, unmatch'd, might to the world give Law,
Neptune, yet doubtful whom he should obey,
Held to them both the Trident of the Sea:
The winds were hush'd, the waves in ranks were cast,
As awfully as when God's people past:
Those, yet uncertain on whose sails to blow,
These, where the wealth of Nations ought to flow.

(11–20)

Dryden now had what he wanted: as an Englishman, he had found an active asserter of the nation's power at sea; as poet, a subject for the kind of verse he most wished to write, an epic or heroic poem.

James Stuart figures again, briefly but heroically, in *Annus Mirabilis* (xix):

Victorious *York* did, first, with fam'd success,
    To his known valour make the *Dutch* give place:
Thus Heav'n our Monarch's fortune did confess,
    Beginning conquest from his Royal Race.

As for Charles II, he is described rather tamely as the peaceful counterbalance to a martial people; he is much concerned at the vast cost of the naval war, and is persuaded to give battle only by the hope of eventual profit:

He, first, survey'd the charge with careful eyes,
    Which none but mighty Monarchs could maintain;
Yet judg'd, like vapours that from Limbecks rise,
    It would in richer showers descend again.

(49–52)

True as this picture was, and important, it was not nearly heroic enough to qualify Charles as the Agamemnon of an epic.

The picture of Dryden presented in the foregoing pages requires a summing up and clarification. The most striking thing in it is the contrast between his insistence upon the poetically ideal and his venturesomeness in reminding the great of their more practical obligations. Another contrast arises out of his conception of the relationship of past and present. He did not so much associate the heroic ideal with the past as he insisted on asking of his own age how well it succeeded in adopting the hero's stance. His primary sense of the greatness of the "Last Age" was, as suited his own dominant commitment, literary. It was the age before the Civil War ruined arts and manners, the age of Jonson and Donne and above all Shakespeare—to him the hero of all heroes. Men who were insufferable old dotards to a totally modern spirit such as Buckingham were to Dryden the revered companions of genius.

This was his view of Clarendon, and not without reason. In a remarkable letter to Pepys, John Evelyn recalled how the Chancellor had adorned his "stately palace (since demolished) . . . with the pictures of as many of our famous countrymen as he could purchase or procure . . . especially of his [Lordship's] time & acquaintance, & of diuers before it. There were at full length, and as I doubt not but you well remember to haue seene, the greate Duke of Buckingham, the brave Sr Horace & Francis Vere, Sr Walt. Raleigh, Sr Phil. Sidney, the greate Earle of Leicester, Treasurer Buckhurst, Burleigh, Walsingham, Cecil, Ld Chanr Bacon, Elsmere, & I think all the late Chancelors & graue Judges in the reignes of Q. Elizabeth & her successors, James & Charles the First." He goes on to name, among many others, the Duke of Newcastle, "the brave Montrosse,"[14] Mr. Hales of Eton, Dr. Donne, and "what was most agreeable to his Ls general humor, old Chaucer, Shakespeare, Beaumont &

---

[14] Montrose was betrayed in the course of Charles II's Scottish adventure, which Clarendon, as an "Anglican Constitutionalist," had disapproved because it involved invasion of England by a foreign force.

Fletcher, who were both in one piece, Spencer, Mr. Waller, Cowley, Hudibras, which last he plac'd in the roome where he vs'd to eate & dine in publiq."[15] Evelyn went on to regret the Chancellor's death in exile, "in the displeasure of his Majesty & others who envied his rise and fortune. . . . The buffoons, parasites, pimps, & concubines, who supplanted him at Court, came to nothing not long after, and were as little pitied . . . whilst what euer my Ld Chancelrs skill, whether in law or politics, the offices of State & Justice were filled with men of old English honor & probitie; less open bribery & ostentation; there was at least something of more gravity and forme kept (things, however railled at, necessary in Courts): magnificence & antient hospitalitie in his Maties houses, more agreeable to the genius of this nation than the open & avowed luxurie & prophaneness which succeeded, a la mode de France, to which this favorite was a declared enemy, upon my certaine knowledge." Evelyn wrote this letter in 1689. His tone of distorted and habitually censorious recollection does not negate the genuineness of the distinction he makes between Clarendon's style and that of his supplanter, the second Duke of Buckingham. Clarendon's was dignified, sober, and stately; by contrast Buckingham's was mad.

It is also clear from Evelyn's letter that the heroic, with its cult of the past and of the traditional virtues, its love of "gravity and form," "magnificence and ancient hospitality," was much more in keeping with the sober than with the mad style. The heroic was, indeed, an attempted continuation of the former age. Dryden took his stand upon the heroic as a young beginner in 1649, maintained it as long as he could, and came back to it in his old age. We know that he was mistaken in thinking that he could write an epic that would reflect the characters and deeds of his English contemporaries. Milton, who did publish an epic when Dryden's aspirations were at their height, was effectively isolated from, and indeed antagonistic to the age his younger

---

[15] Spingarn, II, 320–321.

admirer hoped to celebrate. It was an unheroic time, and eventually Dryden was forced to admit it. During the early years of the Restoration, however, even a sober man, as the poet considered himself to be, could identify a number of legitimately heroic figures alive and active. There was, obviously, Milton himself, whom he knew intimately; heroically, he defied his blindness and the change of times to forge ahead with the kind of work that Dryden called "the noblest effort of the human soul." There were Dryden's two collaborators, Sir William Davenant, who had helped to preserve Milton's life when he was saved from execution as a regicide in 1660, and the Duke of Newcastle, tutor to both Charles II and Buckingham, who had held the North for the King and was still the model of a Cavalier. Both had been brave fighters and gallant gentlemen who had sacrificed themselves for their King and master. The Duke of Ormond (who, according to his biographer Carte, was an occasional dinner companion of Dryden's), was a hero of Homeric proportions. One of Yeats's "Butlers far back, / Half legendary men," he was viceroy of Ireland, steward of King Charles's Household, and had led not only armies but the Irish people. James Stuart, also, was a legitimate fighting hero, first for France under Turenne, and later as admiral against the Dutch, when he was and deserved to be "the nation's Darling." The Duke of Albermarle, a sturdy old campaigner by land and sea, had also fully deserved his meed of praise in *Annus Mirabilis*, as had captains such as Lawson, brave to the death. These were of the Last Age. When one reads the old editions of Dryden's poetry one sees the bookplates of sons and daughters of such figures of heroic legend. The legend of the haplessly heroic defense of the Stuarts was continued, we should not forget, in the Jacobite movement, in which many of the names of Dryden's friends and patrons keep appearing. It entered the stream of world literature with Dryden's editor Sir Walter Scott, in the legendary form of the most romantic of loyalties—undying loyalty to a lost cause.

With such men in his own eye, the heroic was personal and real to Dryden. The fact that he succeeded in delighting even the most cynical and unsober minds of his time with the heroic—occasionally, at least—was only made possible by his ability to conduct a series of dramaturgical and stylistic tours de force. Yet, although he eventually perceived the emptiness of the heroic as a victorious reality, he never viewed it as merely a poetic ideal. His theatrical success was one that required enormous artistic control to keep these two incompatibles from tearing apart. Even more, it required innovation: a vision of the heroic related to present reality by means of powerful and new feelings.

In the realm of political ideas a similar effort of control was necessary, though one requiring less strain, since Dryden was not working nearly so much against the grain of his own age in politics as in his commitment to the heroic. Politically, in fact, Dryden is often in advance of his audience, but leading them in a direction toward which they were already moving. They agreed with him that the Civil War and the Puritan Interregnum had been a national disaster. Their reaction to the Dutch in the Medway proved their sensitivity to national shame and glory. Their busy prosecution of commerce all over the world showed that they, too, wanted expansion. The really serious threat was dissension over religion and the nature of the royal power—two matters quite different in the abstract but inextricably tangled in the concrete reality of Stuart England. Dryden's stand was for a balanced government and religious toleration. His Montezuma on the rack is an emblem of the inhuman perversity that would use the constraining power of a civilized state to compel assent in religion. He kept saying, however, that for a whole people to be on good terms with each other their energies must be allowed to expand, and he called for active leaders to open up the world to their expansion.

CHAPTER TWO

THE CONTROVERSY WITH
SIR ROBERT HOWARD

IN ALL of his earlier political addresses one could, perhaps, fail to single out a clear-cut statement of allegiance on Dryden's part; one might argue that he was merely following a literary preference while feathering his own nest. In 1667 this situation changed radically. He was compelled to make a choice for or against the heroic in actual political life and not only in poetry.

In the political crisis of 1667 the atmosphere was fatal to heroes. The events of that spring and summer, when the Dutch not only swept the Channel but entered inland waters to capture, scuttle, or burn the best vessels in England's war fleet, must constitute the sorriest debacle in the history of Britain. It led Dryden and many other Englishmen to a taking of sides that proved to be as significant and lasting as any in Charles's reign, and set the stage for the great crisis of 1678–1682, which in turn was the seedbed of politics as we know it today.

That England was without defenses in 1667 was the fault of all concerned. The fault was Parliament's, for failing to grant enough money to pay off the openly mutinous sailors and put the fleet to sea; the King's, for failing to inspire confidence that he would make proper use of money if supplied; Clarendon's, for failing to understand naval matters, frustrating younger men, ignoring economic complexities, and needlessly antagonizing such potential troublemakers as Lady Castlemaine. Also, there had been the Great Plague and the Great Fire. As for the nobility and gentry of Great Britain, besides scheming, conspiring, and offering open violence on behalf of their various interests, many of them were allowing themselves to be governed by unpredictable personal rivalries and piques. England in the summer of 1667 was a political chaos.

The readiest remedy for chaos is a polarization. In this case, although there was no villain and certainly no hero, a scapegoat and a rescuer were supplied in the persons of the Earl of Clarendon and the Duke of Buckingham. George Villiers, son of the "great" Duke of Buckingham, had been brought up with King Charles II, and had a personal following among important opposition groups: rural gentry, the Dissenters, and the London populace, many of them Dissenters. His motives tended to be strongly personal; at that time he wished to injure two main rivals, Hyde the Chancellor and Hyde's friend James Butler, Duke of Ormond and Viceroy of Ireland. Against the former, Buckingham could count upon allies among ambitious members such as Sir Robert Howard, intent on showing how troublesome they could be until satisfied by a lucrative place in government. Against Chancellor Clarendon's friend Ormond, Buckingham found a widely popular measure in the so-called Irish Cattle Bill, which was aimed at keeping all the profit of trade in England by preventing encroachment on English trade "by the Jews, the French or any other foreigner,"[1] including of course the Irish. Buckingham's dislike of Ormond was intensified by the fact that the latter had two sons, of whom the elder, the Earl of Ossory, proved a consistently more successful rival for military glory, and the younger, the Earl of Arran, then actually stood to inherit the childless Buckingham's own estate.[2]

Buckingham's impact might have been negligible, had it not been for Charles II's peculiar style of shifting his royal favor from one minister to another in order to preserve freedom of action for himself. Under this regimen, Buckingham

---

[1] Dennis T. Witcombe, *Charles II and the Cavalier House of Commons, 1663–1674* (New York, 1966), pp. 11–12, 14, and notes.

[2] Winifred, Lady Burghclere, *The Life of James First Duke of Ormonde (1610–1688)* (London, 1912), II, 151. Lady Arran died in July, 1668, and the Butler family ceased to have this claim.

remained a threat to anyone who appeared to be making an important position for himself. Such a person was the Duke of York, who was hardly a political leader but rather an administrator, concerned almost exclusively with the Navy and with commercial expansion. New York had been captured and renamed for him recently; he was a principal figure in the Hudson's Bay, Africa, and East India Companies; and he had been admiral of the fleet at the great victory of Lowestoft in June, 1665. Though Lord High Admiral, his role as "the Nation's Darling" was untainted by the ill success of 1666 and the disgraces of 1667 because, once acknowledged as the Successor, he was kept out of those actions, and because it was well known that his advice in Navy matters had been disregarded. First-class men such as Sir William Coventry and Samuel Pepys worked comfortably under him and found him to be responsive to argument and new ideas, as well as very loyal in supporting his subordinates. One of the many differences between him and his brother Charles was his willingness to master administrative routine and detail, and another was his very rare habit of remembering meritorious people when he could do them some good, even though no one was nearby to speak for them.

James's good qualities, and especially his sense of loyalty, cost him dearly in 1667. Buckingham, who had been his enemy since the early 1650s when both were engaged in the campaigns between France and Spain, was able almost to ruin him by taking advantage of those very traits that the poet Dryden extolled as heroic virtues. When Clarendon was the universally acceptable scapegoat for the Dutch in the Medway, James refused to desert him. The Duke of York's loyalty to Clarendon was not merely for old times' sake, but was also a family matter, for he had contracted a highly imprudent marriage with Anne Hyde, the Chancellor's daughter, in 1660.

The official sacrifice of Clarendon went through two phases, which must be carefully distinguished. In the first, he was required to give up the Seal and Mace and retire from office. All courtesy was used by Charles at the start, but the Chancellor insisted upon justifying himself personally before the King. The notion that a leader of government was *ex officio* responsible for major failures and should be ready to step down was still far in the future. Clarendon was upset and confused by the recent deaths of his friend Southampton, the Lord Treasurer, and of his own wife. He felt his integrity was at stake and took a highly self-righteous stand of injured innocence. Further, he (or his daughter) got the Duke of York to support him with all of his influence at Court—"credit," as it was called. The result was most unfortunate, because King Charles had a very special reason for being unmovable in this one case, and the Chancellor's intransigence encouraged his enemies to go beyond his dismissal and work for his impeachment on charges of high treason. Their argument, evidently sincere, was that unless Clarendon were put out of the way permanently, he would regain power and would revenge himself upon all who had worked for his dismissal. The fact that he had York's backing told heavily in favor of the argument, for York was widely regarded as an implacable enemy. At this point, James was in an impossible position: if he supported his father-in-law, he further antagonized Charles and reinforced the claims of his own enemies; if he abandoned Clarendon he committed the fault he himself thought had cost Charles I his life and throne, failure to secure the trust of his followers by first trusting and supporting them.[3]

The second phase was the drive by Clarendon's enemies to impeach him in both houses of Parliament. In this phase, many who had supported his dismissal opposed his impeachment. Three who were typical were Sir William Coventry, Sir Thomas Clifford, and Andrew Marvell, opponents of Clarendon on almost every matter of policy, but incapable of the cynicism that would make him out a traitor. Buckingham led the fight against him in the Lords, with no great

[3] J. P. Kenyon, *The Stuarts* (London, 1958), p. 129.

success; in the Commons, however, things went badly for Clarendon, and in October of 1667 impeachment was moved on seventeen counts of high treason. No member was more active for his impeachment than Buckingham's right-hand man in the Commons, Sir Robert Howard.

The controlling factor in this second phase was the unusual tenacity of King Charles. Normally he might have felt old Ned Hyde had suffered enough, and Buckingham had triumphed sufficiently. However, Buckingham had persuaded Charles that under his management Parliament would grant him the supply of money the King needed. Buckingham had also helped to persuade him (if persuasion was necessary) that Hyde had been guilty of an unpardonable affront to Charles as a royal person; for the King evidently believed that the Chancellor had meddled in his affair with Frances Stewart by arranging that heroically beautiful and virtuous young lady's elopement with the Duke of Richmond. When it seemed to Clarendon that he would be tried for treason before a commission of the Lords handpicked by Buckingham and the King, he gave up hope and fled to Holland and France, having first obtained Charles's promise that his heirs would not suffer. As for the Duke of York, his credit at Court had been exhausted; had he not been out of action during the crucial two weeks with an attack of smallpox, things might have been still worse. For the next two years he had little influence.[4]

James's protection of his father-in-law had involved no swerving in his duty to the King. After arguing personally against dismissal and getting his friends to add their intercession, he had obeyed Charles's command that he himself inform Clarendon of his removal. Nevertheless, he had incurred his brother's grave displeasure. Personal loyalty, to a certain type of Court mentality that Charles evidently shared, extended beyond mere duty. Since James's personal loyalty

[4] Clayton Roberts, *The Growth of Responsible Government in Stuart England* (Cambridge, Eng., 1966), pp. 155–196. This is probably the best account of the parliamentary struggle.

was obviously divided, Charles let him feel the weight of his positive displeasure. The King was known to have very little affection for his brother at any time.

Buckingham was clever in taking advantage of James's fall from grace, as he had been clever in damaging the reputation of Clarendon. He was intimate with a considerable circle of wits, some noble amateurs like himself, others professional poets and writers, who helped to produce in 1667 a truly extraordinary outburst of lampoon, invective, and satire against the Chancellor, ranging all the way from scurrilous beastliness to brilliant wit and magnificent outrage. James Stuart, as the heir, was much less open to such treatment, but his wife, Anne Hyde, was continually attacked in the more noisome pieces. Buckingham helped diminish James's popularity among the Londoners, who would remember his victory at sea and his good behavior during the Great Fire, by going about the city streets shut off from his admirers in a coach surrounded by a bodyguard armed with guns, on the pretense that James had hired assassins to murder him for his protection of the Protestant cause. Buckingham also took up the intrigue, already a few years old, to supplant James with the Duke of Monmouth, Charles's favorite bastard, as Successor to the crown.

From the spring of 1667, Buckingham's right-hand man in Parliament and out of it had been Sir Robert Howard, Dryden's friend, protector, and brother-in-law. Yet while Sir Robert was leading the Commons in hunting down the Chancellor and his allies, Dryden was in the process of engaging himself to one after another of the Earl of Clarendon's old friends and relatives. After Edward Hyde himself in 1662 and his daughter Anne in 1665, Dryden addressed a dedication to Anne Hyde's friend and companion, the Duchess of Monmouth, and then allied himself to three lifelong friends of Hyde (Sir William Davenant, William Cavendish, Duke of Newcastle, and the Duke of Ormond). Finally, and for the rest of his life, he turned to the Duke of York and the group of younger politicians who continued to align themselves with the Successor, men such as Sir Thomas Clifford, Lawrence Hyde, and John Sheffield.

The breach of friendship between Dryden and Howard has been a mystery of literature for centuries. No one has been able to give a reason why their relationship, so close that they shared lodgings from 1660 until Dryden married Howard's sister in late 1663, and highly advantageous to Dryden (as he himself declared), was disrupted. The poet's deadly, contemptuous attack on Howard's literacy, intelligence, and reliability, in the "Defence of an Essay of Dramatic Poesy," reaches its climax of significance in Dryden's acid comment on Howard's claim he was too busy for poetry: "the corruption of a poet is the generation of a statesman." That Dryden should risk, not so much a duel, but a nasty family brawl, is certainly not merely the result of a dispute over the use of rhyme in stage plays. Rather it signals the throwing off by the poet publicly of a relationship and patronage he felt was no longer acceptable or even tolerable. His reasons, it can be shown, were the usual mixed human reasons: temperamental, moral, political, literary, financial. They involved Dryden's whole sensibility and sense of self, and for that reason it is worthwhile to study them by tracing out the full story.

One of Dryden's earliest extant poems is addressed to "My Honor'd Friend Sir Robert Howard, On his Excellent Poems" (1660). Like the other panegyrical addresses, this poem makes the best of its subject without altogether losing touch with reality. It requires the same sense of chiaroscuro as the others to be seen for what it is: a very generous tribute, from one who sees himself already as a professional poet, to an amateur versifier. It is full of friendly warmth and gratitude, but not lacking in critical perspective. The very first line (of 106) speaks of "music uninform'd by art." Sir Robert's happy effects might arise because "Either your art hides art" (19) or else because they are "fortune's work" (25), but even more likely because he has a good strong horse under him (his Pegasus) that can carry the added weight of such an untrained jockey. He is commended for his moral concern, by which

> We're both enrich'd and pleas'd, like them that woo
> At once a beauty and a fortune too.
>
> (43–44)

This couplet wittily suggests Sir Robert's remarkable skill as a fortune hunter. Imprisoned by the Commonwealth, he emerged well before the Restoration to become one of England's richest men through a series of patronage plums, wealthy marriages, and financial coups.[5] The most overtly prophetic expression in the poem, however, is a general one, which now has an ironic twist. No doubt it was in 1660 a not-yet-despairing instance of what has been called preceptive praise:[6]

> Of Morall Knowledge Poesie was Queen,
> And still she might, had wanton wits not been;
> Who like ill Guardians liv'd themselves at large,
> And not content with that, debauch'd their charge:
> Like some brave Captain, your successful Pen
> Restores the Exil'd to her Crown again;
> And gives us hope, that having seen the days
> When nothing flourish'd but Fanatique Bays,
> All will at length in this opinion rest,
> "A sober Prince's Government is best."
>
> (45–54)

Here, for the first time, is Dryden's obsessive image of the poet who finds himself bankrupt when he comes of age because the guardians of his estate have spent it all. His blame here is not for the giants—Shakespeare, Jonson, Beaumont, and Fletcher—to whom he refers in *Of Dramatic Poesy*, but rather for poets such as Cleveland and Sylvester, mis-

---

[5] Pepys, *Diary*, 8 Dec. 1666, says Howard had got £20,000 since the King came in.

[6] By Ruth Nevo, in her study of praise and satire in the Restoration, *The Dial of Virtue*, Princeton, 1963.

leaders of his own youth as a poet. These had wantoned with conceits in ways that Sir Robert's common-sense fancy would hardly find tempting.[7] The period of sectarian controversy that followed their excesses had also been painful. Another noteworthy point in these lines is the middle course Dryden takes between wantonness on the Cavalier side and fanaticism on the Puritan. In government, the golden mean is a sober prince.

Sir Robert was particularly skillful in finding his way through the jungle of Stuart finance, and it was partly due to him that the Drydens began to receive payments on Lady Elizabeth's £3000 in time to take up residence in London, once the great shortage of housing caused by the fire had abated somewhat. As we have seen, King Charles in 1662 remembered that Thomas, Earl of Berkshire, should receive a warrant of £1000 a year to continue for eleven years, and that separate warrants were issued on 27 February 1662 to the Earl for £8000 and to Lady Elizabeth for £3000 "by £1000 a year." Lady Elizabeth's £3000 was hers, and there was never any reason why her father should "assign" it as a sum to be deducted from his own £8000 (which, in fact, he immediately mortgaged).

This mistake arose from an ambiguity in the meaning of the term *assign* in Exchequer parlance, as Dryden used it in this letter sent from Charlton in August, 1666, to Sir Robert Long, Auditor of the Receipt in the Exchequer:

Honourd Sir,

Since you have been pleasd thus farr to give Your self a trouble in our businesse, the whole profit of which we owe originally to you, when you wrought my Lord to Assign the patent, we hope you will so much own your former kindnesse as to keep what money you receive for us in your hands till we come up. As for the unreasonable proposition my Lord Berkshyre made, & writ us word that you

[7] See also David M. Vieth, "Irony in Dryden's Verses to Sir Robert Howard," *Essays in Criticism*, 22 (1972), 239–243.

approv'd it, we well know it was only to be rid of his importunityes we have sent an Acquittance signd by us both with this inclos'd; & a letter which Sir Robert Howard has done us the favour to write to you, on purpose that the money might be receiv'd by no other then your self in whom we absolutely confide, as becomes,

Honourd, Sir,

Your most obliged, &

most obedient Servants

John Dryden.　　　　Elizabeth Dryden.

The "Lord" first referred to was either the Earl of Southampton, Lord Treasurer, or more likely, Lord Ashley, who was then Chancellor of the Exchequer. To "assign" meant to direct that a warrant for payment be assigned to a particular category of funds received into the Treasury through the Exchequer. Unless a warrant was so assigned, it could not be paid; and such assignment was not automatic, but depended upon the willingness of the proper officer to assign the warrant to a revenue that was in funds at the moment. Such assignment was the function of the Lord Treasurer, or if the Treasury was in commission, of a quorum of the Treasury Commissioners. There is reason to think, however, that in this case Chancellor Ashley (later the Earl of Shaftesbury) acted for his uncle by marriage, Southampton; the evidence appears in a letter from Sir Robert Howard enclosed with the Drydens' letter to Sir Robert Long:

Sr

You will receive with this an enclos'd acquittance signed by Mr Driden and his wife my sister; for seaven hundred sixty eight pounds fifteen shillings wch Mr Sheppeard sent downe to be signd: I beinge entrusted by them both; due desire that you will be pleasd Sr to receive the mony that shall be paid upon it; and allow Mr Sheppeard such deductions and charges as he shall reasonably demand; and this to keep in your hand's till farther order from them, etc.

>pray if Mr Sheppeard need's
>your assistance in any thinge
>be pleasd to afford it for wee
>apprehend some stop because
>my Lord Ushley [sic] is out of towne.

Professor Ward printed these letters. Perhaps because he identified Sir Robert Long as Chancellor of the Exchequer, he did not see that "Lord Ushley" must be "Lord Ashley" who, of course, actually was its chancellor.[8] (Later on, in 1672, Ashley became Lord Chancellor of England and Earl of Shaftesbury.) Ashley tended to do a good deal of the Lord Treasurer's work, especially toward Southampton's death in 1667 and thereafter.[9] Ashley, Sir Robert Long's superior, is the person Dryden refers to as "my Lord." A few lines down he first introduces his father-in-law by his title and name, and refers to the wild financial schemes that the Earl, well into his seventies and perhaps senile, was devising.

It is significant that Dryden gives all the credit to Sir Robert Long for clearing the warrant. Sir Robert Howard expedites matters by foreseeing the practical steps necessary; but his letter also serves his own ends in that it cuts Mr. Sheppeard in for his share, and it shows Sir Robert Long that Howard is to thank for his getting the use of £768.15s. Treasury officials could profit from short-term investments of money left in their hands.

At the death of Southampton in 1667, the Treasury was put into commission, with the old Duke of Albermarle as first lord, and Ashley, Clifford, Sir William Coventry, and Sir John Duncombe as the other lords. A number of Treas-

[8] Charles E. Ward, *The Letters of John Dryden* (Durham, N.C., 1942), pp. 6–7 and 144–145. Cited hereafter as "Ward, *Letters.*"
[9] Stephen B. Baxter, *The Development of the Treasury, 1660–1702* (London, 1957), p. 34. H. J. Oliver, *Sir Robert Howard (1626–1698)* (Durham, N.C., 1963), p. 95, reports Berkshire's mortgage. Cited hereafter as "Oliver." Although my interpretation of the Dryden-Howard relationship differs radically from Oliver's, this is an indispensable study, to which I am greatly indebted.

ury reforms were set in motion in an effort to economize and to improve procedure. King Charles, however, disregarding the officials of the Treasury, attempted to raise a national loan on his own credit. It failed all over England; but some officeholders and place-seekers felt impelled to make a contribution. Pepys, for example, took pains to discover what others were giving and resentfully lent the King £300, thinking the loan a very bad bargain. Sir Robert Howard had no place to protect and was about to begin his campaign against Clarendon in Parliament; he had helped to reinstate Buckingham in the King's favor, and he saw a further opportunity to improve his position by "undertaking" to raise a little money for the King. On 21 August 1667 he moved the Board of Treasury Commissioners to the effect that the two remainders, Berkshire's (on which there is no indication that any payment had been made) and Lady Elizabeth's, be confirmed. This was necessary because of Southampton's death. It was ordered by the Board "that the order for her remainder be put into Sir George Downing's hands to be assigned by the Earl of Berkshire to her." This is a confusing order, but its outcome is clear. There is apparently no record of any payments to Berkshire, but on 16 September 1667, £500 was ordered paid to Lady Elizabeth, on 19 September the warrant was given, and on 16 October the entire sum was confirmed by letters of Privy Seal as lent to the King.[10] Realistically, one can only say that Howard let his brother-in-law and sister in for a very bad investment, and no doubt gained credit for himself by doing so. If, as is at least possible, Dryden was later helped toward the laureateship by this loan, there is no evidence whatever to suggest that Sir Robert Howard had this effect in mind.

Another advantage Sir Robert derived in part at least from his brother-in-law was the rise in his shares in the building company of the Theatre Royal in Bridges Street. In a few years after his investment, late in 1661, Sir Robert's shares

[10] Ward, pp. 52–53; Oliver, p. 95.

had more than trebled in value.[11] Dryden's early plays had helped materially to produce this result, so that one might speak of the financial obligation as mutual—although Dryden, characteristically, spoke of his own gratitude and obligation. It would not be surprising if Sir Robert had sold out his theatre shares by 1668, when Dryden became a sharer in the acting company of the King's Theatre, for it is likely he could find even more profitable uses for the money. In 1665 he had managed to get King Charles to recommend him to a rich widow, Lady Honoria O'Brien, as a husband, and it was from her beautiful estate of Vasterne that Sir Robert wrote the note the Drydens enclosed for Sir Robert Long. By 1665 he had sold his valuable offices of Clerk of the Patents and also of Serjeant Painter to the King.[12]

Whatever the extent and nature of Dryden's obligations to Howard, he himself thought he owed more to two old friends of Clarendon, Sir William Davenant and the Duke of Newcastle. These two Old Cavaliers had been close friends since their Paris exile days in 1646. (Davenant was Newcastle's artillery commander in the Civil War, and earlier had been instrumental in sending Prince Rupert to rescue him when he was cut off by the rebels.) It is reasonable to assume that one of them, probably Davenant, recommended Dryden to the other as a collaborator who bore his full share and somewhat more in a literary enterprise. At the time of Davenant's death (early April, 1668) Newcastle may have added his influence to others' within the Court circle to gain the laureateship for Dryden. Newcastle might also have aided directly in obtaining Dryden's patent as Laureate and Historiographer Royal, issued on 18 August 1670, before which time the post of Laureate had been unsalaried. The patent states the yearly total pension as £200, which had been the salary of the historiographer alone when Howell held that post. By this time, moreover, Dryden had several other influential patrons

---

[11] *London Stage*, I, Introduction, p. 1.
[12] Oliver, p. 38.

at Court. One would thus be able to account for the poet's statement, in dedicating his *An Evening's Love; or, The Mock Astrologer* to Newcastle in 1671: "Amongst those few persons of Wit and Honour, whose favourable opinion I have desir'd, your own vertue, and my great obligations to your Grace, have justly given you the precedence" (*Works*, x, 197). It is also reasonable to assume that Newcastle left the profits of *Sir Martin Mar-all* to the poet, who of course deserved them, and it seems likely that he made no fuss over granting him the credit as well as the cash, for Pepys records that the play was "as everybody says, corrected by Dryden."[13]

Such magnanimity was not always forthcoming from a noble collaborator. It is beyond reasonable doubt, I think, though no one seems to have appreciated it, that in Dryden's relationship with Sir Robert Howard the rift in the lute was Howard's printing of *The Indian Queen*, without any mention of a collaborator, in his *Four New Plays* (1665) and again in *Five New Plays* (1668). The editors of the California Dryden have at last, very rightly I am sure, given *The Indian Queen* back to Dryden almost in its entirety.

In addition to their careful presentation of the external and internal evidence, I shall add two new pieces of external evidence that are fairly conclusive in themselves. First, however, before leaving his collaborations with others, here is a relevant passage in which Dryden comments on his association with Davenant in rewriting *The Tempest*: "It had perhaps been easie enough for me to have arrogated more to my self than was my due in the writing of this Play, and to have pass'd by his name with silence in the publication of it, with the same ingratitude which others have us'd to him, whose Writings he hath not only corrected, as he hath done this, but has had a greater inspection over them, and some-

---

[13] In 1660, Buckingham and Newcastle were close to a duel over their rival claims to loyalty; in 1663 Buckingham forced Newcastle to withdraw the privilege of parole he had granted to Colonel Hutchinson. See Alfred Harbage, *Davenant* (Philadelphia, 1935), pp. 93, 108, 134.

times added whole Scenes together, which may as easily be
distinguish'd from the rest, as true Gold from counterfeit
by the weight" (Works, x, 4–5). What is said here applies
a fortiori to Howard, who took such complete credit for *The
Indian Queen* that Dryden had to insist, in the preface
(1667) to its sequel, *The Indian Emperor,* that "part" of the
earlier play was written by him. He had already made his
claim at the sequel's opening in the spring of 1665, by means
of leaflets distributed to the audience, the ostensible func-
tion of which was to show the plot connection. The "part,"
it has been held on good evidence, amounted to nine-tenths
or thereabouts.[14] I should say it probably amounted to all
of the "written" part.

Yet there are two early and rather conclusive pieces of
evidence that Howard's theft amounted to a bold hijacking
of almost the whole play. The first is in the prologue written
by Dryden for *Albumazar* (an old play by Tomkis, first pro-
duced in 1615; Pepys saw the revival, acted for the second
time, on 22 February 1668 and repeated the false opinion
that Jonson had modeled his Alchemist on the astrologer in
this play). Whereas with Jonson, "What was another's Lead,
becomes his Gold," it is far different, Dryden tells us, with
living authors, such

> As make whole Playes, and yet scarce write one word:
> . . . .
> Nay scarce the common Ceremony use,
> Of stand, Sir, and deliver up your Muse;
> But knock the Poet down; and, with a grace,
> Mount Pegasus before the owners Face.
>
> (16, 21–24)

This refers to robbing one's contemporary, which Howard
had done to Dryden with *The Indian Queen.*

Another passage refers to the fact that Howard had robbed
the dead by presenting, as his own, *The Duke of Lerma,*

---

[14] *Works,* VIII (1962), 283.

based largely on an old play, probably by either Henry Shirley or John Ford:

> Faith if you have such Country *Toms*, abroad,
> Tis time for all true men to leave that Road.
> Yet it were modest, could it but be sed,
> They strip the living, but these rob the Dead:
> Dare with the Mummyes of the Muses Play,
> And make love to 'em, the *Ægyptian*, way.
>
> (25–30)

"Tom," as the California editors note (*Works* 1, 141–142, 344, 345), refers to any sort of criminal, but the opposition of *"Country"* and *"true men"* in the next line suggests a reference to the then amorphous, but in both Court and theatre circles unpopular, "Country Party." At the time, Sir Robert appeared to be serving the Country interest (Marvell praised him for leading in the attack on the Court, though not long afterward he was to rebuke him for a relapse).

It would be very surprising if Dryden were aroused merely because Howard had appropriated a forgotten, never-published old play such as *The Spanish Duke of Lerma*. His real motive will be quite obvious, once we have recognized the strength of his commitment to Clarendon and the circle of the Duke of York. For Howard had so adapted the old play as to make it a piece of political propaganda, justifying the ruin of the Chancellor and making it appear that he had escaped by a trick and still constituted a serious threat to the liberty of Englishmen. This fact can be briefly established:

In Act I, scene ii, reference is made (the scene is the Spanish court) to "our last troubles in the Belgic wars— / Backed by the English." This is intended to remind the audience of the Dutch War of 1667 and thereby to suggest that the King of Spain was in the same position as the King of England and could stand for him for purposes of the play and its political meaning. It goes on to speak of "calling all / To just accounts, that those that have done well /

May be continued, other men removed." This is a clear reference to Sir Robert Howard's famous "proviso" tacked on to a bill in the Commons, 7 December 1666, that a Parliamentary committee of nine examine the use of money for the war. This indeed was seen as a blow at the Court, as Pepys reported the next day. The passage includes another topical reference, i.e., to the issuance of tickets to pay off the fleet: "all the soldiers [be] paid their full arrears." Act I, scene iii, presents Lerma as using his daughter Maria to catch the King. Clarendon was widely accused of using his daughter Anne to entangle the Duke of York. Lerma is dissatisfied with the King because "His temper is too gentle;" "a pity hangs upon his heart." Lerma therefore drafts a paper whereby the King would make himself an "absolute" ruler, that is, a tyrant, and compels Maria to wheedle him into signing it. She, however, exposes her father's design—after the King has signed—and calls the action "unworthy of you." "While he seems," she tells the King, "To make you practise power unlimited, / Just then you have the least, obeying his." And she closes with what might be a Country slogan, "Be everybody's king" (Act III, scene ii).

Pepys saw *The Duke of Lerma* in some trepidation because he had heard that it was designed to chide the King for his mistresses. This it does, very mildly and fantastically, in a fourth act scene to "soft music," wherein Medina enters "as a Genius in a glittering habit" to Maria and her friend Isabella and these lines are spoken:

> Let no good Genius henceforth wait
> Upon such false & such unsteady things
> As adored beauties—or as flattered kings.

This episode might possibly refer to the part played by Castlemaine in enraging Charles against Clarendon. Castlemaine had caused him to surprise the Duke of Richmond dallying with Frances Stewart in the latter's bedchamber after Frances had dismissed the King himself on pretense of being tired. She had then helped to fix blame on Clarendon for promoting the affair and the elopement that followed Charles's discovery. This was her revenge on the Chancellor, who had always treated her with contempt and refused to pass any warrant of hers within England—so that all her favors from Charles had been paid out of Ireland.

The most important political point of *The Duke of Lerma*, and most likely the *coup de théâtre* that caused Howard to adapt it in the first place, is the final scene. Lerma has been convicted and is about to be suitably punished by the King, when he suddenly enters "in a Cardinal's habit" and announces that he is above the law and will henceforth take shelter in a monastery of which he has been the patron for years. This is simply a theatrical statement of the contention by those who insisted on the trumped-up charges of high treason against Clarendon, that if he were allowed to take asylum he would eventually return to power and wreak a great revenge.

One would have expected Pepys to comment upon this aspect of the play, in addition to the chiding of the King for his mistresses. It is quite likely that he missed the point of these other passages, even though they seem broad enough now, just as he missed the obvious satire against Sir Robert Howard in *The Sullen Lovers* a few months later. Political allusions on the stage needed to be fairly blatant, or indeed very blatant, it seems, in order to strike so absorbed a play-goer as Pepys.

The remainder of this passage in Dryden's prologue to *Albumazar* is of considerable interest. It suggests a line of speculation that, though it is short of proof, fits in with many aspects of the whole situation and would round off (if any further rounding-off is needed) the motives Dryden had for being so insulting to Howard:

> . . . make love to 'em, the *Ægyptian*, way.
> Or as a Rhyming Authour would have sed,
> Joyn the dead living, to the living dead.
> Such Men in Poetry may claim some part,
> They have the Licence, though they want the Art,

And might, where Theft was prais'd, for Lawreats
  stand
Poets, not of the head, but of the hand;
They make the benefits of others studying,
Much like the meales of Politick *Jack Pudding*:
Whose dish to challenge, no Man has the courage,
'Tis all his own, when once h'has spit i'th' Porredge.

(30–40)

The speculation hinges upon the state of health of Sir William Davenant when these lines were written, shortly before February 21, 1668. Davenant died on April 7, 1668 (he was born in 1606). The fact that Dryden was granted his laurel on April 10, 1668, only three days later, might indicate that the death was expected and the competition for the reversion had been settled some time before; the fact that Davenant required a collaborator for *The Tempest* in 1667 perhaps points in the same direction. Then the lines just quoted would record, not merely a rather farfetched allusion to Spartan laurels, but an effort by Sir Robert Howard to snatch the laureateship for himself. He certainly was capable of it. Evelyn reported of him, years later, that he was "not ill-natured, but insufferably boasting," and Pepys records that the Duke of York and others spent some time recounting Sir Robert's presumptions to all kinds of abilities—the basis of his takeoff in Shadwell's *The Sullen Lovers* as Sir Positive At-all.[15] Such an attempt would explain his unwillingness to give Dryden any credit for *The Indian Queen*.

[15] See Shadwell's dedication of *The Sullen Lovers* (1668), addressed to Newcastle: "I have the example of some that never yet wrote Play without stealing most of it; and (like men that lye so long, till they believe themselves) at length by continual Thieving, reckon their stolne goods their own too. . . ." Ed. Montague Summers, I, 10. This assertion is directed at Howard, not (as has been supposed) at Dryden.

A passage on the next page refers to Dryden and Howard together: "I must confess it is very ungenerous to accuse those that modestly confess their own errors; but positive men, that justifie all their faults, are Common Enemies. . . ." The two passages may have formed the basis for the charge that Dryden incited Shadwell's takeoff of Sir Robert. In 1668, though Shadwell was devoted to Jonson's comic style and

77

It is considerably less speculative to interpret the phrase "Politick *Jack Pudding*" as referring to Sir Robert's supporting role to the Duke of Buckingham. A jack pudding was the assistant to a mountebank—a rather rough approximation of the relationship between Howard and Buckingham, but good enough for a prologue; the word *"politick"* carries the main weight. A very interesting sidelight may perhaps be mentioned at this point, though to lay much stress upon it would be to carry speculation too far. It is natural to ask why *Albumazar* should have been revived by the Duke's Theatre at the same time that *The Duke of Lerma* was being revived at the Theatre Royal. As we have seen, *The Spanish Duke of Lerma* had been adapted to attack Clarendon. Was not *Albumazar* similarly adapted to attack Buckingham? Astrology was a highly pertinent topic in the discussion involving high treason and designs upon the King. It was high treason to cause the horoscope of the King of England to be drawn: and this is exactly what the Duke of Buckingham was caught at early in 1667. His detector and accuser was another one of his old enemies, perhaps the most astute of them all, the Earl of Arlington, Henry Bennet. The Duke was ordered to prison, but he absconded and remained hidden for some months. A proclamation was made against him: a very serious matter, since it required the revocation of his offices under government and therefore of the income from them. His astrologer, Haydon, most gamely resisted torture out of loyalty to the Duke, and the affair stood still until King Charles had a mysterious change of mind. A paper that he had recognized as in the Duke's hand (which Charles well knew) he now was willing to ascribe to Buckingham's sister, and the whole affair was hushed up. None other than Sir Robert Howard had been the Duke's intermediary while he remained in hiding; an overture to Clarendon had been rebuffed earlier. Buckingham emerged from this scrape in the late summer of 1667, not

---

found some fault with Dryden, he expressed gratitude and respect for the Laureate, who later claimed he had "assisted his rising."

only forgiven, but possessed of the King's approval for a scheme involving dismissal of the Chancellor and Parliamentary "undertaking" to obtain a supply of money.[16]

The other piece of external evidence is a passage in the anonymous *Session of the Poets* written in 1668, which alludes ironically to Dryden's charges against Sir Robert:

> Sir Robert Howard, call'd for over and over,
>> At last sent in Teague with a packet of news
> Wherein the sad Knight, to his grief, did discover
>> How Dryden had lately robb'd him of his muse.
> Each man in the court was pleas'd with the theft. . . .
>> *(POAS, 1, 331)*

These lines mock Howard's pretensions, making use of Dryden's metaphor and applying it to Howard by name (which, of course, the *Albumazar* prologue had refrained from doing). It is important to note that it is the living author, in Dryden's metaphor and in the *Session of the Poets* passage, who is the victim of plagiarism. This negates the suggestion that the *Albumazar* prologue is aimed at Buckingham, who had taken his *Chances* from Fletcher, a dead author. Neither can it refer to Howard's theft of *The Spanish Duke of Lerma*, because the whole point of the living-and-dead metaphor is that Howard steals from living authors too. *The Session of the Poets*, in fact, refers to Buckingham elsewhere (p. 328), in connection with his early collaboration with Matthew Clifford and Thomas Sprat on the piece that eventually became *The Rehearsal*.[17]

There are a few other points, not made by anyone else to my knowledge, which help to explain the unusual virulence of Dryden's *Defence of an Essay of Dramatic Poesy*. It was

---

[16] Burghclere, *Buckingham*, pp. 167–179.

[17] R. Jack Smith, *Review of English Studies*, 20 (1944), 29–44, applies Shadwell's attack on Howard to Dryden. J. H. Smith, *Modern Language Notes*, 69 (1954), 242–245 saw the *Albumazar* prologue as a retort to the epilogue of Buckingham's *The Chances*, but took the latter for an attack on Dryden; also, correct chronology destroys the basis of his argument.

necessary for him to dissociate himself in a public way from his brother-in-law's politics, but the relentless contempt of the *Defence* seems to require a personal explanation as well. Dryden may have been offended by the preface to *Four New Plays* in which Howard said that only Orrery's verse was good, but not very deeply, I should think, and anyway Howard made amends on that score in his preface to *The Duke of Lerma*. He may have disliked Howard's comparing him to a speaker in Parliament who failed to speak to the point, but this seems unlikely too, since it gave him the opportunity for such a clever riposte, namely, Howard's maintaining a contradiction *in terminis* in the face of three hundred persons. Here it may be that Dryden had in mind, as has been suggested by Professor Ward, Howard's use of the term *"nuisance"* during the debates over the Great Cattle Act in 1666, by which he wanted to insure against the King using his Prerogative; even closer to home is Howard's assertion on 11 November 1667, to substantiate the charge of high treason against Clarendon, that "corresponding with the King's enemies is treason. If it be not, treason has neither name nor definition." An old veteran of Parliament, Edmund Waller (one of the poets whose pictures hung on the walls of Clarendon's palace) replied that a man "might hold correspondence with the King's enemies, and not betray him to his enemies."[18] Not only would this incident be fresh in people's minds, but it also bore upon the main political issue over which Dryden disagreed with his brother-in-law.

Yet one needs to look still further, beyond either literary or political issues, for something more personal to explain how Dryden could reconcile his profession of respect and gratitude for Sir Robert with the remorseless exposure that precedes it in the *Defence of an Essay*. The true offense was given, I suggest, in the final paragraphs of the preface to *The Duke of Lerma*. From context, it would seem that Howard is about to make a very generous acknowledgment: "But, writing this Epistle in so much haste, I had almost

[18] Oliver, pp. 134–135.

forgot one argument or observation which that author has most good fortune in. It is in his Epistle Dedicatory before his Essay of Dramatic Poesy, where, speaking of rhymes in plays, he desires it may be observed that none are violent against it but such as have not attempted it, or who have succeeded ill in the attempt—which as to myself and him I easily acknowledge, for I confess none has written in that way better than himself, nor few worse than I." This is genuinely handsome, and excuses the clumsy *praeteritio* that introduces it; but the immediate sequel, obfuscated as it is in Sir Robert's most sententious style, seems meant to put the uppity poet forever in his place: "Fancy may be allowed her wantonness; but Reason is always pure and chaste: and as it resembles the sun in making all things clear, it also resembles it in its several positions. When it shines in full height, and directly ascendant over any subject, it leaves but little shadow. But when descended and grown low, its oblique shining renders the shadow larger than the substance, and gives the deceived person a wrong measure of his own proportion."[19] There can be no doubt as to which person is "deceived" and taking "a wrong measure of his own proportion." It seems clear enough to me that the sixth son of an earl is reminding Mr. John Dryden of his lowly status as a versifier.

At the end of his *Defence*, Dryden answered this innuendo directly, in a paragraph the complexity of which takes into full account the variety of issues (literary, political, social, family, and personal) involved, without failing to maintain its author's rocklike sense of dignity. Elsewhere in the *Defence* he had humbled himself like a proud man who needs no help in naming his defects—"My conversation is slow and dull; my humour saturnine and reserved"—but in the concluding paragraph he responds to Howard's innuendo in such a way as to convince anyone that he has a right

[19] See Dennis D. Arundell, *Dryden and Howard* (London, 1929), pp. 98–99. This book conveniently assembles most of the documents in the Dryden-Howard controversy, including the text of *The Duke of Lerma*.

measure of his own proportion: "His last assault, like that of a Frenchman, is most feeble; for whereas I have observed, that none has been violent against verse, but such only as have not attempted it, or have succeeded ill in their attempt, he will needs, according to his usual custom, improve my observation to an argument, that he might have the glory to confute it. But I lay my observation at his feet, as I do my pen, which I have often employed willingly in his deserved commendations, and now most unwillingly against his judgment. For his person and parts, I honour them as much as any man living, and have had so many particular obligations to him, that I should be very ungrateful, if I did not acknowledge them to the world. But I gave not the first occasion of this difference in opinions. . . . as I was the last who took up arms, I will be the first to lay them down. For what I have here written, I submit it wholly to him; and if I do not hereafter answer what may be objected against this paper, I hope the world will not impute it to any other reason, than only the due respect which I have for so noble an opponent." After this, it is hard to see anything left for Howard to do. To send a challenge to Dryden, after the imagery and the very rhythms of this passage, seems too preposterous for any man unless he were very ill-humored indeed, and devoid of all sense of proportion.

The Dryden-Howard controversy is interesting as literary debate. It is of considerably broader importance as a kind of landmark in the sphere of public ethos. Owing entirely to Dryden's skill at personal reference in print and the unshakable security of tone that came from a genuine self-knowledge coupled with a consummate familiar style, he was able to define the situation into which he and Howard had worked themselves, in terms that no man with the least concern for the good opinion of his fellowmen could gainsay. His sense of what was fitting in this highly complex little social crisis has a positively creative side to it. Dryden was standing up for something new: the right of a professional man and a writer to argue and defend himself with his pen, even against a member of the nobility.

All this did not prevent the rumor, at least, of a challenge from Sir Robert to Dryden. The charge that Dryden declined to fight was made three times in print: first, by "R.F." in his *Letter to . . . Edward Howard*; then by the author of the Cambridge pamphlet of 1673, *A Friendly Vindication of Mr. Dryden*; and finally in *The Medal of John Bayes*, where Shadwell (probably) says:

> Then by th'assistance of a noble knight,
> Th'hadst plenty, ease, and liberty to write.
> First like a gentleman he made thee live,
> And on his bounty thou didst amply thrive;
> But soon thy native swelling venom rose,
> And thou didst him, who gave thee bread, expose.
> 'Gainst him a scandalous Preface didst thou write,
> Which thou didst soon expunge rather than fight.
>
> (*POAS*, III, 86, 131–138)

After this last appeared in print (in 1682), further references, such as the one by Langbaine, are mere echoes and have little authority. The gravamen in all cases is that Dryden's behavior was not that of a gentleman; or, in other words, that a dispute over literary theory and literary competence, if between gentlemen, should be finally settled by the sword rather than the pen.

A further accusation was made against Dryden by the second of these three attackers, namely that he suggested Shadwell's ridiculous takeoff of Sir Robert Howard as Sir Positive At-all in *The Impertinents, or The Sullen Lovers*, which made a great hit in May, 1668. It is most unlikely that we shall ever know for certain whether or not this charge is correct; it is probably more important, anyway, to consider whether Howard believed it. For Howard's chastisement, the timing of *The Sullen Lovers* could not have been better. He had been endeavoring in his bluff, self-righteous way to impeach Sir William Penn in the Commons all through April, 1668; and on April 27 a richly detailed petition from his wife, Lady Honoria, accusing Sir Robert of mistreatment, was presented for consideration by the House. This kind of notoriety, added to his consistently picturesque oratory in the Commons as a self-appointed prosecutor of others' attempts to enrich themselves by methods no different from his own, helped to make *The Sullen Lovers* a *succès de scandale.* Yet Howard, whatever he may have been in other respects, was a first-class knockabout politician, and it is doubtful indeed that he minded this notoriety very much, for he was remarkably thick-skinned. He was, however, true to his class and to the times in that he strongly resented any affront from one who was in his eyes an inferior and a dependent. It would have been very hard for him to forgive Dryden, first, for being disloyal, and second, for giving comfort to his enemies.

Howard's resentment and suspicion emerge rather clearly in a letter he wrote to Sir Thomas Clifford in July, 1668. Clifford had evidently called in question the motives behind the publication of Sir Robert's strange venture into heroic poetry, *The Duel of the Stags.* Printed in mid-1668, it is dedicated "To His Grace the Duke of Buckingham," to whom, Sir Robert says, "I have made so entire a dedication of my self." He credits Buckingham with shaping and polishing the poem: "Your Grace has a farther Title to this, being more yours than Mine; as much as an Image made well shap't and pollish't, is more properly due to him that gave it that perfection, then to him that first dig'd the stone out of the Quarry; it was an ill contriv'd House within, full of entries and unuseful passages, till your Grace was pleas'd to take them away, and make it Habitable for any candid opinion."

The "time when Your Grace made this your own" Sir Robert states, very significantly, " 'twas in your Confinement, where after some Concealment of your self, to weigh the Circumstances and Causes of your persecution, you generously expos'd your self"—that is, in the spring of 1667, when Buckingham was hiding in the lodgings of Sir Henry Bellasis under proclamation for high treason.[20] Sir Robert, it will be recalled, was the one who carried Buckingham's letter of submission to the King, after Clarendon had rejected the Duke's overtures.[21] *The Duel of the Stags* shows to what effect the two put their heads together. It is, piquantly enough, a beast fable in its genre. Although in the letter (dated 26 July 1668) Sir Robert assured Sir Thomas Clifford on his honor that it had been written four years before and really was about two stags in the Royal Park at Windsor,[22] the piece is totally pointless unless given a political interpretation, which furthermore is perfectly obvious by its correspondence with the fable of *The Duke of Lerma*, by its timing, and by the clear reference in the dedication to an inner meaning that Buckingham had helped to shape for "candid opinion." Furthermore, Sir Robert's denial offers no evidence beyond bare assertion and immediately takes refuge in bluster and counteraccusations of his malicious enemies. One suspects that Clifford neither believed him nor cared very much about the affair; denial of such imputations "on the honor of a gentleman" would be a fairly routine matter for a politician of Sir Robert's moral insensitivity; both Clifford's question and Howard's reply were *pro forma*, intended mainly to keep lines of communication open.

The "House within" *The Duel of the Stags* is simply the Buckingham-Howard line, centering on the insulting interference and treasonable ambition of Chancellor Clarendon. The fable concerns two stags, one the king of the herd, the other a budding rival:

> His thoughts as large as his proportion grew,
> And judg'd himself as fit for Empire too.

[20] Sir John Reresby, *Memoirs* (London, 1875), p. 72.
[21] Burghclere, *Buckingham*, p. 179.
[22] Ward, *Modern Language Notes*, 60 (1945), 119–121, prints the letter.

(One notes that Sir Robert repeats the expression he had used to describe Dryden's presumption.) The ambitious stag

> . . . from a Subject to a Rival grows.
> Sollicits all his Princes, fearful Dames,
> And in his sight Courts with rebellious flames.

The king stag meets his challenger and defeats him. "The Rebel weaker" after this setback, "From a Retreat at last steals to a Flight"—which can only refer to Clarendon's preliminary retirement after his dismissal as Chancellor ("retreat"), and then his escape by stealth to the Continent when his impeachment was voted by the Commons ("flight").

What happens next in *The Duel of the Stags* repeats the point made in *The Duke of Lerma*. The beaten stag, banished, recoups his strength and returns for another attempt. The king stag, meanwhile, has grown weaker, and carelessly underestimates "a Slave, he had o'recome before." The poem then ends rather abruptly with the victory of the Rebel Stag over the King, and the hint that he too will meet his match.

Although the little fable could hardly be more inept in conception or composition in the literary sense, it outlines a political myth that had an admirable success. The fact that Sir Robert went to the trouble of publishing it as late as the summer of 1668 shows that he genuinely feared Clarendon's return, and also that he thought political capital might still be made out of the threat of that return. The fear was shared by Buckingham, and also by Arlington, then performing the office of foreign secretary. It explains the savage hounding of the old Chancellor by the authorities in France, so pointedly described in his autobiography, and leads us to agree in placing the blame where Clarendon intended it, on Buckingham most of all, for his influence in France was strong.[23]

[23] Clarendon, *Life* (1827), III, 353. Just how these stags should be related to Denham's stag in *Cooper's Hill*, or Davenant's in *Gondibert* (Book I, Canto ii) is a question too involved to discuss here. Both

There was another reason for the appearance of a collaborative effort from the pens of these two gentleman authors at this time. The Duke of Buckingham and Sir Robert Howard were soon to score a really signal success by means of a joint dramatic composition that never was published or performed: "The Country Gentleman," a comedy intended for the Theatre Royal, in which several of Buckingham's enemies at Court were farcically ridiculed.[24] The chief butt was Sir William Coventry, right-hand man of the Duke of York, who in turn was the focus of resentment and residual support of Clarendon in England. These events amount to a rehearsal for *The Rehearsal* of 1671, as we shall see in due course.[25]

---

earlier poems helped to make the political analogy a commonplace. That it could validly be applied, in 1668, to Clarendon is the important political point, although I accept John M. Wallace's general literary argument that the reader must be allowed a plurality of reference.

As for Sir Thomas Clifford's letter to Howard, his concern was justified by the obvious aura of reference in *The Duel of the Stags* to the King's unhappy affair with "La Belle Stuart," in which Clarendon had been made out to be the villain.

[24] Arthur H. Scouten and Robert D. Hume have recently discovered and edited *The Country Gentleman* (Philadelphia, 1975). The text briefly ridicules the ventriloquialism of Dryden's dialogue *Of Dramatic Poesy* and adds a bit of rhyme to the farcical antics of the two politicians. In their introduction, Scouten and Hume present a thorough account of the Court intrigue based on contemporary sources (pp. 1–10). They are able to show that Clarendon is not personally attacked in the play, but their suggestion that he was pro-French and living high in Montpellier (p. 35) contradicts his own account in the *Life*, with its bitter charges of persecution inspired by his old enemies in England. This continued persecution is what makes sense of Howard's *Duke of Lerma*, as I have shown above. See also P. H. Hardacre, "Clarendon, Sir Robert Howard and Chancery Office-Holding at the Restoration," *HLQ*, 38 (1975), 207–214, especially p. 211.

[25] Burghclere, *Buckingham*, pp. 206–207, notes that Sir William was "a firm ally of the Duke of York's, and James had lately rejected Bucks' advances in terms so contemptuous that the breach between them was appreciably widened." Though that of an amateur, Lady Burghclere's work remains valuable.

CHAPTER THREE

DRYDEN AND HIS BETTERS

I. ALMANZOR AND JAMES STUART

E VEN before he took the public offices of Laureate and Historiographer, Dryden had accepted the prevailing rationale that included poetry, and especially the epic and the drama, among the civilizing arts in the service of the master art of politics. He was convinced that it was part of his function to develop models of human behavior, or "characters," which would be worthy of imitation by the leading men and women of the Court and nation. He drew these characters largely from literary tradition, partly from his own imagination, but also (he asserted) from traits that he observed in real men and women. The process of imitation also involved two other terms of reference: first, to an idealized conception of what the hero or heroine ought to be like in the ceremonial ethos of monarchy as the seventeenth century defined it; and second, notions of what the stage hero or heroine needed to be like in order to conform to current rules for the dramatic genre.

Dryden used his dedications to eminent men and women as a halfway house between their actual personalities and the ideal images that he intended to project of them.[1] In the dedication of *The Conquest of Granada* to James Stuart, he made the unambiguous statement that he had taken the Duke of York's character as his model in the play: "I have presumed to dedicate to your royal highness these faint representations of your own worth and valor in heroic poetry:

---

[1] The best statement on this point is Eugene M. Waith's, "The Voice of Mr. Bayes," *Studies in English Literature,* 3 (1963), 335–343, who also argues that "In the dedications . . . Dryden is creating an ideal audience," "an audience whose taste he believed he knew but also believed he could partly mold" (pp. 340–341). The dedication to York may be found in S-S, IV, 11–17.

or, to speak more properly, not to dedicate, but to restore to you those ideas which in the more perfect part of my characters I have taken from you." In keeping with his highly analytical approach to the drama, Dryden had singled out a number of distinguishing traits in James and had put them on the stage in idealized form. They were concentrated, naturally, in the hero, Almanzor, of whom Dryden says: "I designed in him a roughness of character impatient of injuries, and a confidence of himself almost approaching to an arrogance. But these errors are incident only to great spirits; they are moles and dimples, which hinder not a face from being beautiful, though that beauty be not regular; they are of the number of those amiable imperfections which we see in mistresses, and which we pass over without a strict examination, when they are accompanied with greater graces. And such in Almanzor are a frank and noble openness of nature, an easiness to forgive his conquered enemies, and to protect them in distress; and, above all, an inviolable faith in his affection."

This list of Almanzor's faults and virtues is remarkably close to the portrait of James Stuart that history endorses. Even his personal taste in mistresses seems to be alluded to: he had a notorious fondness for ill-featured but clever-spirited women.[2] Some of the good qualities history recognizes by the different names of gullibility, imprudence, and obstinacy, especially in backing of unpopular men and lost causes. Yet there can be no doubt that James was an intrepid battle leader (never better, his friends claimed, than when under fire) who had known at least two passages of glory, by land at the Battle of the Dunes in 1658, and by sea at the Battle of Lowestoft in 1665. The conclusion of Dryden's dedication probably sums up his own view of James's best qualities: "if at any time [Almanzor] fulfils the parts of personal valor and of conduct, of a soldier, and of a general; or, if I could yet give him a character more advantageous than what he

---

[2] F. C. Turner, *James II* (New York, 1948), 142–143.

has, of the most unshaken friend, the greatest of subjects, and the best of masters, I should then draw to all the world a true resemblance of your worth and virtues." By the standards of history today, this is a fair judgment.

The character of Almanzor matches the view of James that was held by his contemporaries. Gilbert Burnet wrote (about 1683) as follows: "He has naturally a candor and a justice in his temper very great, and is a firm friend but a heavy enemy, and will keep things long in his mind and wait for a fit opportunity. He has a strange notion of government, that everything is to be carried on in a high way and that no regard is to be had to the pleasing the people, and he has an ill opinion of any that proposes soft methods and thinks that is popularity; but at the same time he always talks of law and justice." In addition, Burnet said, "he receives enemies that submit, but tries to ruin those that stand out and cannot tolerate half submission"; "he thinks everyone a rebel that opposes the King in parliament"; "he is very brave and abhors a coward."[3]

There are several remarkable passages in *The Conquest of Granada* that, while conforming to this characterization of Burnet's (who was James's enemy when he wrote it), give it a more favorable application. The largest number reflect the contrast between James and Charles, who was always reluctant to take a firm stand, and who often preferred to rehabilitate an enemy rather than allow a friend to become too strong. In Almanzor's first quarrel with Boabdelin, the king tells him he does not want his counsel or aid. Almanzor replies:

Thou want'st 'em both, or better thou wouldst know
Than to let factions in thy kingdom grow.
Divided int'rests, while thou think'st to sway,

---

[3] Quoted by Turner, p. 64. The possibility should not be overlooked that Burnet (like many others then and since) was influenced by Dryden's imaging of the character of a contemporary. Yet Burnet was closely associated with James for a number of years, and is therefore an independent witness.

Draw like two brooks thy middle stream away;
For though they band and jar, yet both combine
To make their greatness by the fall of thine.[4]

Before 1670 the so-called Country party and the Court party hardly existed; there were indeed only factions rather than parties in the modern sense. During these years the pattern of royal behavior showed Charles devious, slippery, bending to the wind, and uncommitted; whereas the Duke of York, stubborn and inflexible, offered a fixed target for his enemies. James was widely regarded as sincere, loyal, a good administrator, and a man of his word; but in the eyes of history and in the light of his behavior later, he seems to have completely lacked political sense.

As for Dryden, he chose to be loyal to James when he clearly perceived it to be ruinous. It is ironical that, for a century or so, he should have been misrepresented as a timeserver and turncoat by the series of brilliant writers who recast the history of England in a Whig image. Nothing could be more false. Dryden stuck by James Stuart through bad times and good, as Duke of York, as King enthroned, and as "King Over the Water" after James ignored his good advice.

James was duller than Charles, but he was much more dependable, as were the people he chose to dispense his favors. The contrast between the versatility of Charles and the staunchness of James is at least glanced at in *The Conquest of Granada*; it seems to be reflected in Almanzor's indignation when he finds that Boabdelin has revoked the promise of freedom made to the Duke of Arcos:

He break my promise and absolve my vow!
'Tis more than Mahomet himself can do!
The word which I have giv'n shall stand like fate,
Not like the king's, that weathercock of state,

---

[4] 1 CG, I. i. 224–229, ed. George H. Nettleton and Arthur E. Case, *British Dramatists From Dryden to Sheridan* (Boston, 1939). This text (like many other anthologies, unfortunately) contains only the First Part.

He stands so high, with so unfixed a mind,
Two factions turn him with each blast of wind.
But now, he shall not veer: my word is passed;
I'll take his heart by th' roots and hold it fast.[5]

There is reason to suspect that the not very glorious por-
trait gallery of kings in the heroic plays reflects Dryden's
unfavorable judgment of certain aspects of Charles's char-
acter. The composite picture on the whole is that of a will-
ful, pleasure-seeking, somewhat inept chief, who does best to
choose loyal servants and then to leave the management of
affairs in their hands. None of the kings remotely resembles
the molder of men and architect of history Dryden painted
in his funeral tribute to Cromwell. Yet there are repeated
sharp comments upon kings who lose their grip upon a nation
when they fail to exercise power vigorously or when they allow
favorites—especially women—to abuse it.

In *Granada*, the spinelessness of Boabdelin presented Dry-
den with a problem of dramatic structure: how could Al-
manzor serve him without loss of heroic dignity? He solved
it, as he often solved such problems, by means of a turn in
the sex interest of his play. He married Almahide to the
king; Almanzor, who loves her, executes her husband's com-
mands only because she seconds them. Thus James obeyed
orders out of respect for his brother and loyalty to the throne,
even though at times he strongly opposed the advice that
Charles was putting into action. The shameful defeats of
1667 left him anxious to recoup the national honor and
inflict revenge upon the Dutch. Similarly, one of the "good"
persons in *The Conquest of Granada*, the Abencerrago Ab-
delmelech, suggests that foreign war is an effective means of
uniting factions behind the king:

> The two fierce factions will no longer jar,
> Since they have now been brothers in the war.[6]

Almanzor welcomes the opportunity for fighting:

[5] 1 CG, iii. i. 7–14.   [6] *Ibid.*, ii. i. 3–4.

> 'Tis war again, and I am glad 'tis so;
> Success shall now by force and courage go.
> Treaties are but the combats of the brain,
> Where still the stronger lose, and weaker gain.[7]

Almanzor's active, straightforward nature and his disgust with the arts of politics (like the "candor" mentioned by Burnet as a quality of James) are summed up in a rebuke he delivers to one of Boabdelin's courtiers:

> Were I, like thee, in cheats of state grown old
> (Those public markets where for foreign gold
> The poorer prince is to the richer sold),
> Then thou mightst think me fit for that low part;
> But I am yet to learn the stateman's art.
> My kindness and my hate unmasked I wear,
> For friends to trust and enemies to fear.[8]

We also find, as the dedication leads us to expect, that some of Almanzor's faults are James's too. Besides an unwillingness and an incapacity for the game of politics, we find a certain hotheadedness, too much self-confidence, and obstinacy—which, however, is subject to check by wiser counsel or by the gracious Almahide. It seems, indeed, that James's most personal vice is poetically rebuked. He was an even greater womanizer than his brother, with a coarse lust sometimes lacking in decency, let alone gallantry. By 1670 he was bitterly ashamed of his weakness.[9] Thus, Almanzor throws himself unreservedly into his attempt to seduce Almahide; even two appearances of his mother's ghost fail to hold him back. Almahide does her best to dissuade him:

> And would you all that secret joy of mind
> Which great souls only in great actions find,
> All that, for one tumultuous minute lose?

In answer, Almanzor comes out resoundingly for sex:

[7] 2 CG, IV; S-S, IV, 179.   [8] 1 CG, IV. i. 36–42.
[9] Turner, p. 61.

I would that minute before ages choose.[10]

He desists only to prevent Almahide from stabbing herself.

Dryden's boldness, even effrontery, in weaving these critical characterizations into the texture of his play should not prevent us from recognizing them for what they were: the faithful fulfillment of his duty as poet, and especially as Laureate, not only to please, but to instruct and correct the great: in this case, Charles and James Stuart.

II. BAYES AND ARLINGTON

Aside from the mistaken notion that his attitude to patrons was servile, Dryden's worst fortune has been to be regarded as personally the model for Bayes, the boorishly vain poet in Buckingham's antiheroic travesty, *The Rehearsal*. Dryden himself rejected this view: "I answered not *The Rehearsal*, because I knew the author sat to himself when he drew the picture, and was the very Bayes of his own farce; because also I knew, that my betters were more concerned than I was in that satire; and lastly, because Mr. Smith and Mr. Johnson, the main pillars of it, were two such languishing gentlemen in their conversation, that I could liken them to nothing but to their own relations, those noble characters of men of wit and pleasure about the town."[11] Clearly Dryden denies that the caricature fits him and asserts that Buckingham's target was bigger game—"my betters." One of these victims was Henry Bennet, the Earl of Arlington, principal secretary of state for foreign affairs and Buckingham's chief (and finally successful) rival in the Cabal. He always wore a nose patch, but knowing contemporaries applied the whole Bayes characterization to him, not merely the nose patch.[12] The boorishness is Arlington's, not Dryden's.

Of course Buckingham also used Dryden's plays as targets

---

[10] 2 *CG*, IV. iii; S-S, IV, 194.   [11] Watson, II, 77–78.

[12] See my "Political Satire in *The Rehearsal*," *Yearbook of English Studies*, 4 (1974), 120–128. Arlington was seen as an upstart clerk by noble rivals.

almost throughout—Dryden's zeal for the heroic gave Buckingham exactly what he needed for parody—partly because the plays were wide open to ridicule, but even more because they had achieved such popularity. Yet it was, in fact, as an epoch-making mode of combating a certain brand of foolishness in church and state that the Duke's farce was immediately celebrated. Andrew Marvell leaped at the opportunity given him by the new wit. In 1672 he wrote his long *Rehearsal Transpros'd*, imitating "an author of the highest quality [who] has furnished our best wits in all their controversies, even in religion and politics . . . with the most effectual and entertaining method of exposing folly, pedantry, false reason and ill writing."[13]

Indeed, the identification of Arlington is not the most important political identification to be made in *The Rehearsal*, for one cannot escape the conviction that Charles and James Stuart, no less, are centered within the amorphous penumbra of the Two Kings of Brentford. Bayes had explained what he calls—N.B.—"the chief hindge" of his play thus:

> I suppose two Kings to be of the same place—as, for example, at Brentford, for I love to write familiarly. Now the people having the same relations to 'em both, the same affections, the same duty, the same obedience, and all that; are divided among themselves in point of *devoir* and interest, how to behave themselves equally between 'em: these Kings differing sometimes in particular, though, in the main, they agree. (I know not whether I make myself well understood.)
>
> (I. ii)

The "Key" glosses this speech, "Two Kings of Brentford, supposed to be the two Brothers, the King and the Duke."[14] It seems to me that here Buckingham established the basic

---

[13] *Prose Works*, ed. A. B. Grosart (London, 1873), 169–170.
[14] In Buckingham's *Miscellaneous Works*, ii (1705), 34–35. The "Key" has a title page dated 1704, Macdonald, 313b.

donnée of his satire, the ridiculous doubling of two kings in one petty suburb, bowing and scraping to each other like Alphonse and Gaston, unable to cross a threshold without ceremonious yieldings, coming and going with no reason to the strains of soft music. Thus he incorporated his fundamental objection to the regime of Charles II: that it brought confusion, divided the loyalty of the country, undermined its own ministers, and condemned the nation to inaction. Since Charles was unwilling to divorce his barren Queen, the Duke of York as Successor had a greatly enhanced status. Buckingham's attitude toward the brothers struck contemporaries as one of ill-concealed contempt. For example, in March, 1669, the Duke of Ormond had written to his son Ossory: "As for the Duke of Bucks, I am confident, he not only under-values, but hates the King's person and his Brother's; and has designs apart, if not aimed at the ruin of them both."[15] Burnet agreed: "He was bred about the king, and for many years he had a great ascendancy over him; but he spake of him to all persons with that contempt, that at last he drew a lasting disgrace upon himself."[16]

Furthermore, Buckingham had already inspired his political henchman, Sir Robert Howard, with the same line of argument. In *The Duel of the Stags*, Charles and the exiled Clarendon are represented as two rival stags about to join combat. The king stag's subjects look on doubtfully:

> The Herd afraid of Friend and Enemy,
> Shrink from the one, and from the other fly;
> They scarce know which they should Obey, or Trust,
> Since Fortune only makes it Safe and Just.

(202–205)

In *The Rehearsal*, Bayes's further explanations draw a precise picture of confusion:

---

[15] Thomas Carte, *An History of the Life of James Duke of Ormonde* (London, 1736), II, 377.

[16] Gilbert Burnet, *History of His Own Time*, ed. Osmund Airy (Oxford, 1897–1900), I, 137.

Why, look you, sir (nay I beseech you, be a little curious
in taking notice of this, or else you'll never understand my
notion of the thing), the people being embarrassed by
their equal ties to both, and the sovereigns concerned in
a reciprocal regard, as well to their own interest as the
good of the people, may make a certain kind of a—you
understand me—upon which there does arise several dis-
putes, turmoils, heart-burnings, and all that.

(i. ii)

It does indeed seem that Buckingham is beseeching us to
pay attention to the theme of his satire. In this speech, his
suggestion is the standard contention around which the
Country party grew up, that the King should be king of
all the people, with no "own interest" aside from that of the
nation as a whole.

Besides making game of the two-headed ineffectiveness
of the Two Kings of Brentford, Buckingham stages (through
Bayes) a monitory palace revolution. The two usurping kings
(King Usher and King Physician, or Ush and Phys, as Mar-
vell called them), though ridiculously senile, are able to sup-
plant "the right Kings" with no trouble at all, and proceed
to make futile policy in whispers no one, including the au-
dience, can hear. Such, to Buckingham, was the policy made
and kept secret even from the Cabinet Council (to say
nothing of Parliament and the English nation), by Arlington
and before him by Clarendon.[17] These two were politicians
of the old school, companions of Charles in the poverty
and petty intrigues of his Court in exile. Buckingham stood
for the new school of carefully cultivated public opinion and
parliamentary management.

III. BUCKINGHAM, DRYDEN, AND THE HEROIC

There is another kind of ridicule in *The Rehearsal*, less
obvious but even more radical. It is directed against the

[17] *The Country Gentleman* also burlesques close management of
"business" of state by bureaucrats, e.g., i. i. 221ff., ii. i. 249–321.

concept of "place," one which was still strong in 1671, though not so strong as in Shakespeare's time. Arlington wore his patch to show that he had a place among the faithful Cavaliers. Dryden took pride in the Laureate's title of "Servant to His Majesty," as Shakespeare evidently did in his title of "Gentleman." However, the Duke of Buckingham, made a Knight of the Garter when he was still a boy, was perhaps scornful of mere honors and hence closer to the modern attitude. Decorum, or "state" (which an old-timer such as Evelyn missed in the conduct of government after Clarendon's fall), is what the ludicrous Gentleman-Usher and Physician (King Ush and King Phys, Marvell calls them) try to vest themselves with in *The Rehearsal*, and what Clarendon wished to secure for the King by putting him above parliamentary involvement. In a similar way, it was Dryden's strong feeling that the different kinds of writing occupied different places, or levels, of excellence, that caused him to insist upon writing heroic plays in verse, and in a style placed recognizably above the mediocre level of what passed for blank verse in the English theatre of the mid–seventeenth century. The elevation of Dryden's style was a form of "place" that Buckingham refused to seek in his own verse, as he had refused to accept the inflated style and tone of the "Petition" that Clarendon wrote and submitted to the House of Lords in 1668. The Lords, after dealing with the Petition, charged Buckingham to pass it to the Commons. Handing it to Sir Robert Howard (who was filling his customary role of representing the House in the Clarendon impeachment), the Duke asked him to "send it to them again, for it had a Style which they were in love with, and desired to keep it."[18] Indeed, Clarendon's defensive tone of hectoring, strident self-righteousness is intolerable for any kind of business, especially the business of public govern-

---

[18] *The Proceedings . . . Touching the Impeachment of Edward Late Earl of Clarendon* (1700), p. 100. The Duke's request did not prevent Sir Robert Howard from moving that the *Petition* be burnt by the hangman, a motion that passed on 4 December 1667 (p. 115).

·ment. In *The Rehearsal*, the Duke's sensitive ear marvelously captured, in what Eugene M. Waith has called "the voice of Mr. Bayes," one of the authentic tones of John Dryden as he unconsciously patronized some patron (and therefore, unfortunately, the reader too) in one of his dedications. Thirty or forty years later, in a passage published in *Characteristics*, the third Earl of Shaftesbury, who perceived the intolerableness of this tone in general discourse, quoted from the *Don Sebastian* dedication and complimented Buckingham on helping to rid the world of what he contended was a national vice of style, one not limited to Clarendon or Dryden.[19]

Buckingham's thrust at the arrogance of Arlington's patch, therefore, was altogether of a piece with his satire of certain lapses in Dryden's tone and style. The more obvious thrust of *The Rehearsal*, however, is against a self-canceling ineptitude. The audience saw Bayes cut his nose in an attempt to "elevate" himself which he could not sustain; this bit of action at the end of the second act is symbolic. The dramatis personae whom Bayes rehearses are also engaged in antics that contradict their pretensions. The whispering politicians are so politic that they make treaties that remain forever swathed in total secrecy, and they plot palace revolutions that come without a ripple and go leaving not a wrack behind. The heroes' wars not only bring nothing about; they seem intestine and villatic. Drawcansir kills on both sides indifferently—but then the other heroes, Prince Volscius and Prince Prettyman, seem to have no sides to be on. Even the geography is meaningless; the general and the lieutenant general fight each other on a battle map resembling a scrambled jigsaw puzzle of the London suburbs. Especially in its last act, where (like *The Critic*) *The Rehearsal* presents a battle scene that must be seen on the stage to be properly appreciated, Buckingham's farce proved a great precursor of

[19] *Characteristics*, ed. J. M. Robertson (1900, repr. Library of Liberal Arts), II, 328 n. Act I, scene ii of *The Rehearsal* has several excellent specimens, especially lines 133–205.

the distinctive English genre of nonsense. Like *Alice in Wonderland*, it is nonsense that cries out for interpretation; and, since its motifs and archetypes are applicable politically as well as psychologically, interpretation can be—if one pleases—rather specific. Like many bad dreams, *The Rehearsal* is built around a fundamental frustration theme. It accurately reproduces the typical experience of Charles II's ministers of state. The King was known to approve of Louis XIV for his manner of foiling one politician with another. As Charles would say, they were like fire and water anyway, so "God's fish! when rogues fall out, the master is like then to know the truth." However, this stalemate policy condemned England to governmental disunity and national inaction, "doing nothing."[20]

The damage done by Buckingham to the idea of a mythically heroic warrior-king, in Dryden's earlier sense, was total. In *The Conquest of Granada*, as he informs the Duke of York in its dedication, he had gone to the fountainhead of the epic, the *Iliad* of Homer, and modeled Almanzor on the archetypal ideal hero, Achilles. He also speaks of using Tasso's Rinaldo. Both of these he thinks have in common with James Stuart the essential heroic virtue of valor. Dryden admits that other, more political, qualities are necessary, but he fails to go into the question of who, in the real world of English politics, would be the politic Agamemnon or Godfrey to James's fighting Achilles or Rinaldo. In all but one of his heroic plays up to this time, his legitimate monarch had been a very weak presence on the stage, politically speaking. In *The Indian Queen*, he has already been murdered when the play begins; in *The Indian Emperor*, Montezuma, who was a hero so long as he was a youth of unknown ancestry, becomes but an impotent "Old Emperor," needing to be rescued rather than conquered by the young invader Cortez. In *The Conquest of Granada*, Abdalla and Boabdelin spoil one another's claim to legitimate rule, and Ferdi-

[20] Maurice Lee, *The Cabal* (Urbana, Ill., 1965), p. 252. See the picture of Arlington, complete with nose patch, after p. 150.

nand and Isabella appear too late to stand as a powerful royal presence—besides being, again, a doublet. Only in *Tyrannic Love* is the ruler a powerful, active monarch, and then he is an outrageous tyrant. Dryden obviously had some block that prevented him from creating a true hero-king, such as Aeneas, or even an Agamemnon-figure, such as Tasso clearly presented in Godfrey:

> For as the Lord of hosts, the King of bliss,
> Hath chosen thee to rule the faithful band;
> So he thy stratagems appointed is
> To execute, so both shall win this land:
> The first is thine, the second place is his,
> Thou art this army's head, and he the hand.
>   No other champion can his place supply,
>   And that thou do it doth thy state deny.

So speaks the vision of Hugo to Godfrey, explaining his relationship to Rinaldo, in *Jerusalem Delivered*.[21] Such a pairing off, in which King Charles would conceive and direct strategies of national expansion that the Duke of York would execute, eminently suited Dryden. However, with a King whose concept of national policy was that it be a tournament of rogues,[22] and a fighting Duke who had to stay home from the battle because he was the Heir, there was nothing contemporary for Dryden to work with. No wonder his thoughts turned back to the Black Prince, who, though the Heir, had been allowed to fight.

Already in the latter sixties, not long after he had engaged himself with the Theatre Royal, Dryden had begun to rummage in English history for material to use in a heroic poem. While he looked for a hero, he also made overtures

[21] Book XIV, trans. Edward Fairfax.

[22] Here is Kenyon's judgment: "Both Charles II and his father treated their servants with a bland indifference that sprang from the same lack of human sympathy; one was conscious of it, the other not. (James II's studied, acutely self-conscious loyalty to men and institutions was a reaction—perhaps deliberate—against a trait infinitely damaging to his predecessors.)" *The Stuarts*, p. 129. See also Lee, p. 252.

to possible patrons, hoping to find one who would in effect commission him to write an epic poem. However, in his plays Dryden continued (it may be suspected, unconsciously) to avoid dignifying his stage kings by giving them controlled and powerful presences. There is a certain literal mimesis here, as if he thought it his duty to admonish Charles directly by showing him images of figures with defects like his, instead of inspiring him in true Platonic fashion by portraits of kings who were full-blooded conquerors and statesmen. Why else should King Boabdelin be so much more visible in *The Conquest of Granada* than King Ferdinand?

Buckingham's Two Kings of Brentford must therefore be taken as the seal upon Dryden's failure to create a potent and dignified king in his plays. Dryden's block against creating a hero-king, and Buckingham's outright ridicule of the conception, very likely point to a mutual rejection of an autocratic monarch. Of the two, it seems that Dryden had the less regard for a dominating royal figure, for unlike Buckingham he was no admirer of Louis XIV (except as a patron of the arts). *The Rehearsal*, therefore, is a perfectly valid critique of Dryden's failure to equip his heroic structures with a head as well as a hand. Montezuma, Cortez, Porphyrius, and Almanzor are capable young warriors and executors, but where are the rulers and the strategists they should be serving? Moreover, in the absence of political wisdom and planning, do not the valorous fighting men degenerate into Drawcansirs?

Dryden, it would seem, clung to two rather incompatible ideals. One was that the heroic play was "a heroic poem in little" with exalted thoughts and images and actions raised above the life; the other was that the stage must be "the representation of the world, and the actions in it," as he had told the Earl of Orrery. He had thought that the same style could be employed in the little heroic as in the great, in the play as well as the epic poem—at least he had hoped that this might be the case and had manfully tried the experiment. However, lacking a leader and planner for his hero, Dryden had consistently failed to achieve a heroic plot.

The "fable" of each of his plays is a mere piece of romantic gallantry. In *The Conquest of Granada*, the essential dramatic action may be stated as follows: an unknown young warrior rescues a fair and innocent lady from false traitors and discovers that his father is a duke. In *Tyrannic Love*, written immediately after Dryden had made his intensive study of French theatre, he came closest to the headstrong and hardy heroes of Corneille in his characterization, not of the Emperor Maximin, but of Saint Catharine. Her opponent (and lover) Maximin is so monstrous as to turn the audience's sympathy from the pair of them to the gallant lovers, Berenice and Porphyrius. In *The Indian Emperor* Cortez implausibly proves the most *galant* of all Dryden's heroes, and Montezuma is more a rival in love than in war. Montezuma in *The Indian Queen* is only a younger and a more successful *galant*. None of them has a meaningful political role. The politics in the plays—and there is a good deal of it—is left to the old councilors, the scheming villains, and the women. The heroes are lovers mainly, as are the emperors and kings. The result is that their actions lack political significance even when they generate some romantic interest. Their strongest scenes are not the ones in which they exercise power but the ones in which they reject it, usually because it is offered them by a woman who is a rival to their own truly beloved. Yet the resistance of the heroes to temptations of wrongful power is the closest thing to a dramatic experience they undergo. For the rest, what they do or what happens to them does not deserve to be called dramatic plot so much as romantic adventure.

A critic who wanted to rescue these plays might make out a case for a kind of distributive heroic virtue. Instead of placing the necessary admirable qualities in the main hero, Dryden might have divided them among his men and women, old and young, in a way that was allowed, but not usually favored, by the theorists of the epic. He might have preferred

Homer's way in the *Iliad* to his method in the *Odyssey* or Virgil's in the *Aeneid*. Yet if the critic attempts to show that, by allocating a different heroic virtue to each of several different persons, Dryden actually achieved a collective heroic effect, I think he will fail. The true effect Dryden succeeded in creating was variety. He always spoke of variety as something particularly insisted upon by English audiences (in reality it was a universal quality of the baroque in art). Ironically, the exceptional force of the great theatre of Corneille and Racine was owing to their refusal to give in to this demand of their time; by denying variety to their audiences they often achieved intensity; this Dryden sought only once, perhaps, in *All For Love*.

This conclusion brings us back to *The Rehearsal*. The real force of Buckingham's criticism lay in showing that the heroic plays were not heroic in plot. Instead of a serious action that demanded character-making choices in matters of large public importance, Dryden's actions provided ready-made characters with occasions for gallant behavior and eloquent speeches. Wherever they had genuine choices to make, Dryden invariably placed them, not in the public, but in the private sphere, and reduced their motives to the promptings of a ready-made love interest. His heroes are heroes by conception only; by the test of dramatic action, they are simply true lovers. Dryden's plots are not sets of opportunities whereby we see the heroic quality shape itself, but (as Bayes declares) occasions to bring in fine things. That some of these things are truly fine—Almanzor's speech rejecting Lyndaraxa, for example—does not alter the truth of Buckingham's satirical judgment.

The other main critical judgment of *The Rehearsal* was that Dryden's style in his heroic plays was incongruous with the heroic, either by being too namby-pamby (in the "turtles" and "tulip" purple patches) or grossly exaggerated (as in Drawcansir's huffing rants). This judgment is true, but superfluous. Once it has been admitted that the action of the plays is not heroic, Dryden's unheroic style can be seen as not at all unsuited to a drama of varied gallant adventure. Granted that the purpose of Dryden's couplets is to accommodate a wide variety of charming, intriguing, amusing, surprising, and astonishing events (the one word *romantic*, in its broad seventeenth-century sense, would include all these characteristics), then as style his couplet verse is rather wonderful. Even with the help of Butler, Sprat, and perhaps a half-dozen other wits, Buckingham could never rise above weak travesty, either of Dryden's couplet or his lyric style, nor achieve what one could call a decent pastiche. One might safely say that Dryden's style survived *The Rehearsal* intact —but not, certainly, as one suited to any conceivable form of the genuinely heroic.

The message of *The Rehearsal* to Dryden, therefore, was twofold: his conception of an heroic action (with regard to the political aspects necessary to epic drama) was not even serious, much less heroic; and his style, though safe from ridicule and, even, imitation, was only too well adapted to his unserious, unheroic "heroic plays." Dryden, I believe, got the message. Yet, in assessing the effect, good or bad, of *The Rehearsal* upon Dryden, we must recognize that, in addition to offering him some trenchant literary criticism, it gave him that dubious thing we call a public image.

It is very worthwhile to examine into the development of Dryden's public image and its bearing upon his writing. He himself made the point that the beginning stages of a process are the most rich in possibility.[23] This wealth of alternative makes beginnings especially worthy of study. The establishment of Dryden's public image provides an opportunity for reaching some general conclusions on an important literary development, for these were the years when "the public" was coming into being as we know it today, and Dryden was the first author to become a public figure, simply as an author.

His reaction when saddled with the character of Bayes

[23] "The Grounds of Criticism in Tragedy," Watson, I, 246.

was bound to affect what he wrote in future, not merely with regard to literary-theoretical debate, but as reflecting its impact upon his inner self. The Bayes image gave him out as lacking in social sense—so boorish as to be incapable of recalling anyone's name, and so self-conceited as to judge of others only according to whether they approved of his writing or not. Bayes's manner toward others is either an excessive, fawning *bonhomie*, or else an impatient disregard. The players, whom he would have worked with closely for years, are strangers to him, and he holds himself aloof from their company. In turn, they have no respect for him. There is a further suggestion that Bayes is so insensitive to the manners of good company that his only idea of a joke is a vulgar bargain or a beastly, bawdy pun. His knowledge of society's second language, French, though he prides himself upon it, is defective and bookish. (These hints were cruelly developed in the enlarged version of *The Rehearsal* acted in 1674–1675 and printed as the third edition, 1675.)

Such imputations were very serious in the case of an author who, like Dryden, professed to be writing about the real behavior of men and women at a sophisticated and open, but socially elevated level. Obviously, if he had been anything like the insensitive, egotistical boor that Buckingham's play presents, Dryden would not have been capable of dealing with Restoration society at all—he could not have perceived it, much less written about it creatively. Unfortunately for himself, Dryden had given occasion for this misapplied portrait by several confessional asides in his dedications. The drift of these *obiter dicta* was, first, that he was very conscious of his own merit (he never asked for reward, or even payment of his salary, unless he felt he deserved it, and he thought anyone who did otherwise was very bold);[24] second, that he was willing to stand correction by the judgment of others, provided they were persons approved and chosen by himself for the function;[25] and third, that he was perfectly

[24] *Works*, IX, 24, Dedication to *The Indian Emperor*.
[25] Dedication to *The Assignation*, Watson, I, 184.

aware of his own faults and honest enough to state them, as if to make it superfluous for others, less perceptive and less in a position to know, to criticize him. These faults, unfortunately, he had ventured to specify in the middle of his skewering of Sir Robert Howard: "I know I am not so fitted by nature to write comedy: I want that gaiety of humour which is required to it. My conversation is slow and dull; my humour saturnine and reserved: in short, I am none of those who endeavour to break jests in company, or make repartees."[26] These words haunted him almost the rest of his life.

Immediately, in fact, Dryden's self-strictures had been examined and enlarged upon by a certain R.F., in a pamphlet of twelve pages entitled A Letter from a Gentleman to the Honourable Ed. Howard Esq; Occasioned By a Civiliz'd Epistle of Mr. Dryden's Before His Second Edition of his Indian Emperour (1668). (There are reasons for ascribing this Letter to Richard Flecknoe but too complex to be presented here.) R.F.'s Letter is important in any account of Dryden's career in controversy because, as Hugh Macdonald pointed out,[27] many of the charges, true or false, laid against him by later writers appear in it for the first time. R.F. is the only source for the accusations that Dryden's father was a committeeman engaged in expropriating the Cavaliers, and that Dryden worked under him and his relative Sir Gilbert Pickering as a "puny statesman" in Commonwealth times. The author of the Letter represents himself as an acquaintance of Edward Howard's who occasionally converses with him and has overheard his brother Sir Robert refer to difficulties he had been having in Chancery. Despite R.F.'s insinuating tone it does not seem certain that he was on familiar grounds with the Howards (and hardly on grounds of equality), while there is no particular evidence to show that he knew Dryden except as a public figure and from his writing. However, once it became the practice in

[26] Watson, I, 116.
[27] John Dryden: A Bibliography (Oxford, 1939), p. 188.

personal controversy for writers to rake over every shred of published material for possible ammunition, R.F.'s *Letter* proved a small bonanza for Dryden's enemies.

Neither were Buckingham and many of his allies prepared to accept Dryden for what we can see he actually was: an independent, largely self-supporting man of letters, who played a self-chosen role in society without holding any well-defined institutional office. Dryden was what we have in recent years been calling a "public critic," by virtue of his literary criticism and its bearing upon court and town society, as well as of the socially tendentious nature of his plays. Of course, writers before Dryden had not failed to record views, often very severe, especially of the Court—but with the difference that they were clothed in fiction or in generality. Also, their views, if not anonymous, were expressly those of officeholders or aspirants to office, or of churchmen. Writers for the theatre had confined themselves to mirroring manners on the stage itself, not in their nondramatic writing. If they fought theatrical wars, they limited hostilities to a small, professional circle. Dryden had so dramatized himself in his dedications, prologues, and epilogues that not only his discursive judgments and opinions but his attitudes toward himself, his audiences, and his patrons had become well known in print. Mr. Bayes in *The Rehearsal* was taken up by Dryden's enemies as a clever travesty of this self-image.

He was far differently known in another circle, also rather new in character. In some ways, the company at Will's Coffee House, with which Dryden was identified by Pepys as early as 1664, must have been a great advance over the gatherings at the Mermaid and the Devil taverns in Jonson's day. At Will's the wits were to be found—the town wits, rather than the court wits. Young gentlemen from the universities, undergraduates during vacations, recent graduates; men reading law and men hoping for a place or a benefice; budding politicians and rising civil servants: anyone with a literary education or ambitions was likely to come to Will's. They were all authors or potential authors, if only of a collection of sermons or a "Letter to a Friend." The fact that Pepys resolved to return to Will's indicates that in the opinion of that shrewd judge the company was worth cultivating. In this society Dryden gradually achieved a personal dominance. By the reign of William and Mary, it had become complete. In 1671, it must already have supplied him with the many friends Bayes confidently says will serve him as a claque. Yet, if we may judge by several written relics of it, his manner toward these coffeehouse associates and admirers, even in his acknowledged dictatorship, was gentle and exquisitely courteous.[28] This, of course, was after many of his ups and downs, when he may have learned a humility he did not possess in 1671. If so, this is another service rendered him by the severe criticism of *The Rehearsal*.

It seems probable that, even before Will's, a circle of a bookish sort had given Dryden a certain status. If, as Mr. Osborn suggests,[29] he worked for Herringman during the late fifties, he would have been closely connected with the bookseller who had perhaps the largest share of specifically literary works published in the earlier years of the Restoration. His role in the printing of Sir Robert Howard's first book sounds, from Sir Robert's preface, exactly like that of an editor. If he performed the functions of editor and preface writer for Herringman, as seems not unlikely, we can see him as a man "placed" in a way quite new to the profession of literature. His position in the Foreign Secretary's Office, then, and his

[28] E.g., the letter to "an unidentified person," Ward, *Letters*, pp. 14–16.

[29] James M. Osborn, *John Dryden: Some Biographical Facts and Problems* (New York, 1940), 171–183; unchanged in the revision of 1963. I am glad to find that Osborn is open to Masson's natural assumption that it was Dryden the poet who walked with Milton and Marvell among the secretaries of the Latin Office after Cromwell's hearse; everything in the present work accords with it. Although there were other John Drydens alive at the time, I believe the poet is the only one we know of who was known to Milton and Marvell and, most important, had the unusual linguistic ability needed for foreign correspondence.

later appointments as Laureate and Historiographer, or his shareholding in the King's Theatre, were hardly so important in establishing his status in a newly developing literary community as his continuous, day-to-day exercise of a commanding skill in letters through *viva voce* criticism. He was the person to whom literary disputes were submitted for judgment, who could make a beginner's poem respectable by his practiced touch here and there, and who could successfully recommend a "taking" play for performance at either of the houses.

One great merit of Buckingham's attack in *The Rehearsal* was that it focused on Dryden's best work to date, *The Conquest of Granada.* The play, while in hardly any other sense equal to *Le Cid*, did serve as pretext for a decent theatrical quarrel. Battle lines were drawn along an axis with Good Sense and Plain English at one end, and Imagination and the Heroic Ideal at the other. Buckingham's own court of wits entered the combat, in hostility to the Court and especially to the Duke of York. Gentlemen of both universities also joined in. Dryden refrained from defending himself directly, wisely biding his time, and he even took occasion to offer Buckingham a compliment on the last two acts of *The Chances.* Perhaps Dryden had learned a lesson from the experience of his "betters," and thus was able to dissociate himself from his public image.

CHAPTER FOUR

AMONG THE COURTIERS

E ARLY in 1672, feeling the need to vindicate himself from the satire of *The Rehearsal*, Dryden printed "An Essay of Heroic Plays" and "A Defence of the Epilogue," along with the text of both parts of *The Conquest of Granada*. His contemporaries found the "Essay" unexciting, as is the usual fate of literary theory; the "Defence of the Epilogue," however, poured oil on the fires of controversy lit by *The Rehearsal*. To Dryden, the question under debate was whether Jonson's and Shakespeare's language expressed a more valid range of social experience than his and his contemporaries'. This range included the hero considered individually as an exceptional person, not simply as a man or woman of elevated status. To his opponents, poetic decorum excluded rather than cultivated exceptions. They had no place for individuals who found their own categories or achieved their own quality. Dryden's opponents saw human materials differentiated by social status rather than by personality and self-assertion.[1] Thus it made no difference that Jonson's characters were "low" so long as they were "exact." To say that they were confined to the ordinary walks of life was no argument against them. Beaumont and Fletcher's kings and queens were good only in so far as they were equally "exact" —that is, the true expression of a category within the normal range of society. Dryden, on the contrary, insisted, first, that serious poetic drama must extend its range of human experience beyond the current social pattern. Second, as to comedy, he felt that poets of his own time were at a positive advantage over Jonson because the whole breadth of society was open to them. Furthermore, his contemporaries, knowing by their own experience (as Jonson did not) the manners

[1] Rymer's handling of *Othello* is a notorious instance.

111

of society at its most cultivated, could follow the rising curve of life beyond literal actuality and project it—"exactly" but imaginatively—into an ideal dimension.

In comedy there was sanction in classical theory for Dryden's view that the poet should rise above the low level of average conversation. In his discussion of friendship in the *Nicomachean Ethics* (iv, 8), Aristotle considers the question of what makes a man good or bad company. The whole chapter might be quoted with profit, it bears so tellingly on the atmosphere that Dryden sought for comedy. A clear-cut distinction between buffoonery and wit is made. The advantage of good company, where "those who are listening or talking to us have our own code of behaviour," is stressed. Aristotle himself makes the application to comedy: "You can see the difference if you compare the Old with the New Comedy. The masters of the Old Comedy thought obscenity was amusing, the masters of the New prefer innuendo, which is a great improvement from the point of view of decency. Suppose, then, we define propriety in ridicule as the power of saying amusing things that are not unsuitable on the lips of a gentleman and do not wound the feelings of the person who is being made fun of, but perhaps even give him pleasure."[2]

However, the deadly thrust of *The Rehearsal* had been to present a vulgarian Bayes who was also a snob, and therefore incapable of moving off his own dead center in any social direction, up or down. Dryden's insistency in defending his epilogue meant that in effect he allowed the ground of debate to be shifted away from the claims of heroic poetry, to the claims of John Dryden to know more about how his betters should speak and act than they did themselves.

At the time, some readers put together the image of Bayes from *The Rehearsal* and a few passages that leaped to the eye from the preface and postscript to the printed *Conquest of Granada*. First, the opening sentence of the preface on

2 Trans. J.A.K. Thomson, Penguin ed., p. 135.

heroic plays, where Dryden speaks, loud and clear, in the voice of Mr. Bayes: "Whether heroic verse ought to be admitted into serious plays is not now to be disputed: 'tis already in possession of the stage, and I dare confidently affirm that very few tragedies, in this age, shall be received without it" (Watson, I, 156). Second, the self-congratulation of its final paragraph, which seems to set the poet in a kind of sanctuary, aloof from attack: "But I have already swept the stakes; and with the common good fortune of prosperous gamesters, can be content to sit quietly; to hear my fortune cursed by some, and my faults arraigned by others, and to suffer both without reply" (p. 166). Such a claim to immunity is itself a challenge, and one that was soon taken up.

The "Defence of the Epilogue" exposed a wide-open target; it also made available a new technique of attack. Perhaps for the first time in an English book, Dryden undertook to pick faults in the text of a poet. His motive was sound enough on scientific grounds. He wished to show a certain kind of linguistic improvement between Jonson's time and 1672. However, the nature and scope of his linguistic examination of a few pages of *Catiline* were, unfortunately, beneath contempt. It was the stock in trade of the coffeehouse reviewers, as it was of the critics extempore in the pit of the playhouse; but to dignify it with print was still a new thing. In France, where linguistic reform had already occurred, verbal criticism from Malherbe to Bouhours found more appropriate outlets than the few invidious excerpts from Jonson and Shakespeare that Dryden offers, as he says, solely to prove he is not alone in his errors. Yet Dryden knew and respected this French tradition, and plainly envied France the institution it helped to create: the Academy.

Yet there is another side to his vision of the role of language in society, as uncalculated perhaps as his examination of Jonson's *Catiline*, but much more revealing of his deeper motives. It comes toward the end of the "Defence of the Epilogue," and presents Dryden, oddly enough, as the Matthew Arnold of his age,[3] though engaged in a compliment to Charles II:

> Now, if any ask me whence it is that our conversation is so much refined I must freely, and without flattery, ascribe it to the Court; and, in it, particularly to the King, whose example gives a law to it. His own misfortunes, and the nation's, afforded him an opportunity which is rarely allowed to sovereign princes, I mean of travelling, and being conversant in the most polished courts of Europe; and thereby of cultivating a spirit which was formed by nature to receive the impressions of a gallant and generous education. At his return, he found a nation lost as much in barbarism as in rebellion. And as the excellency of his nature forgave the one, so the excellency of his manners reformed the other. The desire of imitating so great a pattern first wakened the dull and heavy spirits of the English from their natural reservedness, loosened them from their stiff forms of conversation, and made them easy and pliant to each other in discourse. Thus, insensibly, our way of living became more free: and the fire of the English wit, which was before stifled under a constrained, melancholy way of breeding, began first to display its force, by mixing the solidity of our nation with the air and gaiety of our neighbours. This being granted to be true, it would be a wonder if the poets, whose work is imitation, should be the only persons in three kingdoms who should not receive advantage by it; or if they should not more easily imitate the wit and conversation of the present age than of the past. (Watson, I, 181–182)

Dryden's "constrained, melancholy way of breeding" is not much different from Arnold's Hebraism, except that Dryden speaks of it out of the bitterness of regret for the loss of his own youth with a nation "lost as much in barbarism as in rebellion." He has Arnold's sense of the need for an open-

[3] Arnold's controversial style was also anticipated by Dryden.

ing of the whole of English society to the culture of Europe. In 1672, he was still willing to ascribe to the Court and to the King the effective role of propagator of that culture to the English people. In less than ten years, his attitude toward the Court was to change. However, a month or so after *The Rehearsal*, while *The Conquest of Granada* was his latest play and a great hit, and he was following it up with *Marriage a-la-Mode*, Dryden had good reason to be pleased with the Court and the King. In the early summer of 1671 the wittiest of courtiers, the Earl of Rochester, had enthusiastically recommended this last comedy to Charles at Windsor, and the King had joined in its praise. At the beginning of 1671 he had received £500, full payment for the arrears of his salary as Laureate and Historiographer.[4] He was, to use his own favorite image, a winning gamester.

A careful reading of the "Defence of the Epilogue" reveals that Dryden did not, after all, delude himself very seriously on the extent of his literary success. In attacking Jonson's ability to reflect the upper range of social intercourse, Dryden never actually puts his own plays into rivalry; in his own mind, he acknowledged his inferiority to Jonson as a comic writer. Yet he contended for others, Etherege and Wycherley especially, who had gone beyond Jonson's comedies in the direction Dryden recommends, and whose knowledge of courts was far beyond Jonson's or his own: "I cannot, therefore, conceive it any insolence to affirm, that, by the knowledge and pattern of their wit who writ before us, and by the advantage of our own conversation, the discourse and raillery of our comedies excel what has been written by them" (Watson, I, 181). He compared the level reached by

---

[4] Ward, p. 79. Many years later, Dryden specifically credited Clifford with securing this payment: "he awakened the remembrance of my royal master. He . . . introduced me to Augustus. . . ." Dedication of Virgil's *Pastorals* (1697) to Clifford's son (Watson, II, 217). In February, 1671, Dryden was also granted an order for repayment of his 1667 loan to the King, which Clifford finally executed for him by a peremptory order dated 17 June 1673, one of his last official acts as Lord Treasurer.

comedy in his time to that of Jonson in the matter of witty dialogue alone, and found the current level higher. From a whole series of self-derogatory references, we know that Dryden did not pride himself upon the "discourse and raillery" of his own comedies, and he freely acknowledged the superiority of "some of my contemporaries," as he said, "in comedy."[5] The favorable testimony he gave to the influence of the Court upon language was, therefore, partly to his own disadvantage, for he readily admitted he was a stranger to Whitehall.

The extent to which Dryden was self-critical appears, in startling fashion, in the same passage of the "Defence of the Epilogue." After finding Jonson's Truewit and Shakespeare's Mercutio lacking in courtly wit, he passes the same judgment on Fletcher's Don John, "and yet I may affirm," he concludes, "without suspicion of flattery, that he now speaks better, and that his character is maintained with much more vigour in the fourth and fifth acts, than it was by Fletcher in the three former" (p. 180). Without suspicion of flattery indeed! For Dryden was praising here his arch-tormentor, Buckingham, who had redone the last two acts of Fletcher's *The Chances* (February, 1667). His praise is just, and undoubtedly sincere, although it was also a piece of good tactics on Dryden's part to indicate in this way that the Duke's satire had not disturbed him. At the same time, he was consistently maintaining his opinion as to the importance of court experience, for Buckingham had that, as well as the other advantages of European travel and culture. Since Dryden had "little experience of a court,"[6] (his own words) and so far as can be seen, no experience of foreign travel, he is quite consciously and on principle barring himself from the first rank of comic writers of his time.

Dryden's English offered a semantic correlate to his idea of a society opened up by a refined language. It appears in the double sense of the word *conversation*. He normally used

[5] Dedication of *Aureng-Zebe*, S-S, v, 195–196.
[6] Dedication of *Marriage a-la-Mode* (to Rochester), S-S, iv, 254.

the term to mean "the company one keeps," or "one's man-
ner of living in society," as in the following passage, where
again he is criticizing himself in criticizing Jonson:

> And this leads me to the last and greatest advantage of
> our writing, which proceeds from conversation. In the
> age wherein those poets lived, there was less of gallantry
> than in ours; neither did they keep the best company of
> theirs. Their fortune has been much like that of Epicurus,
> in the retirement of his gardens: to live almost unknown,
> and to be celebrated after their decease. I cannot find
> that any of them were conversant in courts, except Ben
> Jonson: and his genius lay not so much that way as to
> make an improvement by it. Greatness was not then so
> easy of access, nor conversation so free, as now it is (pp.
> 180–181).

Perhaps the most important extension is suggested by Dry-
den's use here of the term "*gallantry.*" He meant by it the
special tone of conversation that includes women along
with men and that aims at giving them pleasure. Although
Dryden is as "masculine" a writer as Jonson is, he continued
through his whole career to pay court to women, apparently
with good success. Already in 1653 there was his charming
valentine letter and poem to his cousin Honor; at the very
end of his life there is the fine address to the Duchess of
Ormond and the series of lively letters to young Mrs. Stew-
art—one might call them gallant, coming from a man of
seventy to a woman of twenty-seven. In between, he ap-
parently won the favor of Anne Hyde, Duchess of York, as
he did of Anne Scott, Monmouth's Duchess, before making
any impression on their lords.

Another important clue to Dryden's desire to include
women more freely in an extended conversation is his criti-
cism of Fletcher, who was generally accepted as the most
successful English writer in presenting love on the stage. He
accuses him of insensitively allowing his heroes to do vio-
lence to women (p. 172), and declares that "he understood

not either greatness or perfect honor in the parts of any of his women" (p. 182). Dryden, in his own plays, always presented heroes who were chivalrous and women who were equally heroic, though in different ways from the men. His transformation of Shakespeare's Cressida into a virtuous and loyal heroine, albeit a sentimental one, is an example of a consistent effort to include women more fully in his dramatic scheme. A passage written in 1685 sums up Dryden's final attitude on the whole question: "the proprieties and delicacies of the English language are known to few; it is impossible even for a good wit to understand and practise them, without the help of a literary education, long reading, and digesting of those few good authors we have amongst us; the knowledge of men and manners, the freedom of habitudes and conversation with the best company of both sexes; and in short, without wearing off the rust which he contracted while he was laying in a stock of learning."[7]

The "Defence of the Epilogue" states that a playwright who wishes to succeed must stick to comedy, for that is the taste of the age. Dryden did write a comedy, *The Assignation*, but it was the opposite of a success. He also was committed, as Historiographer Royal, to work up material to justify hostilities with the Dutch; the result was the tragedy *Amboyna*, as negligible a piece as Dryden ever wrote, yet quite successful. Neither play could have taxed his mind very seriously. Yet there are no signs, after 1671, that he intended to follow up *The Conquest of Granada* with a similar work. Perhaps he was genuinely set back by *The Rehearsal*: not, of course, converted to prose and common sense by it, but disposed to pause and regroup his poetic forces. There is evidence of Dryden's willingness to accept unfavorable criticism. In the "Defence of the Epilogue" he wrote: "And certainly a severe critic is the greatest help to a good wit. He does the office of a friend, while he designs that of an enemy; and his malice keeps a poet within those bounds which the luxuriancy of his fancy would tempt him to overleap" (p. 173).

[7] Watson, ii, 20; from the preface to *Sylvae*.

Furthermore, *Samson Agonistes* had appeared in 1671, with another heavy blast from Milton against heroic couplets. Dryden's reverence for Milton was of long standing and had caused the remarkable *obiter dictum* that is tacked onto Lisideus's advocacy of heroic rhyme: "I am only troubled when great and judicious poets, and those who are acknowledged such, have writ or spoke against it."[8] This remark can only refer to Milton, whose preface to *Paradise Lost*, attacking rhyme, had appeared just before Dryden's *Of Dramatic Poesy* went to press. Again, Dryden was not converted to the use of a chorus and irregularly rhyming strophes by *Samson Agonistes*, but how could he help comparing Milton's triumph in the handling of Samson with his own rather vulnerable conception of Almanzor?

Yet it is rather academic to speculate about self-doubts and questionings in the face of a real event that forced Dryden to consider new alternatives, whether he would or not. This was the disastrous fire of 25 January 1672, which consumed the Theatre Royal in Bridges Street, the home of Dryden's company. All their costumes and scenery went up in flames, along with much of the surrounding neighborhood. This meant, of necessity, that it would be useless for Dryden to write new heroic plays, because his company could not mount them. Even before the fire, production of his plays had from time to time been held up for considerable periods. Sometimes it was the loss of leading ladies to Court lovers; other hindrances, probably more serious, resulted from the incompetent management of Tom Killigrew and the low morale of the players. It is often pointed out that Dryden failed to live up to his agreement with the King's Players for three plays a year; it would be more true to say that they failed to live up to their expectation of being able to use so many of his plays. After the fire, although he helped out with a large number of extra prologues and epilogues for the patched-up revivals that the company offered, Dryden could hardly have been encouraged to follow his former pattern,

[8] *Of Dramatic Poesy, An Essay* (Watson, 1, 55–56).

if only because it was too expensive to produce a new heroic play of the type of *The Conquest of Granada*.

At the same time, the rival Duke's Company was enjoying occupancy of its fine new theatre, designed by Wren. Its players were younger and better disciplined than the King's, and in 1672 they had an oversupply of capable playwrights, many of them quite young. Shadwell, Etherege, Pordage, Settle, Crowne, Ravenscroft, Wycherley, Payne, Betterton, and Behn all had plays produced there in the years between the destruction and rebuilding of the King's Theatre. Downes states that a couple of successful plays nevertheless "were laid aside, to make Room for others, the Company having then plenty of new Poets."[9]

As his lean years began, Dryden for the first time encountered the unpleasant facts of a life dependent upon King Charles's bounty. Since his marriage, he had supported his family mainly by his income from the playhouses—both of them at first, and then, by means of his full share in the King's Company alone. Out of the indemnity payment due his wife, the £2000 actually received must largely have been spent in setting up house at Long Acre, where the Drydens lived for almost twenty years. The rents from his little estate in Northamptonshire never rose much above £100 a year, if that; he might have earned almost as much from a good third day, if he had not given up third-day profits when he became a sharer in the King's Company. His principal source of income had been, therefore, his share, about 12 percent, of the day-to-day profits of the King's Playhouse, an amount equal to what Hart and Mohun and Lacy received.[10]

[9] *London Stage*, I, 201.

[10] These profits were estimated at between £300 and £400 a year in the well-known document drafted by the players in 1678. Hotson, however, by comparing these figures with the known income of the more successful Duke's Theatre, finds them greatly exaggerated. *The Commonwealth and Restoration Stage* (London, 1928), p. 245; for the document, Osborn, 187–189.

A point never remarked about the 1678 document is that its claim refers only to the period before the burning of the Bridges Street Theatre, i.e., only to the years 1668–1671. There is every reason to believe

Ironically, the money Dryden got from the profits of plays by Buckingham and Shadwell, nowadays considered his two worst enemies, were perhaps the last he received for years, while the company was struggling to regain its solvency. This fact may have helped him to the equanimity required to speak of Buckingham's satire in *The Rehearsal* as "the office of a friend."

Lacking income from the stage, Dryden and his wife found it impossible to exist without his pension from the King. They had three young sons, all bright enough to make their father feel they must have "a literary education." His own way of life, though hardly extravagant, demanded a fairly substantial minimum outlay if he were not to become a sort of hanger-on at Will's. His wife, after all, was the daughter of an earl, though an impoverished earl. On a pension of £200 a year, Dryden should have received, by May, 1672, £800; in fact, he had been paid only £500. Furthermore, the King was still in debt to him for the £500 lent, at Sir Robert Howard's instigation, in 1667. To make matters worse, the King at the beginning of 1672 had profoundly shocked his propertied subjects, Dryden included, by declaring a moratorium on all payments from the Royal Treasury. There was no other way for Charles to accumulate the funds needed to reopen the Dutch War.[11]

Dryden's remarks about the advantages of Court conversa-

---

that Dryden found his association with the King's Theatre a source of debt rather than gain after 25 January 1672.

[11] The war was thought to be a necessity of state policy; it also was an obligation incurred by the Treaty of London, the "secret" cover-up for the "top-secret" Treaty of Dover, signed by Buckingham and the rest of the Cabal in September, 1671. Buckingham's failure in his "undertaking" to obtain subsidies for Charles from Parliament now made it necessary for him to go along with this drastic and unlawful expedient of the "Stop," which was formally proposed to the Council by Clifford and endorsed by Shaftesbury, with the acquiescence of Arlington and Lauderdale. These five constituted the Cabal, as the Committee on Foreign Affairs of the King's Privy Council had been called for some time. (It was sheer coincidence that the initials of this group's titles made up an acronym.)

tion were, to say the least, ambiguous. His personal ac-
quaintance with the Court, as such, was both slight and
distasteful. Several of his plays had been performed at White-
hall by the King's Players, and *The Indian Emperor* was
produced there with a cast made up of ladies and gentlemen
of the Court. On these occasions, and others perhaps, Dry-
den might have spoken with the King and the Duke of York.
He must have coached the Duke and Duchess of Monmouth
in the parts they took for *The Indian Emperor*. He had
worked with the Duke of Newcastle (to some extent at least)
on *Sir Martin Mar-all*. If we can believe the biographer
Carte, he regularly dined with the Duke of Ormond; he may
even have dined with Newcastle's and Ormond's friend
Clarendon, part of whose "state" had been to dine in pub-
lic, so to speak. He had met with Buckingham on a com-
mittee of the Royal Society, for the "Improvement of the
English Language." He had literary acquaintances who were
peers: Rochester and Charles Sackville, soon to become the
Earl of Dorset. His wife's relations were as well connected
as they were numerous. However, the sum of all these associa-
tions fell far short of qualifying Dryden for a courtier. He
disliked, disapproved of, and profoundly resented the typical
denizens of Whitehall. Collectively, they daunted him. As
early as 1667, when he wrote to the Duchess of Monmouth
(a mere girl in age) of the misery of those at Court who
were not beautiful or charming, he gave signs of repugnance
and incapacity for a way of life in which self-seeking, in-
gratitude, and coldheartedness were necessary for survival,
unless one happened to be superlatively insensitive or super-
latively gracious. The slight extent of Dryden's actual pene-
tration into the life of the Court can be seen from what he
wrote in 1683 of his relationship with the Duke of Mon-
mouth, to whom he had dedicated *Tyrannic Love* in 1670:
"The obligations I have had to him were those of his coun-
tenance, his favour, his good word, and his esteem, all which
I have likewise had, in a greater measure, from his excellent
duchess, the patroness of my poor unworthy poetry. If I had

not greater, the fault was never in their want of goodness to me, but in my own backwardness to ask, which has always, and I believe, will ever, keep me from rising in the world."[12]

The man who took such a hangdog attitude was not only no courtier, he was completely alienated from the life stream of the Court, which consisted in seeking and granting favors of a more solid sort than the ones Dryden received from Monmouth.

Yet Dryden's most practical problem in dealing with the Court, although no one has recognized it, was the hostility of specific courtiers, including his brother-in-law Sir Robert Howard. The calculated affront of Dryden's "Defence" of his *Of Dramatic Poesy* was not to be forgiven for many years by Sir Robert, whose position at Court meant that Dryden, despite his repugnance for attending upon the great, had to take care lest he be ruined when he was most in need of favor. Sir Robert had always been a diligent and successful courtier, beginning in June, 1660, when he obtained the place of Serjeant Painter to the King, and (on the petition of Clarendon) was made Clerk of the Patents in Chancery *durante vita*.[13] He had already shown his gift for accumulating money: in 1657 Cromwell himself had authorized him to farm the Post Fines. He continued to farm his own talents so well that by 1694 he and his son Thomas were one of the principal founders of the new Bank of England, subscribing the "huge sum" of £18,000. It was in October, 1671, when he received the strategic place of Secretary to the Treasury, which was then in commission (i.e., supervised by a committee), that he began his lifelong career in the inner circle of Court finance. This was the place for which he had been working so hard and making so much trouble in Parliament. No doubt it pleased him better than the places, one in

[12] *Vindication* of the *Duke of Guise*, S-S, VII, 173.

[13] Oliver, pp. 38–39. On his way to amassing his great fortune, Sir Robert sold these places in 1663 and 1664. In those piping times of expanding commerce, he found more profitable uses for the money; see Hardacre's article already cited, *HLQ*, 38 (1975), 207–214.

Ireland and the other as Governor of the Barbadoes, which he had missed earlier, or the foreign secretaryship that Buckingham had tried vainly to obtain for him.[14]

Fortunately for Dryden, he had already received his £500 payment on his salary, through the aid of Clifford, then one of the Lords Commissioners of the Treasury whom Sir Robert served as Secretary. Dryden received nothing, it seems clear, during 1672, for this was the year of the embargo on payment from the Treasury. That such payment was not altogether impossible, however, appears from a letter Sir Robert sent to the Earl of Rochester from his fine house at Treasury Chambers on 29 May 1672. After speaking of his "advantage" in Rochester's friendship, Howard wrote: "I will with as much speed as I can endeavor to serve you in the particulars of your wages and pension," adding apologetically, "the Kings affairs are at this time very pressinge. . . ."[15] Yet Sir Robert made no such endeavors for his brother-in-law, quite the contrary; of that we have ample evidence in a series of angry protests from Dryden in the next ten years.

Clifford became Lord Treasurer late in 1672, and the committee was discharged. Dryden's advantage from his favor was immediate and substantial. He received £200 on the arrears of his salary in March 1673, and £560 in June to repay the £500 loan made by the Drydens to King Charles back in 1667. Twenty-five years later Dryden was still deeply moved when he recalled this bounty. Writing to Clifford's son, he said: "in the short time of his administration he shone so powerfully upon me that, like the heat of a Russian summer, he ripened the fruits of poetry in a cold climate; and gave me wherewithal to subsist at least in the long winter which succeeded" (dedication to the *Pastorals* of Virgil, Watson, II, 217). The long winter lasted until 1678, when

---

[14] Oliver, pp. 158–159.

[15] *Ibid.*, p. 181. In a very early article, Ward reported a Treasury payment to Dryden during 1672, in seeming conflict with his later account in the *Life of John Dryden*. I follow the latter.

he finally broke away from the King's Company and began to receive an income from the theatre once more.

In three separate dedications written during this time Dryden complained with great bitterness that he was being maliciously persecuted by "courtiers" who did their best to obstruct payments of his salary. A close study of his statements, which were supplemented by continued protests in later years, demonstrates beyond reasonable doubt that the chief offender was Sir Robert.

With an active Lord Treasurer (and Clifford was very active), the Secretary's function was largely that of keeping the accounts straight. Soon, however, Sir Robert Howard was able to exchange this place for one even more to his taste. On 7 February 1673, he spoke in the Commons in favor of a supply of money for the King's use, especially in protecting the nation from the Dutch. Supply was granted, in a subsidy not to exceed £70,000 a month, for an eighteen-month period. Then, most surprisingly, Sir Robert spoke on behalf of the Prerogative and the King's exercise of the right of Indulgence—a complete about-face from the days when Marvell had found him the equal of "many Montezumes" in battling Court pretensions. Not long thereafter, Sir Robert was given the reversion of one of the most sensitive places in government: Writer of Tallies in the Exchequer and Auditor of the Receipt, evidently in anticipation of the death of Sir Robert Long, which occurred on 14 July 1673. As Auditor of the Receipt, Sir Robert Howard became the only officer who knew which of the various accounts, representing sources of revenue, happened to be in funds at any given time—information indispensable to assure prompt payment of any Treasury order, no matter how high its authority. As Writer of Tallies, he might obstruct payment on all sorts of procedural grounds. Money could not be paid without the matching of two tally-halves (long pieces of wood, notched and marked to show accounts and amounts, and then split). One half showed the necessary amount was on deposit in the account named, the other that it was being properly paid out. Sir Robert took it upon himself to assign the warrants, as they were presented to his office, to whichever funds he pleased,[16] and "differences" between him and the payees soon arose.

The official most seriously annoyed by Howard's methods was a former political bedfellow of his, also a supporter of the Duke of Buckingham—Sir Thomas Osborn, who took over from Clifford as Lord Treasurer on 20 June 1673. By the end of February 1674, the Earl of Essex, Lord Lieutenant of Ireland, wrote that "the differences of Lord Treasurer and Sir R. Howard must needs make all matters of the treasury go ruggedly. As for Sir R. Howard I do not much wonder at his misbehaviour, but rather how he kept so long in the station where he is."[17] (Essex's wonderment was shared by many for the next thirty years, for Sir Robert held the auditorship *durante vita*—"charming words," as a contemporary said.) Osborn (who was soon made Earl of Danby) began making strenuous efforts to assign all warrants himself, but Sir Robert's record of receipts was kept in such a state of confusion that it was most difficult to do anything without his concurrence. Besides, he was a dangerous person to antagonize because, whenever Parliament was in session, he made very effective use of his old sounding board; the members were used to him in a watchdog role, especially on financial matters.

Howard seems to have assumed his favorite role of censor and watchdog over Dryden's loyalty as one of the King's servants. In the dedication of *The Assignation* (1673), dating from just about the time he collected the £200 on his pension, Dryden wrote to Sedley: "it is an usual trick in courts, when one designs the ruin of his enemy, to disguise his malice with some concernment of the king's; and to revenge his own cause, with pretense of vindicating the

[16] On Treasury matters, see Stephen B. Baxter, *The Development of the Treasury 1660–1702*, London, 1957.

[17] Oliver, pp. 197–198.

honour of his master."[18] Evidently this trick had been played on him. Dryden had also been accused in print of showing disrespect to royalty in his plays. It is significant to note that the pamphlet that makes the most of this particular charge, *The Censure of the Rota*, dates from early 1673. We know of another courtier who might have assisted Sir Robert in maligning Dryden: Baptist May, also a Buckinghamite of long standing, who was Keeper of the Privy Purse to the King, and against whom Dryden complained by name in a letter of 1677. The pair of them were most unfortunate enemies; Howard could hold up payments out of the Treasury, and May could frustrate gifts out of Charles's personal bounty. Both men, and especially May, had many opportunities to be with the King, and they made full use of them.

Although neither Howard nor May is mentioned by name, Dryden surely has in mind one or both of them in these words from the dedication of *Marriage a-la-Mode* to the Earl of Rochester:

> There are a middling sort of courtiers, who become happy by their want of wit; but they supply that want by an excess of malice to those who have it. And there is no such persecution as that of fools: They can never be considerable enough to be talked of themselves; so that they are safe only in their obscurity, and grown mischievous to witty men, by the great diligence of their envy, and by being always present to represent and aggravate their faults. In the meantime, they are forced, when they endeavour to be pleasant, to live on the offals of their wit whom they decry; and either to quote it (which they do unwillingly), or to pass it upon others for their own. These are the men who make it their business to chase wit from the knowledge of princes, lest it should disgrace their ignorance. . . ." Rochester, he adds, is inspired "with pity for other men, who, being of an inferior wit and

---

[18] S-S, IV, 374; see also Watson, I, 186.

quality to you, are yet persecuted, for being that in little, which your lordship is in great.[19]

These are general and unspecified charges, for Dryden was using the public print and signing his name, but the reference to passing off wit as their own surely applies to the old grudge over *The Indian Queen*. Furthermore, Dryden claimed not to be speaking in general, because he began this blast by saying, "In my little experience of a court (which I confess, I desire not to improve), I have found in it much of interest, and more of detraction. . . ." He is making a charge based on his personal experience, and the limited area of reference (he is thanking Rochester because he has "not only been careful of my reputation, but of my fortune") zeroes it in on Howard, the person more than any other who had both the motive and the position to injure Dryden's reputation and "fortune" (i.e., pension) at once. Dryden did not hold his place *durante vita*, but only *durante bene se gesserit*.

Dryden's savior, for a time, was Clifford, who used to make up the pay lists himself, every Saturday. He had been for several years at the head of the Duke of York's household, and in that capacity must have known Dryden and helped him, for the poet began the dedication to *Amboyna* (1673) by saying: "After so many favours, and those so great, conferred on me by your lordship these many years, . . ." In the heartfelt praise heaped on Clifford soon after his retirement Dryden seems to be looking back on a departed Golden Age:

If any went ill-satisfied from the Treasury, while it was in your lordship's management, it proclaimed the want of desert, and not of friends: You distributed your master's favour with so equal hands, that Justice herself could not have held the scales more even; but with that natural propensity to do good, that had that treasure been your own, your inclination to bounty must have ruined you.

[19] *Ibid.*, 254–255.

No man attended to be denied: No man bribed for expedition: Want and desert were pleas sufficient. By your
own integrity, and your prudent choice of those whom
you employed, the king gave all that he intended; and
gratuities to his officers made not vain his bounty. . . ."

Again the shape of Buckingham and his erstwhile henchman Sir Robert seems to manifest itself: "It is easy to discover, in all governments, those who wait so close on fortune, that they are never to be shaken off at any turn: Such
who seem to have taken up a resolution of being great; to
continue their stations on the theatre of business; to change
with the scene, and shift the vizard for another part—these
men condemn in their discourses that virtue which they
dare not practise: but the sober part of this present age,
and impartial posterity, will do right, both to your lordship
and to them. . . ."[20]

Sir Robert Howard was indeed one who waited close upon
fortune. Men on both sides remarked upon Howard's ability
to land on his feet. Marvell, who had admired the spirit
with which he attacked officeholders (Howard's specialty
was moving impeachments in the Commons), attacked his
defection in 1671, when he "fell to head the King's business";
when he was rewarded by the Treasury secretaryship, Dryden's friend, Sir John Berkenhead, wrote: "We hear Sr Rob:
Howard has wonn all: must hee alwaies gain by being agt
the King?"[21] Before getting the reversion of Sir Robert Long's
auditorship in 1673, Howard had spoken in favor of Supply,
Prerogative, and Toleration in the Commons, reversing his
previous performances in the House before he became a
placeman, and (as Dryden suggests) in contrast to the behavior of Clifford, who had resigned the leading post in government rather than submit to the Test. In the highly versatile English Court, the only periods from 1660 to his death
in 1698 during which Sir Robert Howard did not augment

[20] *Ibid.*, v, 6, Dedication of *Amboyna.*
[21] Oliver, pp. 176, 180.

his wealth by Court grants were those brief years when James Stuart was in the ascendant. James refused to be on good terms with him, no doubt remembering his relentless persecution of Clarendon. Howard, however, survived his displeasure and in 1696 proudly stated "that His Majesty, both when he was King, and while he was only Duke of York, never did him any Favour, nor made him the Offer of any: but on the contrary, shew'd him all the unkindness, that Occasion and Opportunity (at any time) enabled him to express."[22]

Howard's is a very recognizable type of politician or man of business. He had a perfectly unclouded view of where his own interest lay at all times, along with unlimited ability to overlook any conflict between it and the patriotic and religious ideals he vehemently proclaimed. He accumulated as many places as he could get, and gave each of them the minimum amount of attention necessary to maximize his profit therein. Yet while he was highly inefficient as a public servant in these separate functions, he was indefatigable in increasing his property by indirect as well as direct means. Especially he was zealous to keep on the good side of people who might be useful to him. His successful greed is illustrated by the fact that in 1672, the year of the war and the embargo in the Treasury, when (as he told Rochester) the King's affairs were pressing, he managed somehow to get his mistress, Mary Uphill, a Treasury pension of £200 a year.[23]

[22] Ibid., p. 291.
[23] Ibid., p. 280. They were married in 1679; the pension continued. Mary Uphill, for a long time confused with the actress Susanna, was what might be called a common-law wife to Sir Robert during his estrangement from the rich heiress, Lady Honoria O'Brien, whom he had "begged" in the manner of the times, and who was duly given him in marriage by King Charles (1665). It is ironical to reflect that, if Sir Robert had managed to obstruct payment on Dryden's salary, he would have enabled the King to pay £200 a year to Miss Uphill at no extra cost to his Treasury. Perhaps this patriotic thought occurred to Sir Robert, in the same spirit that caused him to promote the Drydens' loan in 1667. In general, Sir Robert might have stood as model for Butler's "Character of a Modern Politician."

With such an enemy at Court, it was most fortunate for Dryden that the next Lord Treasurer proved to be an illustration of King Charles's law on the choice of servants for their incompatibility with each other. The Earl of Danby was an energetic administrator bent upon making the revenue go as far as possible, to avoid the necessity of calling a Parliament. In this effort, as I have pointed out, he quickly ran afoul of Sir Robert Howard, who thus lost his power to damage Dryden in this important quarter. With the good will of Danby, the continued (though apparently rather remote) favor of the Duke of York, and the active help of two or three particular patrons at crucial times, Dryden managed to collect the pension due him at fairly regular intervals. Fortunately, the years from 1673 to 1679 were prosperous ones, especially for the customs, which formed an important part of the King's revenue.[24]

The intercession of a Court patron who took a very personal interest in the poet's well-being was always necessary, for Dryden persisted in avoiding the Court or paying attendance upon the great, and evidently Sir Robert and Bab May continued to attack and annoy him. After the failure of his very tentative overtures to Rochester, Dryden settled upon the Earl of Mulgrave (John Sheffield) as his patron, and in a real sense, protector. Addressing him in the dedication to *Aureng-Zebe* (1676), Dryden repeated his charges against courtiers like Howard and May with a few picturesque amplifications:

> ambition, lust, or private interest, seem to be the only end of their creation. If good accrue to any from them, it is only in order to their own designs: conferred most commonly on the base and infamous; and never given, but only happening sometimes on well-deservers. Dulness has brought them to what they are; and malice secures them in their fortunes. But somewhat of specious they must have, to recommend themselves to princes (for folly will

24 Ward, p. 112.

not easily go down in its own natural form with discerning judges), and diligence in waiting is their gilding of the pill; for that looks like love, though it is only interest. It is that which gains them their advantage over witty men; whose love of liberty and ease makes them willing too often to discharge their burden of attendance on those officious gentlemen. It is true, that the nauseousness of such company is enough to disgust a reasonable man; when he sees, he can hardly approach greatness, but as a moated castle; he must first pass through the mud and filth with which it is encompassed. These are they, who wanting wit, affect gravity, and go by the name of solid men; and a solid man is, in plain English, a solid, solemn fool. . . .[25]

Dryden goes on to praise Mulgrave for his judgment in choosing friends and thanks him for "the care you have taken of my fortune which you have rescued, not only from the power of others, but from my worst of enemies, my own modesty and laziness." Yet the greatest of his favors, he says, are those of "your love, and of your conversation." The latter is of the quieter sort: "How much more great and manly in your lordship, is your contempt of popular applause, and your retired virtue, which shines only to a few; with whom you live so easily and freely, that you make it evident, you have a soul which is capable of all the tenderness of friendship, and that you only retire yourself from those, who are not capable of returning it."

The term *"manly"* above is probably an allusion to the hero of *The Plain Dealer* by Dryden's friend, Wycherley, a character modeled on Mulgrave. What Dryden has to say about Mulgrave's choice of friends and enemies refers to his steady adherence to the cause of the Duke of York and to his rivalries with Buckingham and Rochester. The care

---

[25] S-S, v, 189. Cf. Evelyn's comment on Sir Robert Howard's company: "not ill-natur'd, but insufferably boasting." Dryden would not have conceded the former trait, and was no longer in a position to suffer the latter.

he took of Dryden's fortune was probably to solicit for a peremptory order to pay arrears on his pension, assigned to a Treasury revenue known to be in funds. Danby could write such an order, as Clifford had done on 17 June 1673; and Mulgrave's opportunities to talk to Danby were far greater than Dryden's.

Just before this dedication (1676), there was a serious attempt to impeach Danby in the House of Commons. Most responsible, probably, was Arlington. Danby emerged stronger than before and renewed his efforts to improve Howard's bookkeeping. These were not completely successful, for Sir Robert's total self-absorption and massive aplomb, the qualities that made him so easily recognizable as Sir Positive At-all, had not decreased; indeed, he seemed to have become a political institution and an untouchable. Yet although he fitted so very well into Charles's method of yoking rascals together, even the cynical and indulgent King was moved to censure Sir Robert for complicity in the embezzlement of over £7,000 by a clerk in the Treasury office, and for making personal use of money borrowed from a teller. At the Privy Council inquiry into these crimes, Sir Robert defended himself mightily, though on crutches with his gout—the King, ever courteous, ordered a chair for him. Since it was axiomatic that "to a man of honour nothing could be more grievous than the declaration of His Majesty's displeasure," the Council agreed that Charles should personally rebuke Sir Robert Howard for his concealing the embezzlement and borrowing of Treasury money, while commending Danby for his vigilance in the case. This the King did before the whole Council.

Yet Howard, far from grieving, displayed that insensible invulnerability of self-esteem that Dryden identified as the core of "Dulness," and which Shadwell and he and now King Charles had scourged in Sir Robert, absolutely in vain. The nature of the man is displayed in his reaction to the King's reprimand, as told by his biographer:

Howard and Ormond were writing to each other because Howard had been chosen (either by the King or by the lady herself) to help Nell Gwyn to obtain money due to her from a grant of Irish property made by the King; and Ormond had been asked to assist her cause in the Irish Court of Claims. In the letter in question, Ormond wrote to Howard: "I received yours concerning Mrs. Gwyn's concernment in the pension given her in the name of my Lord of Middlesex" but he had to say that he could not overlook prior patents, and the petition of those holding them. He suggested that Nell's pension should "be put on the Establishment" until prior rights terminated, so that everyone could be satisfied: "Be pleased to let her know of all this, and that I am her most obediant servant." Then he added a postscript: "We have heard of wonders you did upon your crutches—it was no small one in that state to be so nimble. I congratulate your activity."

Ormond's irony was completely wasted on Howard, who replied:

I would not have troubled you with the least mention of what has happened to me, were it not to justify myself why I have not thus long presented the offer of my poor services to your Excellency; but while I lay under the least accusation that could but seem to cast a blemish on me, I thought presenting such an offer to your Excellency would rather seem to beg the protection of a powerful friend than to make a clear tender of an inconsiderable servant. But since I am free from such an objection, which perhaps is by this time presented to your Excellency by indifferent persons, I would use the benefits of such an advantage which I have received by the favour and justice of so excellent a King and master only to entitle myself the better to receive your Excellency's commands, and if you are now pleased to judge anything in my power here that may be useful to your Excellency, your commands would give me the satisfaction of esteeming myself your servant by that mark of your favour, and my obedience and care in the performance should at least justify my endeavour to merit the title.

Mrs. Nelly has commanded me to present her among the number of your true servants, and does think herself so much obliged to your Excellency, that unless within a little time you command her something that she may serve you in, she swears she will pick a quarrel with you, for she vows she loves you entirely. I presume to present her own words to your Excellency that she was pleased to use. . . .[26]

The English of this letter achieves perfection in its horrible kind; a perfection that the most consummate art would not be able to match, because it could not afford to be so maddeningly wordy. Yet for all Howard's dullness it is clear that for certain matters he was a useful instrument, whom King Charles did not like to bruise too badly.

The passages just described occurred late in 1677, when *All for Love* was being performed, with a third day for Dryden by special agreement with the players—a badly needed augmentation of his pension and his rents. He had recently moved somewhat closer to the Earl of Danby by making the acquaintance of his son, Lord Latimer, and asked his help in getting permission (which Dryden always seems to have made certain of in advance) to address a dedication to the Lord Treasurer, his father:

My Lord

I am so very bad a Sollicitor, that they who will give them selves the trouble of doeing me a kindnesse, must almost do me good in spight of me: Your Uncle [i.e., Robert Bertie, third Earl of Lindsay] can beare me witness I make but little benefit of his Neighbourhood; for he is commonly up and gone, an houre before I can be at his doore: and my modesty makes me commonly the last

---

[26] Oliver, pp. 209–210, quoting the Ormond MSS.

to assault him, if he do not call upon me him selfe; and
then too I am so easily answered; & so long before I come
againe, that my little business cooles, in spight of his good
will to befriend me. This is the first fit of Coldnesse that
ever seyzd me, when I take on me to write to your Lord-
ship. But the Kings Comedy lyes in the Sudds till you
please to send me into Northamptonshyre: it will be al-
most such another piece of businesse as the fond Husband,
for such the King will have it, who is parcell poet with
me in the plott; one of the designes being a story he was
pleasd formerly to tell me; and therefore I hope he will
keep the jeast in countenance by laughing at it. I heare
My Lord your father will suddenly go out of Town; & I
desire not to be long heere after him; if he please to give
order for the producing that hundred pounds, which is
due on My Sallary from Christmasse to Midsummer, last
[i.e., 25 December 1676 to 24 June 1677]. Your Lordship
will perhaps be troubled with some of the scenes at your
own house; and as farr as two bottles I dare venture to be
a good fellow. The other part of my business depends upon
the Kings memory, & your fathers kindnesse, who has
promised My Lord Mulgrave, that I shall not fare the
worse for Mr Mayes persecuting me. I have a farther hon-
our to beg, that my Tragedy, which will be acted at Mi-
chaelmasse, & is already written, may have the honour to
be addressed to My Lord Treasurer; and that your Lord-
ship and My Lord Mulgrave will I hope beg together for
me: for I must not presume to use so great a name as My
Lord your fathers without his licence; nor do my self that
honour with posterity to be reckond his Servant except he
will give me the same favourable permission, which you
have granted me of being most humbly and most faith-
fully your Lordships Creature

John Dryden.[27]

27 Ward, *Letters*, pp. 11–12 and notes. Professor Ward (who discov-
ered and published this letter) notes that the "Uncle" was appointed
gentleman of the King's Bed Chamber in place of Buckingham in

At the time of this letter (c. July 1677), Dryden was forty-six years old and young Edward Osborn was twenty-two. We can see that Lord Treasurer Danby's son was used to entertaining Dryden; perhaps had extended an invitation to him to which this letter is in part a reply. Also, Dryden was used to entertaining Latimer and other young men with readings and with literary gossip. He was serving, whether this was his chief purpose or not, as his own advance agent in publicizing his new plays where it would do most good. Getting the King to take a collaborator's interest in the plot of a play was a clever means of forestalling any suggestion that he was attacking Charles; he had used it in connection with *Aureng-Zebe* already. Also, we see something of Dryden's habits: he was a late riser, and he liked to work on his plays in the country during the summers. Most clearly, though, we see the amount of leverage Dryden had to employ in collecting half of his year's salary: along with appeals through an earl and principal court favorite, and the Lord Treasurer and his son, he had to throw a major dedication into the hopper before he could count upon what was (supposedly) his due.

Like the one to Mulgrave, the dedication of *All for Love* to Danby is one of Dryden's most forthright and important statements. Even at this level, he takes the time to castigate Sir Robert once again, as he praises Danby:

> His Majesty, the most knowing judge of men, and the
> best master, has acknowledged the ease and benefit he

March, 1674; Lord Latimer was also a Gentleman of the Bed Chamber. Charles Bertie, their kinsman, was Secretary of the Treasury under his brother-in-law Danby, and it was he who discovered the embezzlement for which Sir Robert Howard was reprimanded before the Council by King Charles (Baxter, pp. 64, 152). "Mr. May's persecuting me," as we now would write it, refers to the notorious Baptist May. Like Sir Robert Howard he was a man of wealth. The King had given him a valuable tract of London real estate, which he built upon and sold. He raced his horses at Newmarket against the King's, and in all other ways that concerned his master's pleasures was very close to Charles. See the *Dictionary of National Biography* article on May by Thomas Seccombe.

receives in the incomes of his treasury, which you found not only disordered, but exhausted. All things were in the confusion of a chaos, without form or method, if not reduced beyond it, even to annihilation; so that you had not only to separate the jarring elements, but (if that boldness of expression might be allowed me) to create them. Your enemies had so embroiled the management of your office, that they looked on your advancement as the instrument of ruin. And as if the clogging of the revenue, and the confusion of accounts, which you found in your entrance, were not sufficient, they added their own weight of malice to the public calamity, by forestalling the credit which should cure it.[28]

There is a double reference here to Sir Robert—to his mismanagement of his place as Auditor of the Receipts, and to the philosophy he professed in the preface to *The Duke of Lerma*, where he said he wrote either in rhyme or blank verse, just as chance would have it. Furthermore, the praise recently given to Danby by Charles before the Privy Council, to which Dryden alludes here, had been coupled with his rebuke to Howard.

By the time *All For Love* was published, Dryden had left the King's Theatre and had begun to write for the Duke's Company, not as a sharer but, so far as is known, on the usual terms. Although *Limberham* was stopped, *Oedipus*, *Troilus and Cressida*, and *The Spanish Friar* were all hits during 1679 and 1680. Financial stress had inflamed his resentment against Sir Robert Howard, and financial success evidently cooled it. In the dedications and prefaces of these plays his targets are, as always, the "little critics," with no further references to persecution at Court.

[28] S-S, v, 318–319, with a final reference to the 1672 stop of the Exchequer. C. D. Chandaman, in his recent *English Public Revenue 1660–1688* (Oxford, 1975), p. 244, finds Sir Robert's figures accurate in comparison with Danby's, but makes it more a matter of politics than of accountancy.

CHAPTER FIVE

AMONG THE WITS

F INANCIALLY, as has been shown, 1672 was the first of a series of seven lean years for Dryden. Economic distress partly explains the unusually defensive tone of the dozen prologues and epilogues that, aside from *The Assignation, Amboyna*, their dedications, and the prose apparatus that went with *The Conquest of Granada*, are all Dryden had to show for the years between *Marriage a-la-Mode* and the end of 1675[1]—his "most barren period," as George R. Noyes called it. Even when, more than two years after the fire, the company opened its rebuilt theatre, he was still far from happy, as the prologue he wrote for the occasion shows:

> They who are by Your Favours wealthy made,
> With mighty Sums may carry on the Trade:
> We, broken Banquers, half destroy'd by Fire,
> With our small Stock to humble Roofs retire,
> Pity our Loss, while you their Pomp admire.
>
> (*Works*, I, 149; 12–16)

This complaint is followed by a comment (its irony may be intentional) on the regime of austerity decreed for His Majesty's servants after the ill success of the most recent Dutch War:

> Our Royal Master will'd it should be so,
> What e're He's pleas'd to own, can need no show:
> That Sacred Name gives Ornament and Grace,
> And, like his stamp, makes basest Mettals pass.
>
> (30–33)

The truth seems to be that no help was forthcoming to the

---

[1] Robert D. Hume, "The Date of Dryden's Marriage A-la-Mode," *Harvard Library Bulletin*, 21 (1973), 161–166, dates this play in the fall of 1671.

King's Theatre from the King or the Court, except for the gift of cast-off clothing and perukes for the women to wear when they donned men's breeches in the most fetching of the various attempts by the King's Players to make do. In March 1674, Dryden, as a shareholder in the acting company, was assessed £200 to help underwrite the new expenses of the building company. If he did not carry out the agreement entered into by the players at that time, Dryden was liable to loss of his right to share in the profits.[2] A new agreement was drawn on May 1, 1676, when Tom Killigrew finally retired in favor of his son Charles, and this document lacks Dryden's signature. He could probably have raised the necessary £200 in the spring of 1674. Yet it would square with the attitude toward the theatre as an outlet for poetry that he was then expressing, if he should also have dropped his financial interest in the King's Players.

One cause of that dissatisfaction is indicated by Dryden's apparent loss of conviction that the heroic play could satisfy his need to be a poet. As long as he believed his heroic plays really were heroic poems in little, Dryden was not too unhappy in the theatre; but that faith seems to have been badly weakened between 1671 and 1676, when he gave vent to his feelings of discouragement:

> The truth is, the consideration of so vain a creature as man is not worth our pains. I have fool enough at home without looking for it abroad; and am a sufficient theatre to myself of ridiculous actions without expecting company, either in a court, a town, or playhouse. 'Tis on this account that I am weary with drawing the deformities of life and lazars of the people, where every figure of imperfection more resembles me than it can do others. If I must be condemned to rhyme, I should find some ease in my change of punishment. I desire to be no longer the Sisyphus of the stage: to roll up a stone with endless labour (which, to follow the proverb, gathers no moss) and

---

[2] Hotson, *Commonwealth and Restoration Stage*, p. 254.

which is perpetually rolling down again. I never thought myself very fit for an employment where many of my predecessors have excelled me in all kinds; and some of my contemporaries, even in my own partial judgment, have outdone me in comedy. Some little hopes I have yet remaining, that I may make the world some part of amends for many ill plays by an heroic poem. (Watson, I, 190–191)[3]

Other, personal causes of Dryden's loss of enthusiasm for the stage existed and are worth stating. The story is important, for it underlies the rivalries of his great satiric period from 1678 to 1683. More important still, it enables us to perceive a second polity, the little world of letters, which meant a great deal to Dryden—as their professional activity does to most people. Not only does each of us participate to a greater or less degree in these smaller, personal polities; they tend to reflect the state of the larger national or international political organisms. In 1673, besides lacking the outlet to which he had been directing the bulk of his writing for years, Dryden began to suffer from the harassment of several of his fellow writers. From some of them whom he had generously acknowledged and even helped, he deserved better; others were merely retorting upon him in kind. Yet it was an unhappy falling-off from the vision in *Of Dramatic Poesy*, where he had looked for a contribution to the poetic art and its progress from his whole generation, like that of the poets of Augustus's time who advanced so far because they worked so well together in harmony with the special genius of their age.

Dryden's vision of a new Augustan age in poetry was based on a well-articulated theory of the cultural process. Anticipated by many remarks in passing in his early writing, it had been carefully formulated in *Of Dramatic Poesy*.

---

[3] Much later, Dryden wrote that tragedy "is only instructive, [epic] forms a hero, and a prince." "Discourse Concerning Satire" (1693), Watson, II, 96. This realization, that drama, unlike epic, cannot formatively project a prince-hero of an ideal sort, had come to him by 1675.

Speaking out of his own early experiences, Dryden insisted that the old poets' line of march in England had been interrupted during the Commonwealth. Nevertheless, he saw the chance of a fresh start. *Of Dramatic Poesy, An Essay* is a beautiful image in itself of the poets' fellowship that mutually inspires and guides composition. In it he refers, repeatedly, to a passage in which Velleius Paterculus (writing, like Dryden, just after a great age, and describing the literary golden ages of Athens and Rome), had suggested why those eras were so crowded with accomplishment: "Rivalry nourishes genius; at times envy, at times admiration inspires imitation. Eventually, whatever is made the object of the highest striving is brought to the heights. It takes time to do the difficult well; and in nature anything that fails to progress, falls back."[4]

Almost thirty years later, Dryden reechoed the thought in these words: "Great contemporaries whet and cultivate each other; and mutual borrowing, and commerce, makes the common riches of learning, as it does of the civil government."[5] In the interim, he had lived more than any writer before (or since, it may well be) the life of friendly interchange with his fellow poets.

Dryden seems to have been able at all times to retain his equanimity under attacks aimed simply at his productions and his style of writing. He hardly ever answered them with personal attacks in return, but would reply as part of an extended discussion of the principles that he claimed were involved. He consistently managed to maintain a dignified serenity that in itself seemed a good rebuttal, even to contemporaries.[6] Nevertheless, he had his Achilles' heel: it was money, and most understandably, for after the first few years of his married life in London (i.e., 1668-1672) he was

---

[4] Watson, I, 26, 30, 32, 56, 77; *Historia Romana*, I, 17 [my translation].

[5] "A Discourse Concerning Satire," Watson, II, 81.

[6] *Raillery-a-la-Mode Consider'd* (1673) praises Dryden for his expressed determination to keep silent while his detractors scolded on.

continually in need of about half the money required for the maintenance of his family. He had always made a particular point of expressing his sense of obligation to anyone who helped him in what he called his "fortune," and by the same token he reacted strongly against anyone who offered what he considered to be uncalled-for threats to his livelihood. One of the most attractive traits in Dryden is his élan, his good spirits, and his lack of defensiveness; anxiety about his income is perhaps the only breach in his confident, cheerful approach to literature and the world. He probably was dissatisfied with himself for being so awkward at the game of success, for missing many opportunities that had been the making of several of his friends and dozens of his acquaintances.

With such feelings, Dryden could allow *The Rehearsal* to pass without comment, and even save face skillfully with a compliment to Buckingham over his last two acts of *The Chances*. He could pass off as pedantry the series of four "letters" in the nit-picking manner of his own "Defence of the Epilogue,"[7] addressed to him and circulated in manuscript by Matthew Clifford, a well-beneficed member of Buckingham's writing corps. He could dismiss with a curt sentence or two such attacks as the Oxford *Censure of the Rota* and its Cambridge continuation, ironically called *The Friendly Vindication of Mr. Dryden From the Censure of the Rota. By His Cabal of Wits.* Even better, Dryden could refer his readers to a rebuttal of these pamphlets, called *Mr. Dreyden Vindicated in a Reply*, written without his previous knowledge by a critic who was not even an acquaintance. That an author's work should be attacked and defended

---

[7] *Notes Upon Mr. Dryden's Poems* (first printed in 1687, but circulated in 1672). Clifford signed and dated the fourth letter from the Charter House, of which he had recently become Master, 1 July 1672, and began: "Since I cannot draw you to make a reply to me. . . ." He was, like Dryden, a Westminster and Trinity College, Cambridge man, d. 1677. Clifford's *Notes*, and much of the kind of comment I discuss here, have been reprinted in *Dryden: The Critical Heritage* (London, 1971) by James and Helen Kinsley.

without his having to enter personally into the fray was obviously a new thing in 1673, when these three essays appeared. Dryden had stated his intention of leaving his books to the critics to deal with as they saw fit, and now at last there was a two-way discussion of the merits of his case, by presumably disinterested students of the art. It obviously disappointed the authors of two of the attacks, Clifford and the writer of *The Friendly Vindication*, who looked for the usual retort from the poet himself.

His critics took offense, above all, at Dryden's professionalism. They took their lead from *The Rehearsal*. The contrast between Johnson and Smith, on one side, and Bayes on the other is that of discerning, liberal-minded amateurs opposed to a dogmatic professional. These "little critics," as Dryden called them, particularly resented his efforts to discover and explain the principles of good dramatic construction. They gave the impression that a well-written play somehow happened and that any clever man about town could manage the trick without fussing over rules. At the same time they subjected the detail of mere lines and phrases to the most rigorously logical examination. A morbid, pettifogging rationalism, devoid of literary awareness, is typical of most of these attacks. Only a minority are relieved by a broad, though often grossly unfair, sense of the ridiculous. Yet all this outpouring has its good side; it seems to indicate a great deal of interest in the theatre and a great deal of interest in literary criticism.

If, in the literary sense, there proved to be less at stake in the quarrel over *The Conquest of Granada* than in the controversy over *The Cid* in France, socially at least, and in the developing relation between literature and its audience, the attacks and defenses of Dryden were significant. They emanated from those new centers of public opinion, the coffeehouses, and they brought into focus the attitudes of that new dictator who in English-speaking countries has seemed to function in the place of an Academy: the common reader or playgoer. He is represented in *The Rehearsal* by Smith and Johnson, "two gentlemen of wit and fashion about the town," who exhibit a genuine fondness for the theatre and especially for the players, and who obviously have learned to formulate and express their opinions in the informal give-and-take of the coffeehouse. Their literary philosophy is that of the average man; it is limited to common sense and what seems to them proper and fitting. They handle poor Bayes as the public likes to handle those who have won public success by means of talent and hard work: they patronize and belittle him.

This phenomenon, so familiar to us, was taking shape in 1671. Although a "public" in the modern sense of the word was only beginning to come into being, the essential note that distinguishes the modern public from older types of community was present in the London of that time. In a society rapidly growing more bourgeois, journalism and the theatre provided everyone with the same new topics of conversation, the coffeehouses provided the setting, and a flood of play texts and pamphlets assisted the bulk of the new public to arrive at their opinions second-hand.

The Rehearsal established a manner in coffeehouse criticism and started a brisk flow of pamphlets. In most of these, Dryden came in for some smart handling. *The Censure of the Rota, on Mr. Driden's Conquest of Granada,* by Richard Leigh, conveys an impression of the intense interest the habitués of coffeehouses felt in Dryden's entire output, lit up as it had been by the success of his last heroic play: "Amongst severall other late exercises of the Athenian Vertuosi in the Coffe-Academy instituted by Apollo for the advancement of Gazett. Philosophy Mercury's, Diurnalls, &c.:" it begins, "this day was wholly taken up in the Examination of the Conquest of Granada." The criticism adopts a cultivated manner, speaking of Almanzor as a free hero, since "the poet represented men in a Hobbian State of War." There is a reference to *Of Dramatic Poesy,* and the usual retaliation in favor of Jonson. An arrow is shot at a favorite butt, the "tulip image." "You may be sure [it] grew no where but in a Poets Garden," says Leigh. Leigh also pounces upon

> Like Tapers new blown out, the fumes remain,
> To catch the light, and bring it back again.

He finds this "blowing a candle out, and blowing in again, in two verses," offensive. (Since Sir Samuel Tuke had used this phenomenon for a successful stage effect in the dark scene of *The Adventures of Five Hours*, Dryden's image was social and scientific as well as "natural.") Leigh even objects to the lively "tart and cheese-cake time" phrase of the epilogue to *Tyrannic Love*, because a similar phrase had been used somewhere in *Sir Martin Mar-all*. This is a not unusual sign of the thorough knowledge Dryden's critics had of his whole body of plays.

Leigh also takes exception to "such mean couplets as this in Maximin, 'O my dear Brother, whom Heav'n let us see / And would not longer suffer him to be!'" This couplet is typical of Dryden's style of classical reminiscence, combining echoes of the Marcellus passage of *Aeneid* VI and Catullus's tribute to his dead brother, two of the most famous places in Latin verse. Yet Leigh is typical of most of these "little critics"; either he could not reconcile himself to this kind of imitation, or, more likely, he could not recognize the allusions. The most telltale abuse is directed, not at the lines of any of the plays, but at the preface of *The Indian Emperor*, where Dryden had boasted that the subject of that play was the greatest possible one, being the discovery of a new world. "This Zany of Columbus," snorts Leigh, "covering the known and unknown earth, and the heavens too."

Hugh Macdonald raised a fascinating question as to the special virulence behind these attacks, which continued until Dryden's death. "Indeed it is not easy," he said, "to find any parallel in English literature to so much violence and ridicule directed against one man of letters in his lifetime. . . . some of the pieces are almost incomprehensible in their fury, as though the writers did not clearly know what it was that had angered them." He suggested that "there was in his character some shade of ineffectiveness which, when it is combined with the possession of extraordinary powers, is apt to be met by resentment."[8]

A different answer, in my opinion closer to the truth, was supplied by an unknown author who wrote a defense of the Laureate in reply to the pamphlet by Leigh. This writer suggested that the hostility shown Dryden is natural, coming to "such an Authour who seems to command his fame rather than receive it from the world." The inherent aptness of this remark is strengthened by the historical fact that Dryden was the first man of letters to come prominently before the public in his simple character as writer. He was the first to suffer from the vulnerability of the unburied talent, the exposure of those whose achievement of public status is based upon their success in pleasing the crowd, but who yet try to preserve their independence of the crowd. Dryden had the courage to move along several new and different lines of his own choosing, and the genius to succeed in each, dragging his public behind him; this success proved hard to forgive, either to less successful rivals or to those critics who refused to be pleased along with the rest of the world.

It would be worthwhile to know who this defender of Dryden was. His pamphlet is a very well-written piece, which strikingly anticipates the urbane manner of the best Augustan essays. It is entitled A *Description of the Academy of the Athenian Virtuosi: with A Discourse held there in Vindication of Mr. Dryden's Conquest of Granada; Against the Author of the Censure of the ROTA* (1673). In it, the Athenian Virtuosi meet at a coffeehouse. They prepare for their critical examination of Dryden's play by issuing a pair of claws to each member, and in a private chamber they employ them at the task of tearing it apart line by line, even word by word. When our visitor has listened to as much as

[8] Hugh Macdonald, "The Attacks on Dryden," *Essays and Studies . . . of the English Association*, XXI (1935).

he can stand, he speaks out in protest. He shows himself enough of a classicist to quote Longinus in the original Greek (a year before the appearance in France of Boileau's translation, which practically resurrected Longinus from oblivion), making the point "that criticism must be the deliberation of much experience." He recognizes and sympathizes with allusions to the classics: "If Mr. Dryden applys an happy epithete 'tis traduc'd, as in these excellent verses, speaking of Almanzor,

> A gloomy smile arose
> From his bent browes, and still the more he heard,
> A more severe, and sullen joy appear'd,

Which I am certain is in imitation of Virgil, where fierce Mezentius stands,

> Olli subridens, mixta Mezentius ira."

Very perceptively, he asserts Dryden's piety toward the great writers of "the Last Age" in answer to those who resented his attitude toward Jonson in particular. However, he finds that the Athenian Virtuosi are altogether unresponsive and ignorant of literature, and gives up: "I will no longer give my humanity the trouble, in reclaiming, if it were possible, your folly. . . ." It is a very effective tribute to Dryden's own humanity that he should find such an admirer, whose witty serenity recommends his critical judgment.

Dryden also appeared able to take with aplomb the retorts, by way of preface, prologue, and epilogue, of rival playwrights such as Shadwell, Edward Howard, and Ravenscroft. They objected to his claims for heroic verse or gentlemanly conversation on the stage, or to his taunts against farce and empty spectacle at the relatively prosperous Duke's Playhouse. By the fall of 1673, however, Dryden was obviously disturbed by Elkanah Settle, one of the numerous young poets of the rival company. Thus began a personal disagreement that was to continue and proliferate years later, during the Popish Plot and Exclusion Crisis, and help to bring into being and to shape some of Dryden's best satire.

It was not the extraordinary success of Settle's *Empress of Morocco* that aroused Dryden. Throughout his whole life his record clearly shows a pattern of generous encouragement to younger writers, beyond a parallel in our literature until Ezra Pound came along. He showed no jealousy over the triumph of Settle's play in its premiere at Court during March 1673. After all, its success when performed by the ladies and gentlemen of the Court served to confirm his claims for the heroic play in rhyme. Probably, however, he did oppose Settle's attempt to jump from his parent company, the Duke's, and have *The Empress of Morocco* produced by the King's Company. It was not unreasonable that he should feel the money involved ought to be invested in a play by himself rather than by a poet previously associated with the rival theatre. Yet in fact Dryden's feelings did not hurt Settle; it was the Duke's Company that protested his attempt and secured a decision from the Duke of York himself that the play was theirs. Settle is our witness here; he explained that his motive for wishing to change theatres was a conviction that only Mr. Hart could do justice to his heroic couplets.[9] Since Betterton's style, much more restrained than Hart's, really was less suited to the egregious rants of *The Empress of Morocco*, and since Settle always appears as something of an ass, this sounds like a genuine enough reason for what amounted to an attempt to come aboard a sinking ship.

Earlier in 1673, Dryden had been blamed in *The Friendly Vindication* for fending off other poets from his company. This pamphlet, although it bore a Cambridge imprint, has no printer's or bookseller's name on the title page, and it hardly seems to be a university production; it is informed by gossip of a Grub Street order, perhaps at second hand, but nevertheless reasonably circumstantial and up-to-date. The timing of the piece falls between *The Censure of the Rota*,

[9] See *A Supplement to the Narrative* (1683), p. 18; *A Narrative* (1683), Dedication p. A^v.

which it echoes by name, and Charles Blount's reply to both, *Mr. Dreyden Vindicated*; all three appeared in time for Dryden to take notice of them in a dedication he must have put through the press by May, 1673. In *Friendly Vindication* the reader is introduced, rather vaguely, to a scene in which Dryden is surrounded by his young disciples—his "cabal of wits." The author, however, seems incapable of maintaining dramatic distance. He provides marginalia and other bookish details, such as this one on the phrase "a sawcy Boldness" used in *The Maiden Queen*: "Some say his first Copy had consuming instead of sawcy, not much a better Epithet join'd to Boldness" (p. 4). This comment, at its microscopic level of pedantry, hardly seems sane. A passage on the next page, having very obscurely brought up the subject of ghosts, is at best highly incoherent. Dryden, it states, "had merited from them, by his most ingenious converse and writing (besides some more secret obligations) as also to cry up and preserve the honour of the Laurel conferred on him." On page 6 the pamphlet begins to make sense of a kind, telling the reader that Dryden urged his cabal of "flourishing ingenuities" to form a claque, "that whatsoever was his, might be reverenced as a Play, and so voted, though without Intrigue or Wit." Then "adding, that nothing less could square with his profit, than wholly appropriating the fame and perquisites of Wit, (at least of one Play-house) to himself: for which purpose, he could not but with all humility, implore their Embargo on all other Poets that might possibly impair his repute, and Trade of Writing, though their Consciences were so guilty as to believe his Plays the worst." The notion of an attempted "Embargo" by Dryden on new plays at the King's House (at least ambitious, expensive ones like *The Empress of Morocco*) has some plausibility. An assortment of revivals and a few new pieces by the house poets Dryden and Duffet made up the entire offering of the King's Company during their two years in the dingy and remote Lincoln's Inn Fields Theatre where they took refuge after their disastrous fire. Actually, their impoverished condition, rather than any embargo by Dryden, was a sufficient cause. The last new play before their fire, in fact, had been by a poet associated with the Duke's Company—*The Miser*, by Shadwell (*London Stage*, I, 191). Yet Dryden may very well have urged, one must admit, the necessity of such a policy against the plausible argument that a sure hit such as *The Empress of Morocco* was worth the financial risk. He was, indeed, already known to hold such an attitude, for according to a prologue of his that Hart spoke in 1672, the company could "neither raise Old Plays, nor New adorn."[10]

The pamphlet continues thereafter to make statements that read like those of a well-informed insider. They could just possibly, once again, be the gleanings of a stage-struck outsider extracted from an industrious conning of Dryden's whole printed works to date. In other words, the writer might be a fanatically interested member of the public intruding upon the private life of a public figure. The pamphlet might thus be more or less accurate, but only as a combination of fiction, guesswork, and feedback from printed materials. The subjection of a writer to this kind of fictional invasion of privacy was a relatively new phenomenon in 1673 (it had long been going on in the form of *romans à clef*, dealing with court figures at Versailles and Whitehall). Dryden was its first major victim in our literary history. We cannot ignore the possibility, in certain problems related to his biography, that what seems an authentic contemporary source is really a work of the imagination, and one produced, perhaps, by a member of the general public whose only involvement is that he is what we now know as a "fan."

Having entered this caveat, it does seem to me that *The Friendly Vindication* is genuinely rooted, in its bumbling way, in a knowledge of more or less intimate details of Dryden's earlier writing (not personal) career. An example can be found in this reported speech of "Mr. Dryden" to his disciples: "In the beginning of his undertaking he sufficiently

---

[10] "Prologue to Arviragus Reviv'd," *Works*, I, 145, line 4.

observed as was evident to them and the World, in his Prac-
tises to gain Proselytes to his Muse. As also his humble and
supplicant addresses to Men and Ladies of Honour, to whom
he presented the most of his Plays to be read, and so passing
through their Families to comply their Censures before-
hand: confessing ingeniously, that had he ventured his Wit
on the Tenter-hooks of Fortune (like other Poets, who de-
pended more on the merit of their Pens) he had been more
severely intangled in his own Lines long ago" (p. 6). This
seems to describe Dryden's early successes with Castlemaine,
Anne Hyde, and Anne Scott. On the other hand, it echoes
the business in *The Rehearsal* where Bayes says, after he
rises up hastily and falls down, "A plague of this damned
stage, with your nails and your tenter-hooks, that a gentle-
man cannot come to teach you but he must break his nose,
and his face, and the devil and all."[11] Feedback from printed
works continues to be a possibility on page 8, where "Dry-
den" tells his cabal, "He had found a way not only to Libel
mens persons, but to represent them on the Stage too: That
to this purpose he made his observations of men, their
words and actions, with so little disguise, that many beheld
themselves acted for their Half Crown." This could be an
echo of Edward Howard's protest, printed in the preface
to *The Women's Conquest* (1671): "I cannot chuse but
censure the unpoetical, and no less offensive license in
particularly designing the persons of any, an abuse that de-
serves to be severely resented, since (if permitted) no man
can be secured, but that he may give his money to observe
his alliance, friend, or himself, made his injurious enter-
tainment on a publick stage" (p. 7).

Next, *The Friendly Vindication* plunges us back into the
angry imbroglio when Sir Robert Howard's *Duke of Lerma*
divided him from his brother-in-law on the issue of Claren-
don's impeachment and persecution: "Besides, that he had
been so frankly obliging as (where he could not use a Char-
acter, or apprehended the License) *to assign it to some other*

[11] II. v. 33–36, ed. Nettleton and Case.

poet of his Cabal, or exchange one Part for another, it may be Club-Wit too, the better to set men forth: That this was a Sir Positive Truth Mr. Dryden had not fore-head enough to denie" (p. 8). Here is an obvious reference to Shadwell's character in *The Impertinents, or, The Sullen Lovers,* Sir Positive At-all, which was widely recognized as a legitimate takeoff of Sir Robert Howard. It asserts that Dryden furnished Shadwell with this characterization, early in 1668. It will be recalled that Edward Howard, also, was mimicked in *The Sullen Lovers,* as Poet Ninny. The charge that Dryden invented or "clubbed wit" (i.e., collaborated) on these caricatures may not have been true, but it seems to be stated with complete, if awkward, sincerity by someone who was rather outraged at the crime.

The rest of the passage reaches the bottom of the tunnel, and we seem once again to be in the dark world of the "R.F." who wrote *A Letter From a Gentleman To the Honourable Ed. Howard Esq.* That letter had spoken of a craven evasion by Dryden of a challenge to a duel by Sir Robert Howard. *The Friendly Vindication* offers what purported to be additional details of this episode, now five years past: "besides, that Mr. Dryden had made his submissions and recantations most ingeniously both by word and writing: that he conceived a person of Honor, had a Letter dedicated to the Fire, even by the hangmans hands, if the injur'd should think it necessary; Therefore what was done was candid enough as to that particular. If Mr. Dryden courted more his security than honour, he was not to be blamed, if his temper found it convenient: Or it might be interpreted his Kindness, in not being willing to put so much Wit as his own to hazard . . ." (p. 8).

This labyrinth of innuendo continues and extends to remoter times: Mr. Dryden "was a Poet in Olivers time, and something more subservient to his Principality" (p. 15). "Something" probably means, Dryden performed a function other than poet under the Protectorate—i.e., he had a government place. This, too, echoes the letter of "R.F." It would be tempting to suggest that both attacks were written by the same person, probably Richard Flecknoe. *The Friendly Vindication*, however, is ascribed to "Sr Robert Howard" on the Bodleian copy (Mal. B. 288[9]; Oliver, p. 118). He might have written it; so might his brother Edward. Yet whether either of them, with their experience in the theatre, could have done such a feeble job of dramatization seems doubtful. Also, one wonders whether they would have debased themselves and their family by printing either of the following phrases: "his Imagination (whatsoever his person is) was sufficiently lascivious" or "the Dildo of Mr. Drydens Muse, so neatly applied to all the females of the Town" (p. 12). Nor would either of them, probably, have invited a prolonged exchange of pamphlets, as does the conclusion of *The Friendly Vindication*: "Finis or not Finis as Mr. Dryden pleaseth" (p. 17). In all charity, although Sir Robert and Edward Howard could both write prose that was "mighty silly" (Pepys's term for R.F.'s *Epistle*), they do deviate into sense from time to time, whereas the reader of both the *Epistle* and *The Friendly Vindication* gets a nagging suggestion of a meaning, so involved with the vain and confused gestatory process of the author's mind that it is never born into the open air. Both pieces show an obsession with trivia and an indiscriminate proclivity to mix the important with the microscopic; it approaches imbecility or at least senility.

Dryden's answer to the author of *The Friendly Vindication* was curt: "He is only like Fungoso in the play, who follows the fashion at a distance, and adores the Fastidious Brisk of Oxford."[12] Only a year before he had dismissed "R.F." by saying that the "little critics" in their ignorance or malice "would accuse me for using *empty arms*, when I writ of a ghost or shadow. . . . Some fool before them had charged me in *The Indian Emperor* with nonsense in these words: *And follow fate which does too fast pursue*, which

[12] Dedication to *The Assignation*, fin.

was borrowed from Virgil. . . ."[13] The "fool" was R.F., and it is worth noting that R.F. the author of the *Epistle* is linked in this passage with Dryden's "ghosts," otherwise inexplicably referred to in *The Friendly Vindication* (p. 5).

While we are back on the subject of ghosts, there is a personage mentioned both by Dryden and by the author of *The Censure of the Rota* who may or may not be a creature of flesh and blood. *The Censure of the Rota* was identified by Anthony à Wood as the work of Richard Leigh, a member of Queen's College, Oxford. It introduces "a grave Gentleman that us'd to sup in Apollo and could tell many Storys of Ben Johnson, who told them, that in his opinion Mr. Dryden had given little proof of his Courage, since he for the most part combated the dead; and the dead—send no Challenges. . . ." This might be a mere fiction elaborated from Dryden's brief satirical "character" in the "Defence of the Epilogue": "The memory of these grave gentlemen is their only plea for being wits. They can tell a story of Ben Jonson, and, perhaps have had fancy enough to give a supper in Apollo that they might be called his sons; and because they were drawn in to be laughed at in those times, they think themselves now sufficiently entitled to laugh at ours. Learning I never saw in any of them, and wit no more than they could remember. In short, they were unlucky to have been bred in an unpolished age, and more unlucky to live to a refined one. They have lasted beyond their own, and are cast behind ours: and not contented to have known little at the age of twenty, they boast of their ignorance at three-score" (Watson, I, 181). This revenant, on the other hand, might well be a real person. The fact that *The Censure of the Rota* refers to a charge of cowardice resting upon Dryden because he had failed to answer a challenge, and ascribing this charge to "a grave personage" exactly like Dryden's "character," makes it likely that the *Epistle* of R.F. was

[13] In a paragraph tacked on to the preface of *Tyrannic Love* for the second edition (1672); Watson, I, 142.

being freshly circulated in 1672, and suggests that someone, possibly R.F. himself, was spreading the story of a challenge by Sir Robert Howard to Dryden—a "grave gentleman" who fitted Dryden's rather circumstantial description. (In passing, it should be pointed out that the use of the plural—"these grave gentlemen," for example—does not of necessity mean that Dryden had more than one actual person in mind. Plural reference was a convention of personal controversial writing throughout this period, especially when the passages appeared in signed prefaces and dedications, where personal polemics were theoretically out of place.)

Once again, it makes little difference whether this "grave gentleman" was R.F., or Richard Flecknoe, or whether he was a living person at all. The really important thing is that whatever he was, Dryden had to live with him. In Dryden's existence he was a "man of the crowd," like Dostoevsky's figure, who had unluckily fastened upon him; a thorn in the flesh of the first English writer to have a public. The twisted envy that seems a necessary side-effect of public fame transferred itself smoothly enough from R.F. to Richard Leigh if (and once again it makes little difference) Leigh was the author of *The Censure of the Rota*.

Back in 1668, R.F. had attacked Dryden's use of the title of Esquire. *The Censure of the Rota* now took up a new target on the same range, furnished it by "The Defence of the Epilogue." Speaking of Beaumont and Fletcher, it says sarcastically, "this was the unhappiness of their Education, they were not so well bred, nor kept so good company as Mr. Dryden" (p. 12).

There was no direct way in which Dryden could rebut this line of attack without appearing ridiculous. His tactics of ignoring *The Rehearsal* were clearly the right ones. Yet the imputation that he was really ignorant of the ways of good society was one that he would not allow to stand. This was one of the reasons for the choice of Sir Charles Sedley as the dedicatee of *The Assignation*. Sedley was notorious for his knowledge of courts, although by 1673 he had become disaffected with Charles II's.[14] In the dedication Dryden pressed hard (perhaps a bit too hard) the perfect community of interest he shared with Sedley as a fellow wit. His chief reliance, however, was upon his own skill as a writer of English prose. He managed to weave the notes of his "other harmony" so as to conjure up a warmly nostalgic picture of his favorite social scene—the generous intercourse of those great Augustan poets, critics, and patrons, who figure in his pages as longtime friends and familiars. Thus launched, he begins to fly in marvelously cadenced prose, carrying Sir Charles on his back as he goes: "We have, like them, our genial nights, where our discourse is neither too serious, nor too light, but always pleasant, and for the most part instructive: the raillery neither too sharp upon the present, nor too censorious on the absent; and the cups only such as will raise the conversation of the night, without disturbing the business of the morrow" (Watson, I, 186). This is one of the high points of Dryden's encomiastic style in the dedications. That it is an accurate description of a typical evening in the company of Sir Charles Sedley, one may doubt; but as a statement of attractive possibility, one could hardly reject it. We have to believe in it here as we believe in any consummately successful piece of art. The passage does suggest, however, what a typical evening in Dryden's company would be like. After this passage, it is not easy to belittle the conversation of Dryden.

He was however, under attack in more than one quarter; that is evident from what follows in this dedication to Sedley. Again speaking of "these wretches" who misrepresent wits, Dryden says: "Oftentimes it so falls out, that they have a particular pique to some one amongst us, and then

---

[14] Sedley had accompanied Buckingham and Dorset to Versailles in 1670, along with Sprat, Butler, and Jo Haines (the latter three associated with Buckingham in *The Rehearsal*); V. de Sola Pinto, *Sir Charles Sedley* (London, 1927), pp. 14–18. On Sedley's retirement from Court, see J. H. Wilson, *Rochester-Savile Letters* (Columbus: Ohio State Contributions in Language and Literature no. 8, 1941), p. 78.

they immediately interest heaven in their quarrel; as it is an usual trick in courts, when one designs the ruin of his enemy, to disguise his malice with some concernment of the King's, and to revenge his own cause, with pretence of vindicating the honour of his master" (Watson, I, 186). Leigh, in a rather jolly page of *The Censure of the Rota*, objected to the way Dryden heightened Almanzor's character by bringing in "a sheepish King with a Guard of poultrons to be kick't by him, as often as he thinks fit his Miss. should be a witness of his Gallantry." Dryden took care not to recognize this charge; instead, he vigorously denied to Sedley that he was a contemner of universities. It is a bit like Falstaff, who dismisses a charge of cowardice by a ringing denial that he is a whoremaster. Yet it is clear that Dryden wanted to lodge a countercharge of malicious calumny against a person or persons at Court who were accusing him of disrespect for the King in his plays.[15]

His poor standing at Court troubled Dryden's relations even with the wits, the dedication of *Marriage a-la-Mode* to Rochester shows. In the late spring of 1671 Rochester had taken a fancy to the play, helped Dryden touch it up, and had recommended it to the King at Windsor.[16] Also, he had defended Dryden's writing from the detraction of certain courtiers:

> and, what I never can forget, you have not only been careful of my reputation, but of my fortune. You have been solicitous to supply my neglect of myself; and to overcome the fatal modesty of poets, which submits them to perpetual wants, rather than to become importunate with those people who have the liberality of kings in their disposing, and who, dishonouring the bounty of their master, suffer such to be in necessity who endeavour at least to please him; and for whose entertainment he has

[15] Probably Bab May as well as Sir Robert Howard.
[16] S-S, IV, 253.

generously provided, if the fruits of his royal favour were not often stopped in other hands.[17]

Dryden also lets us know that Rochester's help in 1671 was voluntary and unsolicited, when he had received £500 overdue on his pension and also a warrant for repayment of his £500 loan to the King. Although Clifford was mainly responsible, Rochester had helped by defending the Laureate's wit and loyalty. A word from him would persuade Sir Robert Howard to intermit his wrath. It is strange that Dryden should need to feel grateful to Rochester for what he had earned by his own talent and hard work.[18] The concluding sentences of the dedication do in fact seem very strained:

> Wit seems to have lodged itself more nobly in this age, than in any of the former; and people of my mean condition are only writers because some of the nobility, and your Lordship in the first place, are above the narrow praises which poesy could give you. But, let those who love to see themselves exceeded, encourage your Lordship in so dangerous a quality; for my own part, I must confess, that I have so much of self-interest, as to be content with reading some papers of your verses, without desiring you should proceed to a scene, or play; with the common

[17] *Ibid.*, v, 254–256. In the whole passage, the prevalence of *if* clauses reminds one of the dedication to another slippery patron, Sunderland.

[18] The Sedley dedication, which must have been written at the same time or shortly before the one to Rochester, credits Clifford as "a better Maecenas" among "some great persons of our court who have taken care of me, even amidst the exigencies of a war" (Watson, 1, 185). Dryden refers here to a payment made on 10 March 1673, before the end of the third Dutch War. Ward, p. 94, suggests that Sir Robert Howard helped. On the contrary, the fact that Dryden required the aid of Clifford and Rochester (whom he thanks by name), as well as "great persons" unnamed—the Duchess of Monmouth, very likely, or someone of the highest rank, perhaps the Duke of York—shows that there must have been strong opposition to overcome, and Sir Robert is the likeliest opponent. Moreover, in mid-July Howard was to succeed Sir Robert Long as Auditor of the receipts.

prudence of those who are worsted in a duel, and declare they are satisfied, when they are first wounded. Your Lordship has but another step to make, and from the patron of wit, you may become its tyrant. . . .

Rochester replied to the dedication, in a letter now lost, with what Dryden called "the most handsom Compliment, couchd in the best language I have read." His letter containing these words, perhaps the most interesting of the seventy-odd we have left, refers to the Oxford Act of July 1673.[19] It speaks of "the shame of seeing myself overpay'd so much for an ill Dedication," referring probably both to the £560 he collected on June 19 and to Rochester's compliment, which Dryden describes as saying "all those things to me, which I ought to have say'd to you."

Dryden was apparently unclear as to the extent of Rochester's recent help. We know that the £500 authorized in 1671, plus interest, was ordered by Clifford himself, as one of the last acts of his ministry, "to be paid forthwith out of any money that comes to your hands of his Ma[jesty's] customs" on June 17, 1673. If Rochester had helped, Dryden's dedication would then seem ungracious,[20] especially in view of the compliment that followed. If he had not helped, his compliment might be a hoax. Why else should Dryden write, "I am so much my own friend, as to conceale your Lordships letter. for that which would have given Vanity to any other poet, has onely given me confusion," or feel that "shame . . . has made me almost repent of my Addresse"? If Rochester's praise was overdrawn (and we know his approval of Dryden was mixed with contempt), then there is a hidden meaning in Dryden's phrase about Rochester saying "all those things to me, which I ought to have say'd to you." Without Rochester's letter no

---

[19] *London Stage*, I, 206. Ward, *Letters*, pp. 7–11 and notes.

[20] Irène Simon perceived this lack of confidence in the dedication to Rochester; see her excellent discussion of the prose of the dedications in *Revue des langues vivantes* (1965), 513–527.

more can be proved than that Dryden was uneasy and suspicious that Rochester was now no longer a helpful patron but one of his persecutors. Dryden may have sensed, in his attempt to characterize Rochester as a courtier, a wit, and a generous patron, his own inability to avoid a note of irony. Rochester's counter-characterization of Dryden as a poet has beaten him, he says, at his own weapon. Dryden's letter is in part, therefore, a protest against the supposition that he is the equal of Bayes in vanity. This, I believe, explains the ironical nature of one of the most uncharacteristic things he ever said, "Because I deale not in Satyre, I have sent Your Lordship a prologue and epilogue which I made for our players when they went down to Oxford. I heare since, they have succeeded; And by the event your Lordship will judge how easy 'tis to passe any thing upon an University; and how grosse flattery the learned will endure." This remark, which has rightly shocked students of Dryden, is prompted (as the preceding analysis shows) by Rochester's assumption, in writing his letter, that Dryden, a poet who insisted upon the learned nature of his calling, would endure flattery that was somehow gross.

Yet it is clear from the ambiguity of these expressions that Dryden was still not sure about Rochester's attitude. The rest of the letter can best be read as his attempt to end the uncertainty. It is a frank and cheerful communication in which Dryden seems to throw off the constraints of decorum as between earl and commoner, patron and client, greater wit and lesser, and writes to Rochester as between man and man, in the spirit of good fellowship. Besides his own prologue and epilogue, Dryden communicated a couplet out of a satire translated by Etherege from Boileau. Whereas the prologue might have offended Rochester by its slighting mention of Epicurus (Dryden actually acknowledges Rochester's fondness for Epicurus elsewhere in the letter),[21] the couplet as amended would have pleased him:

[21] *Letters*, p. 9. One might see a further impertinence in lines 22–38 of Dryden's Oxford prologue, enclosed with his letter to Rochester:

I call a Spade, a Spade, Dunbar, a Bully
Brounckard a pimp, and Aubrey Vere a Cully.

Dunbar and Rochester had recently quarreled and had been prevented from fighting a duel.[22] So far Dryden showed his willingness to take sides with Rochester. He closed his letter, grown familiar and chatty, with a clear invitation to at least a gossip's intimacy: "If your Lordship had been in Town, and I in the Country, I durst not have entertain'd you with three pages of a letter; but I know they are very ill things which can be tedious to a man who is fourscore miles from Covent Garden. Tis upon this Confidence that I dare almost promise to entertain you with a thousand bagatelles every week; and not to be serious in any part of my letter. . . ."

Dryden, as this letter shows him, is something of a Tartar. His final offer might have been taken up by Rochester in several different ways, from real sympathy and friendship to an indulgent sufferance, without Dryden's needing to feel rebuked or disappointed, so insouciant is his parting. However, another paragraph betrays his tendency to push his luck —a trait he himself called the "plain openness of my na-

Th'illiterate Writer, Emperique like, applies
To minds diseas'd, unsafe, chance Remedies:
The Learn'd in Schools, where Knowledge first began,
Studies with Care th'Anatomy of Man;
Sees Vertue, Vice, and Passions in their Cause,
And Fame from Science, not from Fortune draws.
So Poetry, which is in *Oxford* made
An Art, in *London* only is a Trade.
There Haughty Dunces whose unlearned Pen
Could ne'er Spell Grammar, would be reading Men.
Such build their Poems the Lucretian way,
So many Huddled Atoms make a Play,
And if they hit in Order by some Chance,
They call that Nature, which is Ignorance.
To such a Fame let mere Town-Wits aspire,
And their Gay Nonsense their own Citts admire.
                    (*Works*, I, 146–147, lines 22–37)

Dryden perhaps felt that a play by Rochester would be an unplanned, Epicurean work of chance.

[22] Wilson, *Rochester-Savile Letters*, p. 11.

ture,"[23] but one that comes through from time to time in his dedications as a tendency to be rather aggressive in fitting people into his pictures of what they should be like. In the middle of this letter, he proposed the rather breathtaking idea that Rochester should join with him in a good laugh at the expense of "the Great Duke of B——, who is so oneasy to [him]self by pursueing the honour of Lieutenant General which flyes him, that he can enjoy nothing he possesses. Though, at the same time, he is so unfit to command an Army, that he is the onely Man in the three Nations who does not know it. Yet he still picques him self, like his father, to find another Isle of Rhe in Zealand; thinkes this disappointment an injury to him which is indeed a favour, and will not be satisfyed but with his own ruine and with ours. Tis a strange quality in a man to love idlenesse so well as to destroy his Estate by it; and yet at the same time to pursue so violently the most toilesome, and most unpleasant part of businesse." Rochester and Buckingham perhaps were not ideal friends, but they had been boon companions for years, and remained so. Although Rochester did not meddle in politics, he had registered his protests on Buckingham's side during the struggle to impeach Clarendon.[24] There was no reason, except for an extraordinary respect for Dryden's wit (his letter, therefore, must have professed such a respect) why Rochester should laugh at Dryden's bidding here.

The suggestion cannot be proved, but I think it is inescapable that Dryden was putting Rochester's good will to a sort of test, as if in Falstaff's spirit of "Out upon this half-faced fellowship!" It seems that he genuinely was grateful for the good word that Rochester gave him at Windsor

[23] In a letter (1697) to his sons in Rome, Dryden wrote: "dissembling, though lawfull in some Cases, is not my talent: yet for your sake I will struggle, with the plain openness of my nature. . . ." Ward, *Letters*, p. 93.

[24] The Lords' *Journals* and *Protests* record them consistently on Buckingham's side. David M. Vieth calls Rochester (in 1678) "a moving spirit in the Whig campaign to exclude the Duke of York," *Attribution in Restoration Poetry* (New Haven, 1963), p. 195.

in 1671 and probably once again at least in 1673. Yet he was not certain as to the latter; Rochester's letter of praise made him uneasy; and it may be doubted whether he set a very high price on the continuance of their relationship unless he could change it into a much less tentative one. The only time Dryden permitted himself to mention Rochester clearly and unfavorably in print, he spoke of his "self-sufficiency" as preventing him from feeling admiration for anyone else;[25] probably, therefore, he found his compliments suspiciously out of character. At any rate, he owed it to his own self-respect to express his gratitude to a benefactor as well as to show, politely, that he had "smoked" Rochester's letter. If, beyond expectation, his saucy boldness should not be taken amiss, then all would indeed be well. Rochester, however, was not amused. The low opinion of Dryden's adroitness he wrote to Henry Savile in 1676 had no doubt been confirmed by this exchange: "I have ever admired [him] for the disproportion of him and his attributes; He is a Rarity which I cannot but be fond of, as one would be of a Hog that could fiddle, or a singing Owl. . . . the blunt . . . is his very good Weapon in Wit."[26]

It is questionable whether Rochester alienated Dryden by the support he gave to Elkanah Settle. Dryden had no complaint at the Whitehall success of Settle's *Empress of*

[25] In dedicating the *Satires* to Dorset (1693): "an author of your own quality (whose ashes I will not disturb) has given you all the commendation which his self-sufficiency could afford to any man: 'The best good man, with the worst-natur'd Muse.'" (Watson, II, 75) Dryden goes on to liken Rochester's praise of Dorset to Jonson's praise of Shakespeare, claiming that both missed the "good nature" in the writings of poets they only praised for candor in their personal lives.

[26] Wilson, *Rochester-Savile Letters*, p. 41. There might, I suppose, be a play here both on Dryden's "conquer me . . . at my own weapon," and on the opposition of "blunts" (practice swords) and "sharps" (fighting weapons); if Dryden would neither offer nor accept a challenge, yet would pursue the quarrel, Rochester would resort to the cudgel of a servant. See Scouten and Hume's gloss on "blunts" and "sharps," *The Country Gentleman*, p. 128. The term "disproportion" should perhaps be compared with Howard's application of its idea to Dryden's behavior earlier in similar circumstances.

Morocco, for which Rochester wrote a prologue (Mulgrave wrote one also). The play was produced by the Duke's Company on Thursday, July 3, 1673, before Dryden wrote his letter to Rochester. There is no sign that Dryden was displeased because it had been embellished by a masque to the music of Matthew Locke, or because it was again successful. If he had lost the favor of Rochester, Settle had not stolen it away from him—he had rejected it himself, with a strange combination of openness and irony.

Rochester showed his displeasure in a series of anonymous satires, in which Dryden was only one of many targets. David Vieth has gone so far as to speak of "the division of literary London during the middle 1670s into two broad factions, one led by Rochester and the other by Dryden."[27] Since Buckingham was active in Rochester's group of wits who assembled several times at the Ranger's Lodge in Woodstock Park, the political allegiance of the Rochester group might be said to have been anti-Yorkist; while once again we find Dryden associated with James's backers, for the principal target on his side, besides himself, was Mulgrave, one of the staunchest Yorkists among the younger nobility. To their honor, wits in neither of the two circles paid much attention to the factions of politics; their animosities were exuberantly personal. Moreover, their libels represent some advance in the civilizing process, for although duels often inspired sharp satire, it became unheard of for a satire, no matter how vicious, to incite a duel. Verse effusions were allowed to circulate in manuscript (sometimes professionally and very elegantly copied out) without restraint. As in 1667, however, the lampooners' energies were quickly polarized by a national crisis, and satire again became factional rather than personal during the Popish Plot. With this politicization, and its spate of printed lampoon lasting from late 1678 to the end of 1683, the characteristically skillful personal verse, amatory and satirical, of the gentlemen wits seemed to die away.

[27] *Attribution in Restoration Poetry*, p. 138.

Before political factionalism became strong, Dryden had ended his ambivalence over Rochester and had (he says) very deliberately chosen Mulgrave for his patron. In the dedication of *Aureng-Zebe* early in 1676, Dryden praised his new patron for a succession of qualities opposite to those of his several enemies—Howard's, Buckingham's, Rochester's—and very much resembling those he had praised in James Stuart four years earlier. Unlike Howard (and, it must be admitted, unlike James), Mulgrave had wit. Unlike Buckingham, he had "always been above the wretched affectation of popularity." Unlike Rochester, having "a soul which is capable of all the tenderness of friendship," Mulgrave's kindness, "where you have once placed it, is inviolable." Mulgrave is stable and loyal; one knows exactly where he stands. Dryden is plainly speaking out of his own open nature in these lines:

> From this constancy to your friends, I might reasonably assume, that your resentments would be as strong and lasting, if they were not restrained by a nobler principle of good nature and generosity; for certainly, it is the same composition of mind, the same resolution and courage, which makes the greatest friendships, and the greatest enmities. And he, who is too lightly reconciled, after high provocations, may recommend himself to the world for a Christian, but I should hardly trust him for a friend. The Italians have a proverb to that purpose, 'To forgive the first time, shows me a good Catholic; the second time, a fool.' To this firmness in all your actions, though you are wanting in no other ornaments of mind and body, yet to this I principally ascribe the interest your merits have acquired you in the royal family. A prince, who is constant to himself, and steady in all his undertakings; one with whom that character of Horace will agree—
>
> > Si fractus illabatur orbis,
> > Impavidum ferient ruinae;—
>
> such an one cannot but place an esteem, and repose a

confidence on him, whom no adversity, no change of
courts, no bribery of interests, or cabals of factions, or
advantages of fortune, can remove from the solid founda-
tions of honour and fidelity—

> Ille meos, primus qui me sibi junxit, amores
> Abstulit; ille habeat secum, servetque sepulcro.

Dryden's remark about Prince James, above, produced this
note, the most egregious blunder in the whole Scott-Saints-
bury edition of his works: "On perusing such ill applied
flattery, I know not whether we ought to feel most for
Charles II or for Dryden." Scott wrote this and Saintsbury
let it stand—which shows how much the misrepresentation
of Dryden wronged him, when two of his best friends could
blush for him over a passage which actually is as favorably
applicable to Dryden as it is to James or Mulgrave.[28] The
spirit of the "faithful few" celebrated in *Absalom and Achito-
phel* is present already in these lines.

Yet Dryden's best wish for Mulgrave is that he, unlike
his ancestor, may escape the need to immolate himself "in
the quarrels of his sovereign." The passage that follows con-
tains a very important matrix of feeling wherein Dryden
makes known the inner effect of his association with the
Court. His feelings as he presents them here are the basis
for *All For Love*, and for a revolutionary change of emphasis
in his serious drama from exterior "greatness" to an explora-
tion of the elements of more purely personal anguish and
joy:

> I do not remember that any of the sects of old philoso-
> phers did ever leave a room for greatness. Neither am I
> formed to praise a court, who admire and covet nothing,
> but the easiness and quiet of retirement. I naturally with-
> draw my sight from a precipice; and, admit the prospect

[28] S-S, v, 191–192. As Scott notes (p. 193) Mulgrave's ancestor was
clubbed to death in a ditch by a butcher during the Pilgrimage of
Grace in 1548/49.

be never so large and goodly, can take no pleasure even in looking on the downfall, though I am secure from the danger. Methinks, there is something of a malignant joy in that excellent description of Lucretius—

Suave, mari magno turbantibus aequora ventis,
E terra magnum alterius spectare laborem;
Non quia vexari quenquam est jucunda voluptas,
Sed, quibus ipse malis careas, quia cernere suave est.[29]

I am sure his master Epicurus, and my better master Cowley, preferred the solitude of a garden, and the conversation of a friend, to any consideration so much as a regard, of those unhappy people, whom, in our own wrong, we call the great.[30]

Dryden, however, was making a distinction between the "practicable virtue mixed with the frailties and imperfections

[29] Dryden agreed with Miranda:

O, I have suffer'd
With those that I saw suffer! A brave vessel,
Who had, no doubt, some noble creature in her,
Dash'd all to pieces! O, the cry did knock
Against my very heart. . . .
(The Tempest, I. ii. 5–9)

Dryden quotes the famous lines from Lucretius, of which Miranda's speech seems a kind of rebuttal. The humanity of Shakespeare (and Montaigne) very strongly attracted him.

[30] Cf. the dedication of All For Love to Danby: "Yet after all, my lord, if I may speak my thoughts, you are happy rather to us than to yourself; for the multiplicity, the cares, and the vexations of your employment, have betrayed you from yourself, and given you up into the possession of the public. You are robbed of your privacy and friends, and scarce any hour of your life you can call your own. Those, who envy your fortune, if they wanted not good-nature, might more justly pity it: and when they see you watched by a crowd of suitors, whose importunity it is impossible to avoid, would conclude, with reason, that you have lost much more in true content, than you have gained by dignity; and that a private gentleman is better attended by a single servant, than your lordship with so clamorous a train. Pardon me, my lord, if I speak like a philosopher on this subject: the fortune which makes a man uneasy, cannot make him happy; and a wise man must think himself uneasy, when few of his actions are in his choice" (S-S, V, 324–325).

of human life" that was proper for drama, and the ideal virtue proper to the ideal world of a heroic poem. In this Mulgrave dedication he gave his most circumstantial account of the attempt he had been making to gain support for the composition of an epic. Unlike Cowley's *Davideis* or Milton's *Paradise Lost*, Dryden's epic would have been overtly political, with an English subject, and it was to honor "my king, my country, and my friends; most of our ancient nobility being concerned in the action." Mulgrave, he says, was obligated to promote the attempt, because he was "the first who gave me the opportunity of discoursing it to his Majesty, and his Royal Highness: they were then pleased, both to commend the design, and to encourage it by their commands." Since Dryden thought ten years' time little enough for the writing of an epic, he wanted a subsidy, guaranteed for that period and amounting probably to at least £300 a year—the sum he seemed to need to maintain his family while he moved back and forth from London to the country in order to live separately while he planned and wrote. He also needed assured protection against the hostility of courtiers such as Sir Robert Howard or Mr. May, especially since there would be nothing to show, at first, for his hours of "study" (as he called it) on an historical epic.[31] This protection the King and Duke of York had given him orally by their "commands" to pursue his design; but lacking firmer support than this, Dryden says, "the unsettledness of my condition has hitherto put a stop to my thoughts concerning it. As I am no successor to Homer in his wit, so neither do I desire to be in his poverty."

One cannot help feeling that this is not the way an inspired poet would approach a great heroic theme. That Dryden felt so too is evident from the words that close the paragraph: "It is for your Lordship to stir up that remembrance in his Majesty, which his many avocations of business

---

[31] The years 1673–1674 must have been spent in such study, of which the result is *The State of Innocence* and Dryden's "new taste of wit."

have caused him, I fear, to lay aside, and, as himself and
his royal brother are the heroes of the poem, to represent to
them the images of their warlike predecessors; as Achilles is
said to be roused to glory with the sight of the combat
before the ships. For my own part, I am satisfied to have
offered the design, and it may be to the advantage of my
reputation to have it refused me." The last sentence sug-
gests that Dryden's reiterated offer was by then *pro forma*
and more an expression of his sense of duty as Poet Laureate
than of a pressing urge to create a conquering hero. He may
well, after three Dutch Wars, have begun to question the
advisability of stirring Charles and James to glory with a
story of combat. The dedication of *All For Love* in 1678
confirms this view: "we cannot win by an offensive war,"
he says then.

On this matter of more "practicable virtue," Dryden had
moved, via his reading of Montaigne, to a position surpris-
ingly close to Rochester's in *A Satyr Against Mankind*, and
out of his former patron's words and those of Homer, Cicero,
and Montaigne, he distilled the astringent wisdom of this
remark: "An ill dream, or a cloudy day, has power to change
this wretched creature, who is so proud of a reasonable
soul,[32] and make him think what he thought not yester-
day." Here is an acknowledgment of that inner change the
poet referred to in the prologue to *Aureng-Zebe* as "another
taste of wit." The earlier passage in which he handed over
to his patron all further responsibility for setting up his he-
roic poem, is like a washing of hands, ridding himself of a
difficult responsibility. Having used his new, elevated style
of couplet verse in "many ill plays" designed to come as close
as possible to a heroic poem, Dryden was getting ready to
write a play for himself instead of for king and country, and
to show "that vain animal / Who is so proud of being ra-

---

[32] Cf. Rochester's *Satyr Against Mankind*, "that vain *Animal*, /
Who is so proud of being rational" (lines 6–7), and cf. lines 12–30
with the opening of *Religio Laici*. Dryden's preface was probably writ-
ten very soon after Rochester's *Satyr*.

tional" how it is that those "people whom, in our own wrong, we call the great" are unhappy. Their "wisdom" is indeed only pride, in the form of an insatiable thirst for power, which, because it can never be quenched, dries them to stone and prevents them from enjoying that world over which they domineer. The "wisdom" of Rochester's *Satyr*, elaborated by "the reas'ning engine," would soon become the statecraft of Octavius in *All For Love*. Antony, following the "certain instinct" of his five senses and his heart, will enjoy the world, happy in the affection of one other person, whereas Octavius will be but a cold and merely verbal presence, removed physically from the scene.

This rather Epicurean insight of Dryden's into the life of the Court was not, perhaps, his deepest and most characteristic response to his personal experience in ten years of success and celebrity; but it certainly continued to be one pole of his feeling, over against his delight in the intercourse of a broadly comprehensive society and in the exercise of his great powers of writing to affect and sway the public. When one thinks of it, it was amazing that he should have spread in the public print the account of his proposing an epic to Charles and James, and it was ironic that he should also have included the expression of his personal need for intimacy and ease and affection, to say nothing of his need for money. Dryden, having become the object of a public, which to a great extent he had helped to create, had for some time been offering his inner self to that public in his prefatory essays. The development seems to have been unconscious. Although these passages serve very well the rhetorical purpose of making him seem the "good man" of Cato's definition,[33] it seems that no such intention was on Dryden's mind. He was giving himself immediately to the public, as Montaigne had never done. Both, however, have something of the same sense, not so much of addressing a single and therefore ephemeral audience, but rather of speaking to

[33] "*Vir Bonus, peritus dicendi*" ("a good man, skilled in speaking") was the famous definition of the orator attributed to Cato by Cicero.

humanity at large. Dryden quotes Terence's great line, *Homo sum, humani a me nihil alienum puto*, as if to justify himself in confessing that awareness of mortality and weakness that is the common human lot.

Having learned to question the practicality of heroism in politics, from the Epicureanism of Montaigne and perhaps of Rochester too, Dryden was still capable of being strongly perturbed by the wit of the latter. There is a fairly long passage in the preface of *All For Love* in which Dryden, as Rochester foresaw, attacked him "at the blunt." The attack, like Rochester's in his satires, has several targets in mind, and Dryden is much more concerned with the politics— or economics, rather—of the theatre than of the nation. The preface was written early in 1678, before the fanciful Popish Plot disclosures of Tonge and Oates, and while Shaftesbury was still imprisoned in the Tower. Dryden was anxious to restrict the intervention of what he called "the herd of gentlemen," first of all to comedy, and then to composition alone, not criticism. He rejected their taste as being Frenchified, effete, and lacking in common sense: tolerable, perhaps, in lyric and light comedy, but hardly in serious drama. "There are many witty men, but few poets; neither have all poets a taste of tragedy." Those who qualify to be judges of tragedy, normally, are the tragic poets themselves: "I shall think it reasonable, that the judgment of an artificer in his own art should be preferable to the opinion of another man; . . ." Meanwhile, both Buckingham and Rochester had engaged themselves in the writing of tragedies, and at Whitehall Saint-Evremond (a kind of oracle in residence) was writing favorable critiques of Racine while neglecting the dramas of his host nation, which had to be translated to him because he would not bother to learn English. This state of affairs accounts for Dryden's amusing, if disastrously mistaken, satire on the character of Hippolytus in *Phèdre*. It also explains his vehemence in this passage: "A poet is not pleased, because he is not rich; and the rich are discontented, because the poets will not admit them of their number.

Thus the case is hard with writers: If they succeed not, they must starve; and if they do, some malicious satire is prepared to level them, for daring to please without their leave. But while they are so eager to destroy the fame of others, their ambition is manifest in their concernment; some poem of their own is to be produced, and the slaves are to be laid flat with their faces on the ground, that the monarch may appear in the greater majesty."

Buckingham's *The Restoration*, an adaptation of *Philaster*, was produced, apparently, in 1683.[34] Considering his deliberate pace of composition, he may have been engaged on this project when Dryden wrote the preface to *All For Love*. Rochester's *Valentinian*, adapted from Fletcher's play, was intended for the King's Company when its complement was about the same as when it performed *All For Love*; we have, therefore, a repeat of the dilemma presented in 1673 by Settle's *Empress of Morocco*, with the same likelihood that Rochester's interloping play would be a success. (As indeed it was, when finally produced in February, 1684, largely because of "the vast Interest the Author made in Town," although Rochester had been dead over three years.)[35]

More pertinently, it would seem that Rochester was actively engaged, at exactly the time when Dryden wrote this preface, on a second tragedy, and in collaboration with—of all people—Sir Robert Howard. This play was "The Conquest of China." It had a very curious history, and it is no wonder that it was never finished. Sir Robert had evidently begun it years before 1678. This, however, appears to have been the date when Rochester was collaborating with him, to the extent of writing a scene of 268 lines. Twenty years later, when John Dryden, Junior, the poet's second son, had succeeded in reconciling his uncle and his father, Dryden himself undertook to complete "The Conquest of China" from Howard's scenario—only to abandon the project a few months later to finish work on his *Virgil*.[36]

[34] LS, I, 319. [35] *Ibid.*, pp. 238 and 326, quoting Downes.
[36] Oliver, pp. 215–217 and 297–298.

Rochester's scene is printed by Pinto from BM Add. MS 28692, ff.70–75, a small folio that also includes Rochester's *Valentinian* (the same contents appear in another small folio in the Folger). We know that the scene was intended for Howard's play from a letter that Sir Robert wrote to Rochester, dated "April: 7th," but without the year. Howard's letter rather clearly refers to passages in the dedication of *Marriage a-la-Mode*, where Dryden expressed his reservations over any attempt by Rochester at dramatic composition; and therefore it seems a link between those apprehensions and his fear in 1678 that "some poem of their own is to be produced, and the slaves are to be laid flat with their faces on the ground, that the monarch may appear in the greater majesty." This striking image in itself also harks back to the admonition of 1673, that Rochester "had but another step to make, from the patron of wit, to become its tyrant." Howard, however, is fearless of such threats. His letter, after beginning with compliments upon Rochester's recovery from a very serious illness in the winter of 1677–1678, goes on to play upon these words in Dryden's 1673 dedication, "let those who love to see themselves exceeded, encourage your Lordship to so dangerous a quality; for my own part, I must confess, that I have so much of self-interest, as to be content with reading some papers of your verses, without desiring you should proceed to a scene, or play; . . . It is a barren triumph, which is not worth your pains, and would only rank him amongst your slaves, who is [etc.] John Dryden." Sir Robert retorts Dryden's words as follows:

> in this modest towne, where the worst men and women censure the best; and the silent knave is sheltered under the Charracter of A sober person; The Criticks on men's Actions, are like the ill naturd ones of the stage, most busie where there js greatest ingenuity; beinge Commonly more provokt by there envie then their judgment; but I forgett how ill I entertaine though upon A good subject; and am sure I shall be better by you though upon an ill one.

I mean by the sceen you are pleasd to write, nor shall I
repine to see how far you Can exceed mee; noe more then
I doe to see others that have more wealth then I live by
mee with A greater plenty; I have tooke [?] pleasure that
you exceed all that can excell mee; and those advantages
of my Lord Rochester must needs be pleasinge to me that
is soe perfectly his

most faithful and humble servant
Ro Howard.[37]

Sir Robert's phrase, "nor shall I repine to see how far you
Can exceed mee" alludes directly to Dryden's "let those who
love to see themselves exceeded encourage your Lordship."
He rather smugly retorts to the other, economic, reproach of
Dryden's *All For Love* preface with his "noe more then I
doe to see others that have more wealth than I live by mee
with A greater plenty," being wealthier by far than Rochester.

Dryden had written, "is not this a wretched affectation,
not to be contented with what fortune has done for them,
and sit down quietly with their estates, but they must call
their wits in question, and needlessly expose their nakedness
to public view?[38] Not considering they are not to expect the
same approbation from sober men, which they have found
from their flatterers after the third bottle." Whereas Dryden
saw himself as a sober man (he stopped at the second bottle,
as he warned Lord Latimer), Sir Robert saw him as a silent
knave, envious of his wealth and Rochester's "ingenuity,"
taking shelter "under the Charracter of A sober person."

It is very easy to free Dryden of the charge of envying
Rochester's critical wit, at least. He obviously found it des-
picable, if only because it was unsupported by learning. This
explains why he includes Rochester with "the rest of my

[37] *Ibid.*, p. 215.
[38] Frank Livingston Huntley, "Dryden, Rochester, and The Eighth
Satire of *Juvenal*," *Philological Quarterly*, 18 (1939), 269–284, asso-
ciated Dryden's reference to "nakedness" with an escapade of Roches-
ter's in September, 1677. See *The Rochester-Savile Letters*, p. 45, for
Savile's statement that it was public knowledge.

175

illiterate censors," in one sentence, and in the next defers to the "judicious" Mr. Rymer. Although Rymer also was threatening the stage with his *Edgar*, Dryden then and always respected him for his learning.

So long as we view Dryden's *All For Love* preface as only a rejoinder to attacks in Rochester's satires, it must seem an overreaction. The picture changes when we realize, first, that Rochester was collaborating with that watchdog of loyalty, Sir Robert Howard. The preface of *All For Love* contains the last of many references by Dryden to his abuse of his Treasury position; "they who should be our patrons are for no such expensive ways to fame; they have much of the poetry of Maecenas, but little of his liberality. They are for persecuting Horace and Virgil, in the persons of their successors; for such is any man who has any part of their soul and fire, though in a less degree." Second, we know that when Dryden wrote this preface he was in the process of cutting himself loose from the King's Players and setting up as an independent playwright. The marketplace was as crowded with talent then as in 1673, with the difference that the stiffest competition was in tragedy. Yet Dryden maintained good relations with his chief competitors, Otway and Lee; in fact it was their mutual cause that he fought for in attacking the dramatic pretensions of the noble wits and asserting the need for well-informed and disinterested criticism. He merely wished to defend the marketplace for tragedy against the working of Gresham's Law, lest bad tragedies drive out good ones.

At the end of 1677 or early in 1678, Dryden had made up his mind to move to the Duke's Theatre. The situation of 1673, when Settle had tried to change theatres, was now reversed; and Thomas Shadwell, Dryden's collaborator in the *Notes and Observations on the Empress of Morocco*, was understandably annoyed, especially since Dryden was going to make his debut at Dorset Garden with a comedy somewhat in his own vein of humors writing. Shadwell had a high regard for his own gifts as a comic writer; in ten years at the

Duke's he had enjoyed a goodly number of successes, and had earned the right to his position of first comic poet to the company. Worse yet for Shadwell, his comedy *A True Widow*, which was meant for performance in March 1678, was being withdrawn in favor of his new rival's *Limberham*.

Shadwell seems to have taken immediate revenge. Following the lead given by Dryden's imitation of *Antony and Cleopatra*, Shadwell was about to put onto the Dorset Garden stage an alteration of *Timon of Athens*. In Shakespeare's *Timon* there is a minor role, the Poet; he is honorably treated, and one of his speeches contains a memorable passage on the meaning of art's imitation of nature. However, Shadwell turned this Poet into a figure of ridicule, and added another stupid and vain Bayes to the gallery opened by Buckingham in *The Rehearsal*. He was certainly aiming at Dryden in the following dialogue between his Poet and the cynic Demetrius:

> *Demetrius.* What d'ye mean by style? That of good sence is all alike; that is to say; with apt and easie words, not one too little or too much: and this I think good style.
> *Poet.* O Sir, you are wide o' th' matter! apt and easie!
> Heroics must be lofty and high sounding;
> No easie language in Heroick Verse;
> 'Tis most unfit: for should I name a Lion,
> I must not in Heroicks call him so!
> *Demetrius.* What then?
> *Poet.* I'de as soon call him an Ass. No thus—
> The fierce Numidian Monarch of the Beasts.
> *Demetrius.* That's lofty, is it?
> *Poet.* O yes! but a Lion would sound so baldly, not to be Endured, and a Bull too—but
> The mighty Warriour of the horned Race:
> Ah!—how that sounds!
> *Demetrius.* Then I perceive sound's the great matter in this way.
> *Poet.* Ever while you live.[39]

[39] Ed. Summers, III, 200.

Verse sound and loftiness of expression, the two qualities at which Shadwell's ridicule is directed, were at this time peculiarly associated with Dryden. The sound of his verse had always been his hallmark. The lofty style he had recently urged at length in his preface to *The State of Innocence*, published early in 1677. Shadwell, in fact, appears to have in mind a particular passage in the last paragraph of this preface: "the definition of wit (which has been so often attempted, and ever unsuccessfully by many poets) is only this: That it is a propriety of thoughts and words; or, in other terms, thoughts and words elegantly adapted to the subject. . . . No man will disagree from another's judgment concerning the dignity of style in heroic poetry; but all reasonable men will conclude it necessary that sublime subjects ought to be adorned with the sublimest, and (consequently often) with the most figurative expressions."[40]

In the speech of Demetrius, Shadwell offers his own definition of wit, for which he had been contesting rather amicably with Dryden ever since the widespread controversy over rhyme in 1668. Now he ridicules the adaptation of figurative language to heroic subjects, which was precisely the Longinian principle so enthusiastically recovered by Dryden in his most recent preface. The parallel continues as Demetrius and the Poet carry on their discussion of lofty language:

> *Demetrius.* Do you make good morrow sound loftily?
> *Poet.* Oh very loftily!—
>> The fringed Vallance of your eyes advance,
>> Shake off your Canopy'd and downie trance:
>> Phoebus already quaffs the morning dew,
>> Each does his daily lease of life renew.
> Now you shall hear description, 'tis the very life of Poetry. . . .

Shadwell rakes up an old charge here: making "good morrow" sound loftily goes back to Sir Robert Howard's taunt

---

[40] Watson, I, 207.

of 1668 about putting "shut the door" into heroic verse. The line "The fringed Vallance of your eyes advance," contains a significant change from Shakespeare's "The fringed curtain of thine eyes advance" (*Tempest*, I. ii. 408), which had been only slightly altered in the Dryden-Davenant version of 1667,[41] and which Shadwell retained in the operatic version he made a few years later. The change is in the crude echo between "*Vallance*" and "*advance*," meant to parody Dryden's later style of reinforced sound.

Finally, Shadwell's ridicule of the claim that description was the life of poetry strikes to the heart of the difference between Dryden and himself. Dryden was convinced that wit must be spirited, and that even in comedy it must rise above the flat humors style that Shadwell professed. In the *State of Innocence* preface he had written: "Imaging is, in itself, the very height and life of poetry. . . .[42] If poetry be imitation, that part of it needs be best which describes most lively our actions and passions; our virtues and our vices; our follies and our humours: for neither is comedy without its part of imaging; and they who do it best are certainly the most excellent in their kind."[43] As a matter of fact, Dryden had used his comedy of *Limberham* to demonstrate this principle of comic language.

The two rivals, after ten years of sharp but not unfriendly debate over dramatic style and the claims of Ben Jonson to superiority over Shakespeare, were thus set completely at odds. It is impossible to tell how successful Shadwell may have been in getting the actor Jevon, who played the poet in *Timon*, to ape Dryden in the performance in January; but his ridicule soon appeared in print, dedicated to no less a person than "the Most Illustrious Prince George, Duke of Buckingham," and with the following significant compliment: "I am extremely sensible what honour it is to me that my Writings are approved by your Grace; who in your own

[41] Act III, scene v, *Works*, x, 59.
[42] Watson, I, 203.
[43] Cf. Shadwell's "description, 'tis the very life of Poetry. . . ." in the passage just quoted.

have so clearly shown the excellency of Wit and Judgment in your Self, and so justly the defect of 'em in others, that they at once serve for the greatest example, and the sharpest reproof. And no man who has perfectly understood the *Rehearsal,* and some other of your Writings, if he has any *Genius* at all, can write ill after it."[44] Shadwell then took up service with the Duke of Buckingham and his ally Shaftesbury as a Whig pamphleteer. As for Dryden, he took advantage of the timely death of Father Richard Flecknoe to give his resentment, which he had been brooding over since 1673, its final comic form in the poem known immortally as *MacFlecknoe,* with its deadly turn against Shadwell.

[44] Summers, III, 193. For Shadwell to refer to Buckingham as "Prince" in itself indicates that he was taking a stance opposite to Dryden's in politics. Probably this is the "northern dedication" Dryden ridiculed in *MacFlecknoe*: Buckingham was Lord Lieutenant of Yorkshire; this was his only pretense to the title of "Prince."

PART TWO

THE SUCCESSION CRISIS
AND ITS CRITIC

THE latter part of the reign of Charles II has always been recognized as probably the most significant period for the development of parliamentary and party politics. The period, a century later, of the American and French revolutions was no doubt of greater practical importance; but in the ideological sphere the originality of the English political imagination was as great as their commercial energy and industrial inventiveness was in the economic world. England was the first nation to generate the notion of a public as an articulated political entity to be represented, to be informed, to be responsible to. Writing to King Charles's sister in 1669, Buckingham felt the need to explain one great difference between England and France, that the English had such a thing as public opinion, which politicians and even the King had to take into account.

The theatre was certainly one of the most important channels of developing and giving specific form to public opinion. Directly, the stage offered language, situations, characters, and ethos to a relatively small but very important part of the public; indirectly, the fictions and feelings presented in the two London theatres shaped every form of political argument or propaganda, from parliamentary speeches to sermons, from treatises on government to scurrilous broadside ballads. Granted this phenomenon produced a great deal of literature that hardly deserves the name, from a social viewpoint one can only admire the surprising vigor of an institution, bound up as it was with a corrupt court, that managed to signify, not referential reality to be sure, but a counterpart adequate for the imagination and the feelings of people to

181

see themselves more clearly in the midst of a confusing and perhaps revolutionary change in their world.

The principal actor on the political scene, of course, was Shaftesbury. He seized the essential routes of power, the House of Commons and its control of the supply of money. He understood the value of an enemy who might serve both as ogre and scapegoat to the public, while signifying to them whatever Shaftesbury wanted to destroy. He cast James Stuart in this role and thus precipitated a struggle much too big for any politician to determine. For James was both a Roman Catholic, which brought religion in along with a host of imponderables, and also the legitimate inheritor of the crown; inheritance brought in the most weighty and ponderable of all considerations, the system of wealth in inherited property (including former church property) that was the basis of aristocratic society. Shaftesbury meant James to signify popery, expropriation, servitude, France, and wooden shoes, but he lost the game when his tactics came to signify instead the disinheritance of a lawful claimant to his royal property. For this reason, the whole historical episode is properly known as the Succession (or Exclusion) Crisis.

It is interesting to find that Dryden's *Aureng-Zebe*, written after Shaftesbury had succeeded Buckingham as the opposition leader, is the first of his serious plays to present the perennial question of legitimate kingship from the angle of the succession to the throne. Hitherto it had been the issue of usurpation or conquest. Now Dryden's plays will deal with the lawful transfer of power to, or lawful retention of power by, a legitimate king.

CHAPTER SIX

AURENG-ZEBE: THE CHARACTER OF A LOYAL SUCCESSOR

A FTER *The Conquest of Granada,* Dryden took almost six years to produce a serious drama, *Aureng-Zebe* (November 1675). The play is as skillful a composite of heroic motifs in character, story, and ethos as one can find among the "tragedies" of the Restoration theatre. However, Dryden was now intent less upon exploiting old structures of dramatic action than upon developing new structures of dramatic feeling. Of these latter, perhaps the most important development is in the new conception of the hero and the heroine as victims of politics, rather than triumphant practitioners. The truth seems to have been that the astonishing hero, so much a part of Corneille's conception of tragedy, was the product of a feudal and aristocratic tradition that burned up brightly for the last time in France during the Fronde.[1] Long before this tradition flickered out on the borders of England in the Jacobite uprisings of 1715 and 1745, it had already lost much of its meaning in the commercial metropolis of London, and especially with the departure of Charles I early in the Civil War. When, not many years after the production of *The Rehearsal,* Buckingham became the open opponent of royal power both in and out of Parliament, he and Shaftesbury worked to make Charles II and his Successor the creatures of a government conceived according to the as yet nascent Whig pattern. Their principal weapon was English fear and resentment of

[1] Paul Bénichou, *Morales du Grand Siècle* (Paris, 1948) discusses this development; see pp. 61, 75–76, 98, 101. The effect upon the English heroic play was due, perhaps, less to a loss of popularity by Charles II, as Merritt Y. Hughes suggests in "Dryden as a Statist," *Philological Quarterly,* 6 (1927), 335–350, 343, than to the other factors stated in the text.

the idea that an arbitrary monarch, supported by a standing army, should occupy the throne of England. The national attitude forced Charles II (without much reluctance on his part) to play an unheroic role. The King became well aware that stirring deeds on the international scene tended to exhaust the Royal Treasury, while the opposition in Parliament developed as its strongest issue the contention that Charles, and James even more, cherished absolutist notions like those of Louis XIV. In France, meanwhile, the ideal of active heroism had been reduced by 1675 to become a mere ritual attribute of the monarch.

Dryden began to work out a new kind of hero, not only obeying a dramatist's impulse, but also responding to new political and social conditions. First, during the years that intervened between *The Conquest of Granada* and *Aureng-Zebe*, he covered himself from the burlesque of *The Rehearsal* by thoroughly rationalizing the hero's language and demeanor.[2] Also, he followed the new line in Stuart politics by toning down the conquering activism that had been characteristic of Montezuma, Cortez, and Almanzor. He no longer left the question of the hero's legitimate origin up in the air until the very last scene of the play, for the question of the succession had become altogether too precarious in the real-life struggle of the Duke of York against the attempts of his enemies to exclude him in favor of some newcomer such as Monmouth.[3] Dryden's hero from then on was already a prince, a king, or a king in exile, rather than a young man from nowhere. Characteristically, the hero is unambitious and by nature most unlikely to turn into an absolute monarch. He is forced by his position to be concerned with power,

---

[2] Such changes occasionally meant a loss in topical freshness, as when Dryden dropped these lines from the second quarto (1673) of CG:

> It was your fault that fire seized all your breast;
> You should have blown up some to save the rest. . . .
>
> 1 CG, v. iii, 269–270

See George H. Nettleton, "Author's Changes in Dryden's *Conquest of Granada, Part I*," *Modern Language Notes*, 51 (1935), 360–364.

[3] Turner, pp. 105, 120–123.

but his attitude toward it is not grasping: he resents its usurpation and abuse more keenly than he desires its restoration, and he almost never aims at the extension or aggrandizement of his own power. He will not stoop to crime or indeed even to minor baseness such as flattery, even to preserve or restore his dynasty. He chooses the noble way. The result is that, in the nine serious plays Dryden wrote after *The Conquest of Granada,* heroism is to be found chiefly in the moral order, and in restraint rather than activity.

Thus, the situation in *Aureng-Zebe* is the familiar one of the besieged monarch; its political idea is also familiar, the reconciliation of enemies after a civil war. From his source in Bernier's *Voyages* (1671), Dryden took a modicum of local color, and enough history to justify his calling *Aureng-Zebe* a tragedy. He nevertheless presented the struggles of his Indian potentates in an altogether unhistorical light, drawing only slightly upon the interesting details reported by Bernier. Aureng-Zebe in Bernier was an unscrupulous, ambitious schemer who played one brother off against the other in a single-minded lust for power—a perfect political hero. In Dryden's play he becomes instead an ideal hero of the gallant variety, tenderhearted and generous. The emperor, who in history was the great Shah Jehan, builder of the Taj Mahal in memory of his first empress (Aureng-Zebe's mother), is presented by Dryden as an old man without a remnant of real power, beleaguered by his sons and despised by his second wife. Only the rather conventional generosity of Aureng-Zebe prevents him from being slaughtered. The status of this young prince is also precarious, for by Indian custom younger sons are executed upon the father's death and the succession of the eldest to the throne. Yet when he defends his father against the rebellion of his two elder brothers, it is not from self-interest or love of power—power seems to disgust him—but from loyalty to principle and to his own sense of integrity.

Like all of Dryden's heroes at this stage of his dramatic career, Aureng-Zebe's strongest impulse is a desire to possess the woman he loves. Changes in the character of the heroine, however, and in the nature of the hero's relationship to her, alter the dramatic effect of this desire. Aureng-Zebe's love is entirely legitimate, for it was by his father's arrangement that he was betrothed to the beautiful captive, Indamora, queen of Cassimere. When this promise is betrayed and his father makes senile overtures to Indamora, Aureng-Zebe suffers a deep disillusionment. It awakens him out of the naive idealism that characterized the earlier heroes, as if he undergoes a sudden maturation. For the first time he becomes aware of the disparity between the value of services rendered and the rewards allotted to them by the world. Suffering from a sense of injustice and betrayal, he becomes resentful and unhappy. In this inverted Theseus situation, if Aureng-Zebe proves immune to the example of his father and the temptation of his stepmother, it is not because he is in love with chastity as is Hippolytus, nor is it because his instincts have been put in order by the charm of his captive queen. Aureng-Zebe's character is such that he will remain true to himself and to his noble ideal. He will endure his distress of spirit, unless he should be betrayed by the hasty impulsiveness to which his youth makes him subject. In opposition to his hedonist father, Aureng-Zebe stands out as a noble sufferer, the first of a line of suffering heroes that was to run through Dryden's later plays.[4]

Sensing from the beginning that an inactive hero would be a much less interesting, though more credible, figure than an Almanzor, Dryden set him off against a second male character of almost equal importance, who was uninhibited by the checks and balances of morality, and who plunged into action as the result of simple motives of love or hate. Splitting the hero in two in this way was not, perhaps, a particularly

[4] After commenting on the "serious intellectual purpose" informing Dryden's plays, especially the later ones, John A. Winterbottom pointed out their growing stress upon an unselfish devotion, based on Stoic principles of the inner kingdom. "Stoicism in Dryden's Tragedies," *Journal of English and Germanic Philology*, 61 (1962), 868–883, 882.

artistic expedient, but it was serviceable to the political theme and theatrically effective. The second male figure, or deutero-hero, met the demands of the epic pattern for an Achilles, allowing the tragic hero to be a more responsible and ambivalent leader like Homer's Agamemnon. Also, it gave tragic stature to the hero by making him a victim, rather than a monster, like Maximin or Almanzor, or a weakling like Boabdelin.

In *Aureng-Zebe*, the young prince is thus set off against his half-brother Morat. Although Morat, while he is unscrupulously ambitious and self-interested, warlike and perhaps cruel, has no political goals except conquest, the old emperor is eager to resign "the drudgery of power" to him.[5] At this point Dryden brings out the contrast between the activism of Morat and the cynical hedonism of the emperor in order to pose a striking parallel with the England of 1675. Morat speaks in a way that may have struck Charles II, sitting in the Royal Box at his own theatre, as being painfully naive:

> Me-thinks all pleasure is in greatness found.
> Kings, like Heav'n's Eye, should spread their beams
>   around.
> Pleas'd to be seen while Glory's race they run:
> Rest is not for the Chariot of the Sun.
> Subjects are stiff-neck'd Animals they soon
> Feel slacken'd Reins, and pitch their Rider down. . . .
> Luxurious Kings are to their People lost;
> They live, like Drones, upon the public cost.
> My Arms, from Pole to Pole, the World shall shake:
> And, with my self, keep all Mankind awake.[6]

Morat's bloodlust is, in fact, sheer satire on the war-making impulse, which Dryden (like most Englishmen) had learned

[5] III. i. 172. I use the text in *John Dryden: Four Tragedies*, ed. L. A. Beaurline and Fredson Bowers (Chicago, 1967); in I. 150, I read "sabre" for "sable."
[6] III. i. 166–171, 176–179.

to associate with ambitious conniving for generalships, and, worse, an empty treasury. The cynical realism of the emperor's reply makes it evident that the world of the play, like the world of Whitehall, afforded no backing for "stirring" heroism:

> Believe me, Son, and needless trouble spare;
> 'Tis a base World and is not worth our care,
> The Vulgar, a scarce animated Clod,
> Ne'r pleas'd with ought above 'em, Prince or God.
> Were I a God, the drunken Globe should roul:
> The little Emmets with the humane Soul
> Care for themselves, while at my ease I sat
> And second Causes did the work of fate.
> Or, if I would take care, that care should be
> For Wit that scorned the World, and liv'd like me.[7]

One cannot help thinking of King Charles's own attitude toward "the drudgery of power" and of the atmosphere of the English Court as we find it reported in Pepys or the *Memoirs of Grammont*. The old emperor's hedonism makes him a very effective contrast, not only to the battle-lust of Morat, but also to the ethical, serviceable heroism of Aureng-Zebe, which would otherwise seem gratuitous and even a bit stuffy.[8]

The emperor can only recognize beauty as a force, to be dealt with by an equal or greater force. The exercise of this kind of power in love still fascinates him now that he is old. The perversion of eros into brute force in this aging sensualist appears in his dialogue with Indamora:

> *Emperor.* Force is the last relief which Lovers find:
> And 'tis the best excuse of Womankind.
> *Indamora.* Force never yet a generous Heart did gain:
> We yield on parley, but are storm'd in vain.
> Constraint, in all things, makes the pleasure less;
> Sweet is the Love which comes with willingness.

---

[7] III. i. 180–189.   [8] See I. i. 246–270.

> *Emperor*. No; 'tis resistance that inflames desire:
> Sharpens the Darts of Love and blows his Fire.
> Love is disarm'd that meets with too much ease:
> He languishes, and does not care to please.
> And therefore 'tis your golden Fruit you guard
> With so much care, to make possession hard.[9]

This power-psychology appears again as a very effective metaphor in *Absalom and Achitophel*, when the young hero is urged to "commit a pleasing rape upon the crown." As we have seen, Dryden had presented the spontaneous affection of his English subjects as the real mainstay of Charles's overindulgent rule.

The resistance Indamora shows to the emperor is unnecessary with his minister Arimant, whose love she relentlessly exploits. She forces him to act as go-between for the benefit of Aureng-Zebe, with no promise of reward except that he may retain her friendship. Arimant's complaint seems to express the quasi-religious bond between a loyal courtier and a king:

> Why am I thus to slavery design'd,
> And yet am cheated with a free-born mind?
> Or make thy Orders with my reason sute,
> Or let me live by Sense a glorious Brute—
> [She frowns.]
> You frown, and I obey with speed, before
> That dreadful Sentence comes, *See me no more*!
> See me no more! that sound, methinks, I hear
> Like the last Trumpet thund'ring in my ear.[10]

Arimant is a true believer in "state"; he wishes to share it and be placed as close as possible to its source. The terrible force of the phrase *durante gratia*, "during the king's pleasure," made and unmade the happiness of such courtiers. To be frowned upon was to be disgraced, and to be disgraced at court meant that one was humiliated, ostracized,

and rendered impotent. To such a courtier, a fall from the
king's grace was equivalent to final damnation. Arimant's
love for Indamora is an effective displacement for his honest
longing for an orderly, stately, decorous service. He is a loyal
and sympathetic member of a class that has representatives
in most of Dryden's later tragedies: the faithful ministers
who act to serve the self-interest of royalty and not their own.

Indamora's final appeal to Morat is probably Dryden's
most ambitious attempt of this rhetorical kind. Morat begins
the debate on the lowest plane of the Platonic ascent by
offering himself in place of Aureng-Zebe as "more warm,
more fierce, and fitter for your Bed."[11] In what follows, the
Dryden of the great political satires is clearly present. Present
too is a strong trace of the old lion, Milton, whose *Paradise
Lost* had stirred Dryden's admiration in his recent years of
study for an epic.[12] Whatever Morat's success, Indamora
tells him, the world will know him for a villain; he, like
Milton's Satan, will know it himself:

> Ev'n you your self, to your own breast, shall tell
> Your crimes; and your own Conscience be your Hell.
> *Morat.* What bus'ness has my Conscience with
> a crown?
> She sinks in Pleasures, and in Bowls will drown.
> If mirth should fail, I'll busie her with cares;
> Silence her clamorous voice with louder Wars:
> Trumpets and Drums shall fright her from the
> Throne,
> As sounding Cymbals aid the lab'ring Moon.

So far, Morat expresses that sense of the search for and exer-
cise of power as a form of *divertissement*, which was Dry-
den's final charge against Shaftesbury. The rest of his answer,
in the circumstances of England from 1672 to 1683 when

---

[11] v. i. 42.

[12] To the extent, as I have suggested elsewhere, of divorcing Dryden
from rhymed plays.

the succession of James Stuart to the throne was the focus
of partisan strife, is pure contemporary politics:

> Birthright's a vulgar road to Kingly sway;
> 'Tis every dull-got Elder Brother's way.
> Dropt from above, he lights into a Throne;
> Grows of a piece with that he sits upon,
> Heav'n's choice, a low, inglorious, rightful Drone.

"Right comes of course," then says Morat; power *de facto*
very soon becomes power *de jure*. To be great, it is necessary
at the beginning to incur some guilt. The contrast between
"greatness" as achieved by the hero-adventurer, and the all-
too-familiar legitimacy of James, is sharply stated. The ef-
fect is to associate greatness with the arbitrary and the
illegal.

Indamora's reply is a surprise: she invokes the *unum
necessarium* of the Gospel:

> All Greatness is in Virtue understood:
> 'Tis onely necessary to be good.

When Morat repeats that what he wants in life is renown
and power, Indamora's appeal reaches its climax in lines that
combine good stage psychology, the new moral optimism
of the Enlightenment, and the rhythmical throb of Dryden's
best verse:

> Dare to be great, without a guilty Crown;
> View it, and lay the bright temptation down:
> 'Tis base to seize on all, because you may;
> That's Empire, that which I can give away:
> There's joy when to wild Will you Laws prescribe,
> When you bid Fortune carry back her Bribe:
> A joy, which none but greatest minds can taste;
> A Fame which will to endless Ages last.[13]

This lofty challenge, with its perhaps direct evocation of the

[13] v. i. 50–55; 66–70; 83–84; 104–111.

Longinian sublime,[14] is nothing less than a call for the abandonment of self-interest in favor of patriotism. The aristocratic ideal of kudos, pride in a self-centered areté, is opposed to the new ideal of service to a much broader community—the nation, or humanity, or posterity.[15]

We have Dryden's printed statement, never challenged, as evidence that Charles II read *Aureng-Zebe* and stated his opinion that it was the best of Dryden's tragedies so far. This degree of involvement on the part of the Poet Laureate and his master is, after all, impressive, especially since so much of the play bears upon Charles's own personal and political situation. Dryden was, undoubtedly, very skillful in preserving a tactful distance between fact and fiction; yet some topical references are unmistakable, and other more general aspects of the situation in the Agra of Shah Jehan show a daring suggestiveness when paralleled to Charles's London.

For example, when Mrs. Cox as Melesinda invoked the deity in these lines at the Court performance on 29 May 1676, she must have addressed them directly to the King, for, after beginning with a play upon the royal surname, they apply to Charles alone:

> Those who Stuards of his pity prove,
> He blesses, in return with public Love.
> In his distress, some Miracle is shown:
> If exil'd, Heav'n restores him to his Throne.
> He needs no Guard while any Subject's near:
> Nor, like his Tyrant Neighbours, lives in fear:

[14] The idea that there is a sublime joy in the renunciation of greatness appears in Longinus, recently translated by Boileau. See *Traité du sublime* (1674), chap. v.

[15] S-S, v, 197. In this and in several other respects, *Aureng-Zebe* departs from the heroic, and, as Arthur C. Kirsch says, paves the way to a greater stress on domestic piety and compassion: *Dryden's Heroic Drama* (Princeton, 1965), p. 119. It should be added that this tendency was already in evidence in the Ozmyn-Benzayda episodes of *The Conquest of Granada*. The new development is not merely sentimental (as opposed to heroic) love, but a general emphasis upon all the sentiments of "humanity."

No Plots th'Alarm to his retirements give:
'Tis all Mankind's concern that he should live.[16]

Other passages support the feature of Charles's statecraft
that Dryden always singled out for praise, his mercifulness,
presented now, rather paradoxically, as the central prop in
the security of his government:

> What if this death, which is for him design'd,
> Had been your Doom, (far be that Augury!)
> And you, not *Aureng-Zebe*, condemn'd to die?
> Weigh well the various turns of Humane Fate,
> And seek, by Mercy, to secure your State.[17]

These words, from another speech of Melesinda, are ad-
dressed to her savage husband Morat. The political wisdom,
decidedly un-Machiavellian, may seem impractical for the
Mogul empire, but it was proving to be eminently practical
in Charles II's England.

A rebuke (or rather, a warning) is decorously offered to
Charles, tucked away in a speech of Morat, where its satiri-
cal offensiveness is cloaked in irony. That arrogant youth
tells his mother Nourmahal to keep out of politics:

> Pleasure's your portion, and your slothful ease:
> When Man's at leisure, study how to please.
> Soften his angry hours with servile care,
> And when he calls, the ready Feast prepare.
> From Wars, and from affairs of State abstain:
> Women Emasculate a Monarch's Reign;
> And murmuring crowds, who see 'em shine with Gold,
> That pomp, as their own ravished Spoils behold.[18]

Of the King's two principal mistresses, Nell Gwyn and
Louise Kéroualle, the former was known to concentrate on his
pleasure rather exclusively. However, the latter, the Duchess
of Portsmouth, was notorious for using her influence to com-
mit England to Louis XIV in his continental wars. The

---

[16] III. i. 427–434.   [17] III. i. 470–474.   [18] IV. i. 195–202.

Duchess might have resented these lines, and also their reference to her extravagant display; she spent large sums in the most conspicuous manner, such as building and rebuilding her section of the rambling old Whitehall palace.[19]

The central political idea of *Aureng-Zebe* concerns the position and attitude of the Duke of York with regard to the succession. James was careful never to seem in any way eager to take power from Charles; in fact, his deep sorrow when Charles died, coupled with his consistently ruinous behavior as king, suggests he might always have dreaded the responsibility, which the peculiar nature of his religious convictions would make so heavy. James was content for years to be the second gentleman in the nation and a model of loyalty and obedience to the King. He had carried out Charles's order to inform Clarendon, his father-in-law, of his dismissal. He had accepted the decision to withhold him from active fleet command in 1666/67, and the later decision to expose him in 1672/73. His daughters, totally against his personal wish, were being brought up as Protestants. Although he always argued for his point of view and did all he could to protect his friends and supporters, he did not intrigue against his enemies, at least not to the extent that some of them intrigued against him. His interest therefore was honestly subordinated to the wishes of his brother the King. Dryden presents this attitude very favorably, in a speech of Aureng-Zebe to Morat, as a form of magnanimity allied to the Longinian sublime:

> I dare you, as your Rival in renown,
> March out your Army from th' Imperial Town:
> Chuse whom you please, the other leave to me;
> And set our Father absolutely free.
> This, if you do, to end all future strife,
> I am content to lead a private life:
> Disband my Army to secure the State,
> Nor aim at more, but leave the rest to Fate.[20]

[19] See "The Royal Buss," *POAS*, I, 263–265.
[20] III. i. 227–234.

James, indeed, had proved his willingness "to lead a private life" by resigning his offices in 1673 rather than swear to the Test. However, there was never any doubt in anyone's mind that, should something happen to Charles, James would then fight vigorously for the throne. Moreover, he had an excellent chance of winning. He was remembered favorably as an administrator in Navy affairs, and over the years was the most consistent influence in Army matters. Until it was realized that he was a Catholic, he was "the nation's darling," victor (at least by partisan standards) in two great fleet actions with the Dutch. His interest among the armed services and in the nation, therefore, was stronger than that of any rival, and at least strong enough to give him a fighting chance against any plausible combination of rivals.

This is the kind of power that Dryden represents Aureng-Zebe as possessing: a power greater than any rival's, unless the rival be supported by the emperor.[21] It is in the latter's character that Dryden effects the greatest distancing from historical actuality. Shah Jehan is old and incapable of rule; Charles, in the judgment of many historians today, was in 1675 a gifted politician who ruled with skill and energy. It is quite clear, however, that Dryden did not agree with this modern verdict. He, too, thought that Charles was a very good judge of men, but he saw his most characteristic traits as being his good-natured love of ease and an inherited disposition to mercy and forgiveness. Over the years, nevertheless, he had come to recognize that these traits were what the English needed most in their ruler, so that Charles, for

[21] A dialogue involving Aureng-Zebe and two of his followers makes his position clear and shows the parallel to James's (Fazel is speaking):

Know your own int'rest Sir, where e'er you lead,
We joyntly vow to own no other Head.
  Solyman. Your wrongs are known. Impose but your commands;
This hour shall bring you twenty thousand hands.
  Aureng-Zebe. Let them who truly would appear my friends,
Employ their swords, like mine, for noble ends.
No more: remember you have bravely done:
Shall Treason end, what Loyalty begun?

(II. i. 17–24)

all his faults of negligence, was a providential gift to the nation. An important factor in this changed judgment of Dryden's (after all, he had begun by counting upon Charles to be another Henry V) was the King's indulgence to his Laureate in the face of damaging accusations. Dryden had handed himself over to his Court enemies by his characterization of King Boabdelin as a weakling. His portrait of Shah Jehan, though not applicable personally to Charles, would yet allow of the same reproach of dishonoring kings as was brought against him before. Yet Charles, as Dryden said in the dedication to *Marriage a-la-Mode,* was "always more ready to hear good than ill."[22] With Mulgrave's help, Dryden was able to obtain Charles's acceptance of the conception of Shah Jehan, and to receive "the favour from him, to have the most considerable event of it modelled by his royal pleasure." (This suggests that Dryden offered the King the option of a happy or an unhappy ending to his "tragedy," and that the King opted for the present denouement, in which Shah Jehan restores Indamora to Aureng-Zebe and yields up the throne to him.) After he had been a beneficiary, in this episode, of Charles's tolerant understanding, it would have been hard for Dryden to convict the King of excessive good nature.

What happened, evidently, was that the King behaved in a very humane way toward the poet who was loyally endeavoring to instruct his prince. Whereas his trusted political advisers, such as Bab May, and also such self-appointed watchdogs of his servants' loyalty as Sir Robert Howard, raised a hue and cry at Dryden's freedom in handling the behavior of royal personages, King Charles had enough good sense and good taste to approve of his Laureate's fulfilling a well-recognized function: to teach as well as please. Charles expected his preachers to reproach him for his lapses, so long as they did it in gentlemanly fashion; he expected no less from his Laureate. Indeed, he obviously had a very healthy and very modern disregard for *lèse majesté,* as if he

22 S-S, IV, 254.

realized that amused tolerance is a public man's best defense against nonviolent attack.[23] Charles no doubt realized, also, that the old emperor, as played by his favorite actor Major Mohun, would be on the whole a very sympathetic figure.

The important political conception, however, is not the good nature of the old emperor, but the obedience of Aureng-Zebe. His loyalty is total; whatever the emperor commands, he will accept. Yet where his loyalty and his obedience are no longer in question, Aureng-Zebe acts more vigorously against his rivals and asserts his own right with great effectiveness. The evident parallel between this situation and the political situation in England at the end of 1675 may be stated, simply by stating in political terms the subject of *Aureng-Zebe*: the government of the reigning monarch,

---

[23] This toleration appears, perhaps with an overtone of irony, in Rochester's description of the reaction to Mulgrave's anonymous *Essay Upon Satire*: "I have sent you herewith a libel, in which my own share was not the least. The King having perused it is no ways dissatisfied with his. The author is apparently Mr. [Dryden], his patron my [Lord Mulgrave] having a panegyric in the midst, upon which happened a handsome quarrel between his L[ordship] and Mrs. B[ulkeley] at the Duchess of P[ortsmouth's]. She called him the Hero of the Libel and complimented him upon having made more cuckolds than any man alive, to which he answered, she very well knew one he never made, nor never cared to be employed in making. —Rogue and Bitch ensued, till the King, taking his grandfather's character upon him, became the peacemaker." It seems to me probable that Rochester shared, more scornfully than mercifully perhaps, the attitude of Charles and that he was not so likely as was the Duchess of Portsmouth to have caused the Rose Alley ambuscade in which Dryden was badly beaten up. These lines must have been offensive indeed to her:

> Yet saunt'ring Charles, between his beastly brace,
> Meets with dissembling still in either place,
> Affected humor or a painted face.
> In loyal libels we have often told him
> How one has jilted him, the other sold him;
> How that affects to laugh and this to weep;
> But who can rail so long as he can keep?
> Was ever prince by two at once misled,
> False, foolish, old, ill-natur'd and ill-bred?
>   (*POAS*, 1, 404–405, lines 65–73)

The expression "loyal libels" is an interesting one.

though threatened by ambitious pretenders and rendered unpopular by unwise indulgence of women, is adequately supported by a loyal and obedient prince, who stands ready to fill any power vacuum that may develop and fill it legally, so that obedience and power will continue to go hand in hand, rather than being fatally divided.[24] A confidence of this sort is attached to Aureng-Zebe from beginning to end in the play. At the start, the faithful minister Arimant (a reliable spokesman) gives this picture of him to the old emperor:

> You knew him brave, you know him faithful now:
> He aims at Fame, but Fame from serving you.
> 'Tis said, Ambition in his breast does rage:
> Who would not be the *Hero* of an Age?
> All grant him prudent: prudence interest weighs,
> And interest bids him seek your love and praise.[25]

Having been victorious in two campaigns, Aureng-Zebe has a just claim to recognition. To deny it, Arimant warns, would in practical politics only strengthen the young prince's hand:

> At once your People's heart and Son's you lose:
> And give him all, when you just things refuse.[26]

Interpreted, this means that Charles cannot, even if he would, remove the succession from James, who, although he might continue to be personally obedient, would become the

---

[24] As Morat implies in these lines, an arbitrary monarch destroys the principle of duty and obedience in his subjects:

> You cancell'd Duty when you gave me pow'r.
> If your own Actions on your Will you ground,
> Mine shall hereafter know no other bound.
>
> (IV. i. 321–323)

Thus if Charles should abrogate the law of succession and name someone other than James, it would be an arbitrary action destructive of the foundation of government, obedience. It is noteworthy that Dryden is placing continual emphasis upon obedience by the monarch and the subject, rather than force by the state, as the basis of government.

[25] I. i. 219–228.   [26] I. i. 239–240.

object of sympathy among many who would feel their own
security was at stake when hereditary right was denied. At the
very least, a strong—indeed, a just—cause of civil war would
arise, either at Charles's death or before, whenever a different
successor should be named.[27]

The nature of the conquests attributed to Aureng-Zebe
is much more significant than appears at first, so rapidly does
Dryden's verse move in the exposition at the beginning of
Act I. Like his three brothers, Aureng-Zebe raised an army
when the emperor became seriously ill. All four rivals re-
sorted to "open force," but Arimant, the clear-sighted *raison-
neur* throughout the play, rejects the terms "rebels and par-
ricides" for them:

> Brand not their actions with so foul a name:
> Pity, at least, what we are forc'd to blame.
> When Death's cold hand has clos'd the Father's eye,
> You know the younger Sons are doom'd to die.
> Less ills are chosen greater to avoid,
> And Nature's Laws are by the State's destroy'd.
> What courage tamely could to death consent,
> And not, by striking first, the blow prevent?
> Who falls in fight, cannot himself accuse,
> And he dies greatly who a Crown pursues.[28]

What this Hobbesian (or rather Hegelian) speech makes
plain is the all-too-human likelihood of war in the absence
of a powerfully sanctioned rule of state, such as the English
law of succession. The audience is moved to pity for the
three sons who cannot succeed, and who therefore are to be
executed by the inhumane Indian law. In the play, however,
neither Darah nor Sujah die: the more humane outcome,
where nature's laws are in harmony with the state's, is not
precluded. Such a bloodless outcome in England not only

---

[27] James's feelings concerning this possibility seem to be canvassed
in the play; see II. i. 520–547, ending in Aureng-Zebe's

> I neither would Usurp, nor tamely die.

[28] I. i. 38–47.

was heartily wished for by Dryden, but was the goal of his whole political effort as a writer during the next fifteen years.

What Aureng-Zebe overcomes in his eldest brother is suggested in this character:

> *Darah*, the eldest, bears a generous mind:
> But to implacable revenge inclin'd.
> Too openly does Love and hatred show:
> A bounteous Master, but a deadly Foe.[29]

This character is startlingly close to the portrait of James Stuart furnished both by Burnet, his enemy, and by Dryden his admirer and protégé.[30]

Next the second son is overcome; he is described as follows:

> From *Sujah's* valour I should much expect,
> But he's a *Bigot* of the *Persian* Sect:
> And, by a Foreign int'rest seeks to Reign,
> Hopeless by Love the Sceptre to obtain.[31]

This is an even more startling suggestion of the charge against James, that he was a Catholic bigot and a tool of the Pope, willing to be brought in by the might of Louis XIV. (In this connection, the Empress Nourmahal is also a "Persian"—i.e., she suggests Louise Kéroualle, who was a Frenchwoman and a Catholic.)

In the face of these rather daring attributions, one can only feel that Dryden wished to suggest, as part of his rhetoric to princes, that James needed to overcome his proclivity to hold grudges and display hard feelings, and also needed to guard against the loss of his nation's love should be become a papist bigot and a tool of the Pope or the French

---

[29] I. i. 90–93.

[30] Like James as described by Burnet, Aureng-Zebe has little regard for popularity:

> The People's love so little I esteem,
> Condemn'd by you, I would not live by them.
>
> (III. i. 286–287)

[31] I. i. 94–97.

King. The action of Aureng-Zebe does show the hero over-
coming these characteristics in the persons of his older, re-
bellious brothers, as if these stage figures represented bad
traits in himself that James should master before he could
be worthy of the succession. The description of Aureng-
Zebe's character bears out such an expectation:

> But *Aureng-Zebe*, by no strong passion sway'd,
> Except his Love, more temp'rate is, and weigh'd:
> This *Atlas* must our sinking State uphold;
> In Council cool, but in Performance bold:
> He sums their Virtues in himself alone,
> And adds the greatest, of a Loyal Son: . . .[32]

Compared to these characters, that of Morat is somewhat
less explicit, although it might apply to Buckingham:

> Morat's too insolent, too much a Brave
> What he attempts, if his endeavours fail
> T'effect, he is resolv'd no other shall.[33]

Buckingham, on occasion, was something of a bravo. More-
over, that Morat is unwilling to brook others' success agrees
with what Dryden would say of Zimri in *Absalom and Achi-
tophel*:

> He laught himself from Court, then sought Relief
> By forming Parties, but coud ne're be Chief:
> For, spight of him, the weight of Business fell
> On *Absalom* and wise *Achitophel*: . . . .
>
> (563–566)

Perhaps this is a characteristic form of the envy that Dryden
attributes to usurpers and revolutionaries in general. How-
ever, the dramatic situation develops so that Aureng-Zebe,
after overcoming the threat either of a revengeful or a
bigoted successor offstage, is confronted for the rest of the
play with the presence of Morat—as if a psychomachia were
to be developed against cruelty and zeal by suggestion and

[32] I. i. 102–107.   [33] I. i. 98, 100–101.

against overambition by direct confrontation. In the event, Morat is also engaged in the internal conflict of the psycho-machia by the persuasion of Indamora. The real struggle dramatized in the play is an inner one both for the hero, Aureng-Zebe, and the deutero-hero, Morat. So Dryden wished it to be: the only victory he desired in 1675 was an inner victory of loyalty and obedience, and the continuation of government according to law.

CHAPTER SEVEN

ON STAGE: SOPHOCLES, SHAKESPEARE, THE POPISH PLOT

THE five years that followed the premiere of *All For Love* may well have been the most significant period in the history of English politics. Between 1678 and 1683 two parties arose and took names as Whigs and Tories; the continuance of a traditional constitution was assured; the seeds of the peaceful Revolution of 1688 were planted; excess of religious bigotry, instead of leading to armed conflict, helped produce a reaction toward the almost completely secularized state of the next century. Dryden, while playing a leading part in these developments, continued to nourish his political writing upon his activity for the theatre. He drew upon Sophocles and, especially, Shakespeare for a passion and a nature that could match the strain of life in those years, moving away from heroics toward a more humane and, finally, a comic view of English society in turmoil.

At the beginning of this momentous period, Dryden produced a little manifesto. It appeared early in 1678, as part of the dedication of *All For Love*, addressed to Thomas Osborn, Earl of Danby, who had been King Charles's chief minister since 1673. Although Danby's policies were opposed to the ideas of the Duke of York, from the fall of 1677 James and the minister had been on good terms.[1] Dryden gave him a carefully reasoned defense of his administration,[2] which had led England through five of the most prosperous and

[1] See Turner, *James II*, pp. 123–124, 152.
[2] For the text of this dedication (published early in 1678), see S-S, v, 316–325. John Harrington Smith, "Some Sources of Dryden's Toryism, 1682–1684," *HLQ*, 20 (1957), 233–243, spoke of Dryden as "far more a literary man than a scholar or student of political theory," p. 243. True enough; but this dedication, nevertheless, shows him a student of current political developments and an accurate forecaster.

untroubled years she ever knew. After heartfelt praise for Danby's success in improving the collection and administration of the revenue, he goes on to speak of him as an "emanation" of Charles, "a king who is just and moderate in his nature, who rules according to the laws, whom God has made happy by forming the temper of his soul to the constitution of his government, and who makes us happy, by assuming over us no other sovereignty than that wherein our welfare and liberty consists." To this virtue of "moderation," so suitable in the King, Danby, he says, adds "a steadiness of temper that is likewise requisite in a minister of state." An eloquent disjunction: Charles was moderate, but in Dryden's eyes he was not steady. His chief minister, therefore, must be "so equal a mixture of both virtues, that he may stand like an isthmus betwixt the two encroaching seas of arbitrary power and lawless anarchy. . . . to pay what is due to the great representative of the nation [Parliament], and neither to enhance, nor to yield up, the undoubted prerogatives of the crown." Dryden goes on to praise balanced government as an English blessing.

After this he sketches out a foreign policy. Continental expansion, he says, has not made France happier and is doubly wrong for England. The taxes it requires result in "conquering abroad, to be poor at home." By geography, temperament, and government, he says, the English are suited to commerce and defense, rather than to military aggrandizement.

At home, just as it is indefensible to disturb the happy balance of government, so it would be foolish, he continues, to weaken the Church establishment in the name of liberty of conscience. "The moderation of our church is such, that its practice extends not to the severity of persecution; and its discipline is withal so easy, that it allows more freedom to dissenters than any of the sects would allow to it."

Dryden then strikes at Lord Shaftesbury: "He who has often changed his party, and always has made his interest the rule of it, gives little evidence of his sincerity for the public good; it is manifest he changes but for himself, and takes the people for tools to work his fortune. Yet the experience of all ages might let him know, that they who trouble the waters first, have seldom the benefit of the fishing; as they who began the late rebellion, enjoyed not the fruit of their undertaking, but were crushed themselves by the usurpation of their own instrument." No warning could have proved more true in the event. The dedication ends in praise of the devoted loyalty of Danby's father and his wife's grandfather, "fit to adorn an heroic poem."

Soon after the dedication came into print, the storm broke that was to ruin Danby and put the steadiness of Charles to its great test. Since 1673 the Earl of Shaftesbury had centered his management of the so-called Country party in the policy of attacking James Stuart, breaking up the Cavalier Parliament elected at the Restoration, and forcing new elections. In the latter part of 1678 he had a piece of great good luck. One day in August, as King Charles was about to step out for his walk, he was accosted by a man who helped in his chemical experiments, and warned that his life was in imminent danger. The same night he was given the "Narrative" in which Titus Oates and Ezrael Tongue had set down their preposterous concoction of a Popish Plot to murder the King and stamp out the Protestant religion with the aid of France.[3] Charles wanted to suppress the "disclosure" at the source, but his minister felt too vulnerable. Proof that he had taken money from Louis XIV would be produced by his enemies if he showed any lack of Protestant zeal. Hence Danby was tempted to outdo Shaftesbury in harrying the unfortunate people Oates accused. He retained barely sufficient control to have the Duke of York exempted from a new Test Act aimed to exclude Catholic members from Parliament; but in the end of December, 1678, Danby himself was impeached for treason. Charles first prorogued and then finally dissolved the Cavalier Parliament, after a

---

[3] See John Lingard, *History*, ix, 349, with contemporary references.

tenure lasting almost twenty years. Shaftesbury had won, elections would have to be held.

As expected, the newly elected Commons that convened in February, 1679, was hostile to the Court. As in 1667 with Clarendon and 1678 with Danby, they needed a victim and began to concentrate upon the bill to exclude the Duke of York from succession to the throne. Charles tried to pacify them by sending James into exile in Brussels that March, but the Exclusion Bill seemed sure to pass, and he soon had to prorogue the session. Finally he dissolved it in July. Another House was elected, even more hostile; and Charles put off its meeting, by one prorogation after another, until October, 1680. This was a period of great uproar and confusion. The central aim of the Whigs was to exclude James from the succession. They used the Popish Plot, the successive parliamentary elections, and each Parliament itself with its investigating and prosecuting committees, to intensify the crisis, terrorize their enemies, and intimidate the King. The usual licensing requirement had been allowed to lapse, so that a torrent of violent political pamphlets, newsletters, and gazettes spread the direst rumors, and lampoons massacred the characters of all who were engaged in the political struggle. While the uproar was at its height, the King twice fell seriously ill, in late August of 1679 and again in the following May. The Court, frightened at the chance of his death in August, was very glad to see James return from exile full of assurance, as usual, and determined on action. Early in September he and the Earl of Sunderland, who had succeeded Danby as the leading minister, were working together in an attempt to recapture the initiative lost to Shaftesbury.[4] The Duke of York left London late in October, 1679, for Scotland this time, and did not return until the last week of February, 1680. In the interim his faithful adherent John Dryden was severely beaten up by toughs in Rose Alley. Who set them on is hard to tell; Dry-

---

[4] J. P. Kenyon, *Robert Spencer, Earl of Sunderland* (London, 1958), pp. 30–32.

den had made enemies of three of the most powerful persons in England: Shaftesbury, Buckingham, and the Duchess of Portsmouth;[5] his side in politics was at its weakest, and he had done nothing to ingratiate himself with the opposition —quite the contrary, in fact.

Perhaps because of York's absence, Dryden's dedication of *Troilus and Cressida* to Sunderland deals in hypothetical generalities rather than concrete politics. Sunderland's sister was married to Dryden's brother-in-law Thomas Howard, the new Earl of Berkshire—Charles, the godfather of Dryden's first son and a Catholic, had died in disgrace in Paris, foolishly mixed up with Coleman, the only real Popish "plotter." *Limberham*, which had met with some disapproval in the Duke of York's household, was printed during James's Brussels exile and Dryden wrote its dedication in the fall, when the Duke was in Scotland. Dryden made the necessary excuses, indicating a poet's love of his own offspring; but he also proclaimed an unswerving loyalty to the Duke in his adversity: he has "taken a becoming care, that those things which offended on the stage, might be either altered, or omitted in the press; for their authority is, and shall be, ever sacred to me, as much absent or present, and in all alterations of their fortune, who for those reasons have stopped its further appearance on the theatre. And whatsoever hindrance it has been to me in point of profit, many of my friends can bear me witness, that I have not once murmured against that decree."[6]

---

[5] Ward, p. 144. Even if Portsmouth did not blame Dryden for the "beastly brace" slur in Mulgrave's *Essay upon Satire*, or the passage cited earlier from *Aureng-Zebe*, there is a passage in *Troilus and Cressida* that she might have found offensive:

> If parting from a mistress can procure
> A nation's happiness, show me that prince
> Who dares to trust his future fame so far,
> To stand the shock of annals, blotted thus,—
> He sold his country for a woman's love!

(III. ii. S-S, VI, 342)

[6] S-S, VI, 9–10. Susan Staves, in "Why Was Dryden's Mr. Limber-

The summer and fall of 1680, Dryden seems to have remained longer than usual in the country. He was studying history and theology in preparation for the body of poetry that is, probably, the main basis of his reputation today: *Absalom and Achitophel, Religio Laici*, and eventually, *The Hind and the Panther*. In addition, he may have done some pamphleteering on James's behalf.[7] He was now fully committed to the succesion of the Duke of York, and his work in and out of the theatre during the next dozen years is inspired throughout by politics.

Let us return to 1678, a year in which Dryden reinstated himself on the public and the theatrical scene after a kind of semiretirement. It was topped off by the production of *Oedipus*, a tragedy Dryden wrote with Nathaniel Lee, that became a hit at the Dorset Garden Theatre—a success probably owing to Lee in large measure. Dryden, however, says he alone wrote Acts I and III, and "drew the *Scenery* [i.e., the scenario] of the whole Play."[8] The epilogue alludes to the Pope-burning, which that year occurred on Guy Fawkes' Day, November 5. Pope-burnings had begun in 1673, as an aftermath of the anti-Catholic and anti-French sentiment that produced the Test Act.[9] These early examples of "theatre in the streets" took on an entirely fresh significance once the Popish Plot hysteria began with the discovery of Justice Godfrey's body. On 31 October 1678, the day of Godfrey's funeral, his corpse had been escorted by a huge mob of Londoners "so heated that anything called Papist, were it cat or dog, had probably gone to pieces in a moment."[10] Their ardor carried over into the annual Pope-burning a few days later. An all-time climax was reached in the Pope-burning of 1679, which was delayed until November 17 in order to coincide with the anniversary of Queen Elizabeth's succession. This,

---

ham Banned?" *Restoration and 18th Century Theatre Research*, 13 (1974), 1–11, ignores the York relation in an otherwise excellent article.

[7] Ward, pp. 155–156. [8] Macdonald, p. 118.

[9] Lee, *The Cabal*, p. 236.

[10] Bryant, *Samuel Pepys: The Years of Peril* (Cambridge, Eng., 1935), p. 225, quoting a contemporary source.

after church bells all over London had tolled through the darkness of early morning, brought most of the city into the streets to watch a procession that ended at the headquarters of Shaftesbury's Green Ribbon Club.

The political significance of *Oedipus* is concentrated in its scenes of mob violence and in the characterization of Shaftesbury as Creon, mainly discernible in Dryden's Acts I and III. Creon's character clearly anticipates the sinister side of Achitophel in Dryden's great verse satire. He is presented as a clever malcontent, driven by envy, who stirs up the crowd against the king of Thebes by a series of false rumors and accusations aimed at friends to the throne. Dryden was unwilling, during the uproar of the Plot, to continue his strictures upon unsteady government. In the preface to *Oedipus* he even acknowledges past errors by mingling some implicit self-criticism in a rather uncalled-for assault on Corneille. The latter, to develop a subplot, had introduced the figure of Theseus, king of Athens, into his *Oedipe*, thus diminishing the importance of Oedipus, king of Thebes: "He forgot that Sophocles had taken care to shew him, in his first entrance, a just, a merciful, a successful, a religious prince and, in short, a father of his country: instead of these, he has drawn him suspicious, designing, more anxious of keeping the Theban crown than solicitous for the safety of his people: hectored by Theseus, contemned by Dirce, and scarce maintaining a second part in his own tragedy. . . . He introduced a greater hero than Oedipus himself: for when Theseus was once there, that companion of Hercules must yield to none. The poet was obliged to furnish him with business, to make him an equipage to his dignity, and by following him too close, to lose his other king of Branford in the crowd."[11] Aside from this affirmation of royal primacy (which shows again that Dryden had learned the lesson of *The Rehearsal*), the preface contains only one topical reference, to the futility of the long struggle by France for domination on the Continent: "that politic nation . . . who

[11] Watson, I, 233.

have taught their enemies to fight so long, that at last they are in a condition to invade them."[12] It reinforces a wry couplet in the prologue:

> Pray be advis'd; and though at *Mons* you won,
> On pointed Cannon do not always run.[13]

This recalls the British share in William's victory over the French general Luxembourg on 17 August 1678, when Ossory led the English and Scottish regiments. Dryden is obviously not encouraging further exploits of the kind, although Ormond's son Ossory was one of his heroes.

War, in fact, is spoken of as the "other plague" of Thebes in the opening of Dryden and Lee's play.[14] In Oedipus's absence while fighting against Argos, Creon takes advantage of the terrible plague and the confusion it has produced to connive at rebellion. Knowing the people are unsettled, "prone, as in all general ills, to sudden change,"[15] he orders his "creatures" to stir them up:

> you insinuate
> Kind thoughts of me into the multitude;
> Lay load upon the court; gull them with freedom;
> And you shall see them toss their tails, and gad,
> As if the breeze had stung them.[16]

Creon pursues Euridice (supposedly the daughter of Laius, and therefore a symbol of dynastic legitimacy if Creon can marry her) in the manner of Richard III pursuing the Princess Anne. Yet his bodily deformity is also meant to allude to Shaftesbury, and Dryden gives him the essential trait to be found later in Achitophel: he is, in his own words, a "daring" pilot, sinister but sublime:

> And as from chaos, huddled and deformed,
> The god struck fire, and lighted up the lamps
> That beautify the sky, so he informed
> This ill-shaped body with a daring soul.[17]

---

[12] *Ibid.*, p. 234.   [13] Lines 25–26.   [14] S-S, VI, 139.
[15] *Ibid.*, p. 140.   [16] *Ibid.*, p. 141.   [17] *Ibid.*, p. 143.

When Euridice rejects him, Creon accuses her rather preposterously (but no more so than Oates in his charge against Queen Catherine) of conspiring in the killing of Laius with Adrastus—who is represented on his entrance as Oedipus's "brother of the war."[18] This scheme comes close enough to suggest the basic premise of the Popish Plot, that the life of the King was threatened by the Catholics, including his brother James and his own queen. The appearance of the Theban crowd in full cry upon the stage in Act I, Act II, Act IV, and in a battle in the streets in Act V, bears out theatrically the chaos of civil war that peaceable men feared most of all during those years. Since mob violence was Shaftesbury's most intimidating threat, Dryden counted on a cathartic effect from these stage scenes, as he hoped for an increase of tenderness from the impact made by the dreadful suffering of his royal protagonist upon the hard-hearted audience. This barbaric hardness of theirs, so often decried by Dryden as an imposition from Commonwealth days upon the good-natured English nation, is attacked in the prologue on humane grounds:

> For were it known this Poem did not please,
> You might set up for perfect Salvages:
> Your Neighbours would not look on you as men:
> But think the Nation all turn'd *Picts* agen.
> Faith, as you manage matters, 'tis not fit
> You should suspect your selves of too much Wit.
> . . . .
>
> With some respect to antient Wit proceed;
> You take the four first Councils for your Creed.
> But, when you lay Tradition wholly by,
> And on the private Spirit alone relye,
> You turn Fanaticks in your Poetry.[19]

In his next play, Dryden totally reworked Shakespeare's *Troilus and Cressida* according to his newly formulated conception of a catharsis of pity and terror aimed at the pre-

---

[18] *Ibid.*, p. 152.   [19] Lines 15–20, 27–31.

vailing vices of pride and hardness of heart.[20] His adaptation appeared at the very worst stage of Popish Plot frenzy, in the early spring of 1679.[21] In the face of heavy attacks in Parliament, Charles declared he would no longer have a cabinet council or cabal, but would rule instead by the advice of a newly modeled Privy Council, with Shaftesbury as President. "The Opposition had made it plain that it was no mere security against Popery that was sought. That was but the handle: the aim was avowedly the old one of '41— Reformation! Nor were the weapons different: armed Covenanters in Scotland, the rabble loose in London, and the City magistrates refusing to tame it, since, as one worthy constitutionalist declared, the noise of its roaring would do more to persuade Whitehall than all the fine speeches in Westminster."[22]

In these riotous circumstances, Dryden gave a double distance to his *Troilus and Cressida*, by following Shakespeare fairly closely, and by stressing the fundamental idea he himself found in the Tale of Troy as told in Homer's *Iliad*: the need to avoid division among the followers of a ruler, especially in face of disaster.[23] In the spring of 1679 this stress was more hopeful than realistic. Three lines, in which Dryden compresses Ulysses' famous "Degree" speech, apply better to the situation at that time:

> when supremacy of kings is shaken,
>
> . . . .
>
> Then everything resolves to brutal force,
> And headlong force is led by hoodwinked will.[24]

[20] "Rapin, a judicious critic, has observed from Aristotle that pride and want of commiseration are the most predominant vices in mankind; therefore, to cure us of these two, the inventors of tragedy have chosen to work upon two other passions, which are fear and pity." "Grounds of Criticism in Tragedy," Watson, I, 245.

[21] *London Stage*, I, 276.

[22] Bryant, *King Charles II*, pp. 284–285.

[23] In the pertinent passage from "A Parallel Betwixt Painting and Poetry" (1695), Dryden comments that, had Achilles "been less passionate, or less revengeful," Troy would have been captured at once.

[24] S-S, VI, 290.

Ulysses goes on to inform Agamemnon of one source of the distemper, the scurrilous mimicry of the Grecian chiefs by Patroclus for the amusement of his friend Achilles:

Even thee, the king of men, he does not spare,
(The monkey author) but thy greatness pageants,
And makes of it rehearsals. . . .[25]

This can only be an allusion to the Duke of Buckingham, author of *The Rehearsal*, and to his friend the Earl of Rochester, "the monkey author." Rochester's well-known portrait (now in the National Portrait Gallery) shows him crowning a monkey with a laurel wreath.[26] Dryden has in mind the raucous contempt expressed by both Buckingham and Rochester, not only for the Two Kings of Brentford, but for what Bryant calls Charles II's "dream of a united nation."[27] Neither Buckingham nor Rochester was ever likely to accept Charles as an Agamemnon. Furthermore, Buckingham, although he had ceased to serve Charles, still kept his own dream of leadership and command. Dryden rather plainly satirizes him, much in the comic vein of his later portrait of Zimri, at the conclusion of the first scene of *Troilus and Cressida*. He begins with two verses from Shakespeare (I. iii. 161–162) and then manages to effect a skillful merger of the two figures, Achilles and Patroclus, and of his own words with selected phrases from Shakespeare, so as to direct a thrust at Buckingham as an unnatural freak, a buffoon-prince:

Fortune was merry
When he was born, and played a trick on nature,
To make a mimic prince; he ne'er acts ill,
But when he would seem wise:

---

[25] *Ibid.*, p. 291.

[26] Reproduced as the frontispiece of Pinto's edition of the *Poems*, London, 1953. (I cannot help wondering whether Rochester did not assist in the extensive additions to *The Rehearsal* that appear in the 1675 edition.)

[27] *King Charles II*, pp. 259–260. Bryant's chronology in the passage referred to is poetic rather than exact, but he is faithful to the contrast of attitudes between Charles and the Buckinghamites.

For all he says or does, from serious thought,
Appears so wretched, that he mocks his title,
And is his own buffoon.[28]

The next few lines, abbreviated from Shakespeare, carry
the process of allusion along to Shaftesbury. Dryden's audi-
ence, which was unfamiliar with Shakespeare's original on
the stage,[29] would certainly detect a resemblance between
Ajax's keeping of Thersites and Shaftesbury's sponsorship
of Titus Oates, in both cases to act as all-privileged accusers
of men envied by their masters. In early 1679, this was as
close as Dryden dared to come to an attack upon Oates,
then officially entitled "the Savior of the Nation"; even the
King himself could not harm Oates, although he accused the
Queen in Parliament of plotting to murder her husband.[30]

Charles's strategy against Shaftesbury is very well described
by Dryden in a speech of Ulysses, the wise councilor:

[28] S-S, VI, 291–292. Cf. "a mimic prince" and Shadwell's dedication
of *Timon of Athens* to Buckingham as "Prince"—the dedication at
which Dryden took umbrage and (I believe) refers to in *MacFlecknoe*.

[29] Shakespeare's play was assigned to the Duke's Company. However,
it was not performed until Dryden's version appeared. No doubt he
felt he was rescuing—as in redoing *Antony and Cleopatra*—an unknown
Shakespeare work from theatrical oblivion.

[30] Bryant, *King Charles II*, p. 276. There is another pretty direct
allusion to Oates in IV. ii. (S-S, VI, 361), where Thersites describes
Calchas as "that fugitive priest of Troy, that canonical rogue of our
side." In V. i. (p. 375) there is a passage that reiterates Dryden's un-
changing antipathy to the clerical interest; it had, however, a special
point while Oates was leading the London mob like a Pied Piper:

> By heaven, 'twas never well, since saucy priests
> Grew to be masters of the listening herd,
> And into mitres cleft the regal crown;
> Then, as the earth were scanty for their power,
> They drew the pomp of heaven to wait on them.

The same may be said of Troilus' execration in v. ii. (p. 383):

> That I should trust the daughter of a priest!
> Priesthood, that makes a merchandise of heaven!
> Priesthood, that sells even to their prayers and blessings,
> And forces us to pay for our own cozenage!

Oates pretended to be an ordained priest and was lavishly supported
at government expense.

Oppose not rage, while rage is in its force,
But give it way a while, and let it waste.
The rising deluge is not stopped with dams;
Those it o'erbears, and drowns the hopes of harvest:
But, wisely managed, its divided strength
Is sluiced in channels, and securely drained.[31]

It might be said that Charles had no other course to follow, granted that his prime concern was to preserve the continuity of the monarchy, than to ride out the storm or run with it when it became necessary. However, it was not until this crisis over the attempt to exclude James from the succession that the King demonstrated he could be steady on any point of sailing in politics. While Shaftesbury was President of the Council, there was fair reason to believe that, if Charles did not agree to the exclusion of James, his rule would be supplanted by some form of oligarchy or republic. To give in to exclusion would have been the easy way; and Charles notoriously loved his ease. Yet he resisted, remained firm, and won a personal victory in the end. Dryden celebrated this triumph (rather prematurely, perhaps) at the end of *Troilus and Cressida*, in lines spoken by Ulysses:

Hail, Agamemnon! truly victor now!
While secret envy, and while open pride,
Among thy factious nobles discord threw;
While public good was urged for private ends,
And those thought patriots who disturbed it most;
Then, like the headstrong horses of the sun,
That light, which should have cheered the world,
   consumed it:
Now peaceful order has resumed the reins,
Old Time looks young, and nature seems renewed.
Then, since from home-bred factions ruin springs,
Let subjects learn obedience to their kings.[32]

"Obedience" stands as Dryden's guiding principle in the

---

[31] v. ii. S-S, vi, 378–379.   [32] S-S, vi, 390.

nation's crisis: here it means obedience to the King by his nobles and erstwhile servants. Elsewhere, his principle (as strongly) called for obedience by the King too, to the law of the land. As Dryden saw it, mutual obedience to the constitution of the country by king, nobility, and people was necessary to the continuity of England in that state of delicate, sheltered equilibrium he had imaged in the sixties. It was a perilous balance, to be maintained only by the continual practice of reason and forbearance. Its worst enemy was destructive passion, including the passion of patriotism —that cover for unrestrained will and selfish pride.

In his effort to meet wild passion with passion under control, Dryden turned to Shakespeare for a blank verse style better adapted to the expression of feeling than his own heroic couplet. However, to shelter men's minds from factional rancor, he continued to cultivate rhyme in prologues and epilogues, providing a pair of comic parentheses as a means of cajoling audiences into good will. In these short pieces he habitually addressed two audiences in the theatre. The larger one was made up of "the great vulgar and the small," to use the phrase he picked up from Cowley; the other one consisted of the thinking few who were capable of giving a lead to the many. During the riotous times of 1678–1683, Dryden distinguished between the two groups according to their ability to be dispassionate and to suspend certain prejudices. These included insular pride, northern callousness and coldness, and a weakness for the deceits and commotions of fanaticism. The last Dryden linked with empty bombast and silly spectacle; he damned Settle's propaganda plays and Shaftesbury's Pope-burnings under the same rubric of highflying farce:

> Go back to your dear Dancing on the Rope,
> Or see what's worse the Devil and the Pope!
> The Plays that take on our Corrupted Stage,
> Methinks resemble the distracted Age;

Noise, Madness, all unreasonable Things,
That strike at Sense, as Rebels do at Kings![33]

However, for the university audience at Oxford, where the players performed at the Act as usual in July 1680, Dryden reserved a special place of authority. They shared his detestation of the cultural blight the success of factional bigotry would bring:

But 'tis the Talent of our *English* Nation,
Still to be Plotting some New Reformation:
Jack Presbyter shall here Erect his Throne.
Knock out a Tub with Preaching once a day,
And every Prayer be longer than a Play.
Then all you Heathen Wits shall go to Pot,
For disbelieving of a Popish Plot:

. . . .

Religion, Learning, Wit wou'd be supprest,
Rags of the Whore, and Trappings of the Beast:[34]

Dryden saw "Religion, Learning, Wit" as the first victims of anarchic zeal (he had lived through three or four years of it at Cambridge in his youth).

The most important thing to say about Dryden as an author in politics, it seems to me, is that he never gave up the weapons of wit and learning in fighting their opposites, and that he held fast to the sense of inclusive charity that at all times marked his religion. His raillery never had a brighter sparkle, nor his attacks on the foe a more high-spirited humor, than when he was fighting his worst enemies, the dullard and the bigot. His reservations about the limitations and dangers (for him at least) of malicious satire gave way sufficiently in 1678 for him to write *MacFlecknoe*. He found in the mock-heroic style of Boileau and the narrative-dra-

[33] Prologue to Tate's *The Loyal General* (winter, 1679/80), lines 10–15.
[34] See LS, I, 288 for date, July, 1680; lines 9–16, 23–24.

matic form of *Le Lutrin* a perfect mode of defense for his new position in the theatre. It enabled him to avoid lampoon, or mere abuse of particular persons, and to create a genuine poem of the kind he was to call Varronian satire. One of the marks of the new kind is a far greater share of the comic than is to be found in normal Restoration couplet satire. Instead of lashing the ridiculous in a variety of manners and persons, with little pretense of the structure necessary for truly comic fiction, *MacFlecknoe* developed its portrait of the Prince of Dullness so as to make him both peculiar (like Shadwell in some striking ways) and universal (like Settle also, and other bad poets), so making him what Dryden says Shakespeare made of Falstaff, "not properly one humour, but a miscellany of humours or images, drawn from so many several men."[35] The great advantage of this kind of writing was that it produced a work of constructive poetry and not merely an effusion of witty violence and malice, which could be retorted effectively enough by more of the same. Moreover, its Varronian commitment to produce some positive increment of knowledge, good sense, and entertainment made it useful in the arena of politics.

Such is the spirit in which *The Spanish Friar* was written. It was probably Dryden's most popular play after his earlier successes. He worked on it with care and with a degree of liking he seldom admitted, very much inspired by his new fascination with Shakespeare. He called it "a Protestant Play." When it was produced however, about the beginning of November, 1680, the Popish Plot had passed its worst extreme of turbulence and suspicion. As long as critics thought of Dryden as always anxious to give his audience whatever they wanted at any given moment, *The Spanish Friar* was seen as an outright exploitation of the anti-Catholic rage generated by Oates's charges and Shaftesbury's propaganda.[36] Yet, in fact, the play is an attempt to allay that rage

---

[35] Watson, I, 71.

[36] Dedication, Watson, I, 279, and George W. Whiting, "Political Satire in London Stage Plays, 1680–1683," *Modern Philology, 28*

by providing outlets for it in sentiment and in humor, just as Ulysses recommended the deluge ought to be channeled off harmlessly rather than vainly dammed up, and just as *Absalom and Achitophel* would seek outlets in unmalicious laughter, which the ridiculous themselves could share.

Scott thought that "the comic part of this play is our author's masterpiece in comedy,"[37] and it should be noted that the Friar, who belongs in the comic plot almost entirely, gives his name to the work; its subtitle, "The Double Discovery," refers to the serious action, where Torrismond is discovered as the son and successor of the old King Sancho, thought murdered, and then Sancho is discovered to be still alive. Dryden's claim that he did his best to make the two actions "of a piece" was approved not only by Scott but by Johnson as well, although modern critics have not always agreed. I believe it is as much a matter of ethos as of plotting. The action of the serious part, and even more its characterization, is constantly undercut by the cynical, anti-heroic jibes of Pedro (a sort of honest cynic *raisonneur*) and by Dryden's refusal to grant tragic stature to anyone except Leonora, a second-generation usurper whose attempt to mix love and Machiavellian politics fails because she is too ingenuous for her self-serving minister Bertran.

Overall, the most remarkable feature of *The Spanish Friar* is its adherence to the archetypal comic opposition of the young and fertile to the old and sterile. The "death" of Sancho, who is the real father of Torrismond, is willingly accepted by his son and daughter-in-law, Leonora the queen.

(1930), 29–43, who assumes as a point that needs no argument that the play is "a satire upon Catholicism." Bredvold recognized that *The Spanish Friar* is not very anti-Catholic, and that "instead of the vacillating pamphleteer that has been painted, Dryden appears to have been in these years a firm, consistent, and loyal Tory." This paper, "Political Aspects of Dryden's *Amboyna* and *The Spanish Fryar*," *University of Michigan Publications in Language and Literature*, 8 (1932), 119–132, is a landmark in the rehabilitation of Dryden's reputation. In particular, it shows that Dryden's income from the government actually fell during these years of his greatest service to it.

[37] S-S, VI, 399.

The comic hero, Lorenzo, is not only arrayed against old, impotent Gomez (a typical miser and cuckold), but also against his own father, an old courtier who wants revenge upon Leonora. The old man Torrismond always thought was his father, Raymond, also a revengeful courtier of the old king, has incited the mob to attack Leonora's palace. "Both our fathers thrust them headlong on," Lorenzo says, and Torrismond replies, "be / A friend, and once forget thou art a son." As the two of them rush offstage to repulse the mob, Torrismond invokes "Leonora, beauteous in thy crimes," believing that "even my father's ghost [will] his death forgive" (all this at the end of Act V, scene 1). Although Dryden is exploiting the tragic side of the Oedipal myth, the comic alignment of old age and hardhearted revengefulness against youth, lusty sexuality, and loving kindness is more important.

The title role of the Friar is modeled after Shakespeare's Falstaff and Pandarus. Friar Dominic is not young, but he is an abettor of youth and far from impotent himself. He is Lorenzo's agent in the struggle with old Gomez, whom he worsts in the big final scene where, as in comedy, the stage is made to look "as full as possible." The Friar exits with a rabble triumphantly pushing him off, but with a farewell blessing of an old comic sort: "May your sisters, wives, and daughters be so naturally lewd, that they may have no occasion for a devil to tempt, or a friar to pimp for them." The actor who played Friar Dominic in 1680, Anthony Leigh, had recently done Pandarus in Dryden's *Troilus and Cressida* as well as Old Bellair in *The Man of Mode*. His portrait as the Friar shows him very humorous and Falstaffian, not the least bit sinister.[38] Gomez, his antagonist in several rollicking

---

[38] Cibber's account (much later) of Leigh in the role of the Friar indicates a more sinister interpretation than Dryden's lines justify. See the *Apology* (Everyman ed.), p. 80. I think Leigh's portrait in the role (*LS*, 1, facing p. 401) confirms my view. See also Robert D. Hume's account of another hit part of Leigh's, Sir Jolly Jumble in *The Souldiers Fortune* (June 1680), in his important "Otway and the Comic Muse," *Studies in Philology*, 73 (1976), 98.

scenes, was played by the great James Nokes. The comic pos-
sibilities Dryden provided for these two (and many of his
lines are as witty and imaginative as his business is farcical)
were undoubtedly exploited to the full. Lorenzo, the comic
lead, was played by William Smith, who created the part of
Sir Fopling Flutter and also did Edgar in *Lear*. He is rather
prominent in the main plot, too: on three occasions his
interpositions mark happy turning points.

It is not nearly so easy to identify any role in *The Spanish
Friar* with a particular actor on the political scene as it was
to identify Creon with Shaftesbury in *Oedipus*. That, no
doubt, is one reason why Dryden was right to be proud
of *The Spanish Friar* and rather contemptuous of the too-
explicit *Troilus and Cressida*. As John M. Wallace has ar-
gued, the audience needs to be able to exercise its imagi-
nation. Yet *The Spanish Friar* is in every sense a richer
political play, and its contemporary relevance is if anything
closer and more varied. To suggest how this is so, we might
consider Saussure's model of *langue* as a static system of
signs made up by signifiers and signifieds without exact ref-
erents in external historical reality. Each sign has a meaning-
value, not determined by a particular external referent but
rather by its relations within the system to the other signs.
In Dryden's play, for example, the Friar accuses Gomez of
being in the plot to murder King Sancho. The audience
could detect an allusion here to Titus Oates, but in literary
fact the Friar is an entirely different figure. The meaning-
value, therefore, is not that there is an identity between
Dominic and Titus in that both are false witnesses, but
rather that in a time of civil chaos any scamp will take an
opportunity to serve an interest of his own. The "system"
here is not "Titus Oates" but "civil turmoil." Torrismond's
is, perhaps, the most interesting case for imaginative specu-
lation. At first the audience sees him as the son of Raymond;
then as the dead Sancho's son, therefore legitimate king;
and finally as the live Sancho's son, therefore not king but
successor. Actually Monmouth was the son of King Charles;

but Charles was very much alive, and so Monmouth was not king; and finally he was not the successor because he was not legitimate. This last element is apparently missing from the system of the play, where the only "illegitimate" person is Leonora, whose father was a usurper. Dryden, therefore, has linked Torrismond and Leonora. Within the system of the play, her usurpation, their guilty marriage, and the parricidal feelings of both, function to transgress the legitimate child-parent relation. Yet there is a stronger, more inclusive system, as we have seen—the comic, which sanctions youthful unions and sides with them against old and infertile fathers. The richest meaning emerges in relation to this comic scheme, when the marriage of Torrismond and Leonora turns sterile so long as he believes Sancho is dead, i.e., so long as youth is contaminated by usurpation. Thus Dryden establishes a bond between legitimacy and fertility, requiring forgiveness; whereas Sophocles established a bond between parricide and infertility, requiring punishment. On this more basic level of comic feeling, there is a strong structure in *The Spanish Friar.*

In the dedication of *The Spanish Friar,* Dryden showed himself anxious (as he often was not) that the play receive a careful reading to disclose what he calls "the silent graces" of its construction.[39] One of these "silent graces" brings to mind "The Grounds of Criticism in Tragedy," where Dryden had quoted a pathetic passage from *Richard II* to illustrate the difference between bombast and the true Longinian sublime. "Behold King Richard," he had written, "consider the wretchedness of his condition, and his carriage in it; and refrain from pity, if you can."[40] Now he took Shakespeare's description of Richard and made it the basis for the compassion he wished his serious plot to inspire. First he established a similar situation: Sancho, like Richard, is indulgent to a fault; he has been overreached by a calculating poli-

[39] Watson, I, 278.
[40] *Ibid.,* p. 259. This essay was printed with *Troilus and Cressida* in 1679.

tician, deposed, and cast into prison. Torrismond describes
the scene:

> But I have been in such a dismal place,
> Where joy ne'er enters, which the sun ne'er cheers,
> Bound in with darkness, overspread with damps;
> Where I have seen (if I could say I saw)
> The good old king, majestic in his bonds,
> And 'midst his griefs most venerably great.
> By a dim winking lamp, which feebly broke
> The gloomy vapors, he lay stretched along
> Upon the unwholesome earth, his eyes fixed upward;
> And ever and anon a silent tear
> Stole down, and trickled from his hoary beard.[41]

The shock Torrismond receives at this sight first causes him
to plead with Leonora for the old man's life, vainly, and
when he learns Sancho is his father, he avoids intercourse
with her. It turns out, however, that the king has been kept
alive by Bertran, who now is anxious to "end our fears of
civil war" for his own sake. Bertran begs forgiveness. Finally,
Torrismond calls him brother and ends the play with these
pacific lines on the King:

> Oh! fear not him! pity and he are one;
> So merciful a king did never live;
> Loth to revenge, and easy to forgive.
> But let the bold conspirator beware,
> For heaven makes princes its peculiar care.[42]

Dryden makes it quite obvious that he was using the sen-
timental catharsis for a political end. Trust in Charles's pity
is to overcome the rebellious subject's fear. "Oh! fear not
him!" Even the worst offenders in the uproar over the Popish
Plot can count on the notoriously forgiving Stuart disposi-
tion. The experience of suffering, and of being pitiable him-
self, had made Charles kind, as it had done with King Sancho

[41] III. iii (VI, 468). Cf. *Richard II*, v. ii. 23–36.
[42] v. ii (VI, 521).

in the play. Only the hardened plotter should despair. In
The Spanish Friar, therefore, we have a rhetoric directed at
humane feeling. One might call it a metarhetoric, for Dry-
den used every resource of tragic and comic drama to dis-
solve the hostility and terror of the Popish Plot into tears and
laughter.

A new and surprising development, most worthy of com-
ment, is the respect Dryden begins to show for the power of
the London mob. He had seen during the previous year that
Londoners were willing to fight when aroused, and that
courage was not confined to soldiers and cavaliers. As Friar
Dominic and Lorenzo are fleeing from Gomez's uproar, the
Friar says: "Away, colonel; let us fly for our lives! The neigh-
bors are coming out with forks and fire-shovels and spits, and
other domestic weapons; the militia of a whole alley is raised
against us."[43] Raymond tries to persuade Leonora to com-
mission some bold, loyal man to raise the city trainbands:

> You do not know the virtues of your city,
> What pushing force they have. Some popular chief,
> More noisy than the rest, but cries Haloo!
> And in a trice the bellowing herd come out,
> The gates are barred, the ways are barricadoed,
> And "One and all" 's the word. True cocks of
>   th'game,
> That never ask for what or whom they fight!
> But turn them out, and show them but a foe,
> Cry "Liberty!" and that's a cause of quarrel.[44]

London's passion for liberty is shared by Dryden. It may
be surprising in one so devoted to a hereditary monarchy,
but it is true nevertheless that liberty is Dryden's highest
political value. He sets it even above peace and order, and
he attributes the desire for liberty to all human beings who
have escaped corruption. Yet repeatedly he explained his

[43] IV. i (VI, 482).
[44] IV. ii (VI, 488–489). The reference to barricades is a reminder of
the method used by the Paris populace to drive King Henri III from
the city.

conviction that legitimate monarchy and an established church, at least at that time in England, were the most solid guarantees of liberty. In *The Spanish Friar*, nevertheless, he makes it very clear that either an absolute monarch, or the arbitrary use of royal power, is intolerable. In a lively debate Bertran counsels Leonora to "turn the edge of right" in her own defense. She answers:

> You place such arbitrary power in kings
> That I much fear, if I should make you one,
> You'll make yourself a tyrant. . . .[45]

Leonora blames Bertran for suggesting the king's murder, and he complains:

> This 'tis to serve a prince too faithfully,
> Who free from laws himself will have that done
> Which not performed brings us to sure disgrace,
> And if performed to ruin.
>   Leonora. This 'tis to counsel things that are
>   unjust:
> First to debauch a king to break his laws,
> Which are his safety, and then seek protection
> From him you have endangered. But just heaven
> When sins are judged will damn the tempting devil
> More deep than those he tempted.
>   Bertran. If princes not protect their ministers,
> What man will dare to serve them?
>   Leonora. None will dare
> To serve them ill when they are left to laws.[46]

Clearly this discourse, while leaving open the question of sovereign power, rejects the notion that the Crown is not in effect bound by law; in fact, law is presented as the basis of the Crown's security. Human liberty arises out of the willing

[45] IV. ii (VI, 485).
[46] IV. ii (VI, 486–487). A reference to Danby, languishing in the Tower, seems inescapable. His dealings with France or his overcountenancing of the Plot might have lost him Dryden's approval.

obedience to law: this old, paradoxical truth is the corner-stone of Dryden's politics. The law, like the rules of poetry, to be worthy of man must be based on reason and nature and sanctioned by tradition; that is, it must be made in great part by human agency over the years. It cannot be dependent upon human willfulness, passion, or fanaticism. The king, like his subjects and ministers, is under the law.

Dryden's success in creating occasions for all these political allusions by relation to the framework of his plot is quite remarkable. Much more important, he showed the power to invent a fiction and an entire dramatic structure that would carry the weight of topical and satirical comment while functioning in its own right aesthetically and as a work of art. In the sense that it develops political wisdom and tells a story entertainingly, *The Spanish Friar* is an extreme form of what Dryden called Varronian satire. A more normal form like that of *Absalom and Achitophel*, where an episode from the Bible is treated according to a contemporary dramatic formula, would be a natural pattern for him to adopt when he wished to appeal to men's minds more than to their feelings.

CHAPTER EIGHT

ABSALOM AND ACHITOPHEL

I. THE POLITICAL SITUATION

THE new political factor that emerged in 1680 was Charles's statement that Exclusion was the one accommodation that he would refuse to make, backed up at last by convincing evidence that he might keep his word. Resisting the flood of addresses and petitions for another election of the Commons and a new Parliament, the King began to speak privately of his determination to live on his normal revenue. To economize, he spent the whole summer at Windsor. Monmouth, on the contrary, was the object of extravagant hospitality as he made a "progress" like a reigning monarch's through the west of England. External necessity, to defend Tangier and help William of Orange, finally compelled the King to call for his fourth Parliament on October 21, 1680. The majority in the Commons continued to insist upon the present danger from the Popish Plot—brazenly now, for in recent months their witnesses, mostly Irish, had been caving in under cross-examination from the Crown's attorneys and judges (who had become less friendly). By November 15, 1680, another Exclusion Bill had been rammed through the Commons and presented to the Lords. London itself was more than ever governed by Shaftesbury's men. Its mayor, Patience Ward, its sheriffs, Bethel and Cornish, were ready to send the mob to demonstrate at Whitehall as soon as the Lords approved Exclusion. (It was Pope-burning time again, and the preparations were all made.) However, the bill was defeated in the Lords, with Halifax speaking against it some sixteen times between noon and midnight. The Commons majority retaliated by resolving that whoever should advance money to the King, for no matter what purpose, was a national enemy (a move that

227

made explicit the tactics of terror they were using). On January 10, 1681 they further resolved "that whoever should advise a prorogation was a betrayer of the kingdom, a promoter of Popery, and a pensioner of France." On that day Charles prorogued them, a week later he dissolved them, and on January 19 he called for a new Parliament, to meet this time at Oxford.[1]

Once again the better-unified "interest" committed to Exclusion swept the elections, aided in many areas by the intimidation of their opponents. The Exclusionist members rode to the session at Oxford well guarded by volunteers armed with sword, gun, and the "Protestant Flail." On Saturday, March 19, many of them were welcomed in a totally different spirit by an epilogue Dryden wrote for the King's Company, which was there to entertain them. "Spoken to the KING at the opening the PLAY-House at *Oxford*," it was printed within the week:

> As from a darkn'd Roome some Optick glass
> Transmits the distant Species as they pass;
> The worlds large Landschape is from far descry'd,
> And men contracted on the Paper glide:
> Thus crowded *Oxford* represents Mankind,
> And in these Walls *Great Brittain* seems Confin'd.
> *Oxford* is now the publick *Theater*;
> And you both Audience are, and Actors here.
> The gazing World on the New Scene attend,
> Admire the turns, and wish a prosp'rous end.
> This Place the seat of Peace, the quiet Cell
> Where Arts remov'd from noisy business dwell,
> Shou'd calm your Wills, unite the jarring parts,
> And with a kind Contagion seize your hearts:
> Oh! may its Genius, like soft Musick move,
> And tune you all to Concord and to Love.

---

[1] For this summary I have checked Bryant's lively account (pp. 299–308) against Haley: see also the latter's pages 525, 528n., 586, 601.

Our Ark that has in Tempests long been tost,
Cou'd never land on so secure a Coast.
From hence you may look back on Civil Rage,
And view the ruines of the former Age.
Here a New World its glories may unfold,
And here be sav'd the remnants of the Old.
But while your daies on publick thoughts are bent
Past ills to heal, and future to prevent;
Some vacant houres allow to your delight,
Mirth is the pleasing business of the Night,
The Kings Prerogative, the Peoples right.
Were all your houres to sullen cares confind,
The Body wou'd be Jaded by the Mind.
'Tis Wisdoms part betwixt extreams to Steer:
Be Gods in Senates, but be Mortals here.

In this wealth of images each one functions, and all fit to-
gether in a harmony of their own. Love, mirth, and art bring
all together, King and people, gods and mortals, body and
mind—for all men need to allow themselves the pleasure
of art or else be worn into brutishness and lose their sense
of mankind. This harmony is of a piece with the substructure
of feeling that underlies *Absalom and Achitophel*; it is in-
voked again in its preface "To the Reader." A century before
the term was invented by Kant and worked out by Schiller,
Dryden's lines are a statement of aesthetic freedom. They
state a cultural ideal as well: if theatrical shows cannot de-
termine political action, they can at least keep people's minds
clear for action.[2]

The Exclusionist plan was to breathe new life into the
Plot by impeaching their latest "witness," Fitz-Harris, so as
to set up the usual sounding board in the Commons. Charles,
in his speech of greeting, offered extraordinary concessions,

---

[2] Haley, p. 632, records the fact that on Sunday, March 20, the
Whig members who went to church sat apart in the congregation at
St. Mary's Oxford, as a flock unto themselves. I doubt that they seg-
regated themselves the night before in the theatre.

spelled out in private as follows: York would be banished for life, his children brought up as Protestants; Mary would become regent if Charles predeceased James, and Anne would succeed her. Apparently because it was taken as a sign of weakness, this offer was rejected by Shaftesbury's party. Instead they impeached Fitz-Harris, as planned. Yet the House of Lords refused to have him removed to the Commons from the jurisdiction of the court of King's Bench, where he would be tried according to law before his own peers. The Commons majority then voted what amounted to an impeachment of the Lords, and Charles seized the opportunity to dissolve Parliament once again—to the utter surprise of the majority in Commons.

The shock of this dissolution of the Oxford Parliament was really very great. Colonel Cooke wrote to Ormond that day, March 28: "Though I have seen the distractions and dejections of routed armies (a prospect dismal enough), yet nothing ever equalled this day in this place at the surprising dissolution of Parliament."[3] The reason for such consternation was the brand-new likelihood that this time Charles was going to stick to his word. His firmness would mean that most of them, in following Shaftesbury, were staking themselves and their estates upon rebellion. The King, counseled (weakly, it had been thought) by the "Trimmer" Halifax and the inexperienced "Chits," Lawrence Hyde, Godolphin, and Sunderland, had played his enemies out on a long line, and now they were hooked.

During the next month a *Declaration* from the King (possibly written by Halifax) was ordered read from the pulpit of every church and chapel.[4] Along with other arguments, it openly declares that exclusion of the King's brother would "establish another most Unnatural War, or at least make it necessary to maintain a Standing Force for the Preserving

[3] Bryant, p. 315. By then, Charles knew his secret French subsidy would be continued.
[4] The King's *Declaration* is reprinted in *Works*, XVII, 513–516.

the Government and the Peace of the Kingdom." "Establish" meant a regular tax to support that *bête noir* of the propertied class, a standing army. The *Declaration* closes with this reminder: "who cannot but remember, that Religion, Liberty and Property were all lost and gone, when the Monarchy was shaken off, and could never be reviv'd till that was restor'd." Above all, we should note the climactic position of "Property" in the triad of "Religion, Liberty and Property." The unfavorable response of the propertied class to Shaftesbury's schemes determined their failure.

On May 27, 1681, Ormond sent an extraordinary letter to the Duke of York in Scotland remarking upon the good effect of the King's *Declaration*.[5] To this veteran politician the Popish Plot had reached the ridiculous stage: "His majesty seems to have taken resolutions . . . not to suffer his Person, Dignity and Prerogative, nor the liberties, lives and properties of his subjects and servants to be contemned, reviled, invaded, and brought into perpetual danger under the notion of preserving them; things so visibly designed, that a contrary pretence grows ridiculous, to men impartial and of moderate capacities."

Ormond then stated the principle that Dryden stressed in his political writing during the rest of Charles's reign: "if a steddy and prudent and dispassionate perseverance be held, such a course will in all probability set his Majesty at rest for his days. But the least relaxation will undoubtedly produce worse effects (if it be possible) than if he had never gone about to vindicate his just Prerogative." Ormond, naturally, had a clear insight into the social class that dominated the Whig opposition: "Let none that shall rise against the Crown and Government," he urged, "be able to call themselves by any other name than Rebels. Then those that venture to lead the rabble, as far as mutiny and sedition, will think of their estates, persons, and families, before they dare

[5] Thomas Carte, *History of the Life of James, Duke of Ormonde*, III, 108.

to head them in open action." A prudent respect for property was an interest that every respectable person in the party had in common.

At one point Ormond's letter achieves a kind of grimly humorous poetry: "The wrack of the Crown in the King your Father's time is fresh in the memory of many of us; and the rocks and shelves he was lost upon (tho' they were hid to him) are so very visible to us, that, if we avoid them not, we shall perish rather derided than pitied." This is the mood Dryden shared. He made it his task as a poet to show his countrymen how ridiculous the political situation was, and to show the King how his enemies would deride him should he fail to hold "a steddy and prudent and dispassionate perseverance" in his course for the future. One more remark of Ormond's letter applied personally to Dryden as a pensioner of the King, that "no man, that means well to the King, will repine" at the "retrenchments and frugality now made and practised" in the royal household.

Ormond wrote to James again in July, about the trial of Shaftesbury.[6] He was aware that Halifax, who had urged the extreme "expedients" in March, had been counseling Charles to free Shaftesbury (who was, by the way, Halifax's uncle) without making him stand trial for the conspiracy with which he was charged. Halifax, with devious Machiavellian art, argued that the London jury would free Shaftesbury anyhow; why not free him first as a politic gesture of mercy? Yet Ormond sticks to his principle: "His Majesty's proceeding with the Earl of *Shaftesbury*, seems to be an argument of his resolution to pursue the method he has begun, which is the only expedient left him to recover the awe and reverence due to the Crown; without which it was not probable it could long subsist. And though, by the shameful partiality of a Jury, a Bill of Indictment should not be found against him . . . yet the discovery of so horrible a corruption to the world will undeceive all that are rather seduced than engaged

[6] *Ibid.*, pp. 108–109.

in the apparent designs to subvert Monarchical Government." As we shall see, Dryden took Ormond's side against Halifax, agreeing with him that "the King is bound by his high office, and the care he should have of his people's peace, and the safety of his best subjects and servants, to let justice take place in cases of this nature."

It is perfectly clear from this letter that *Absalom and Achitophel* could not have been part of a plan to convict Shaftesbury in November, 1681. The Crown's case would fare all the better in the nation as a whole if it first received obviously prejudiced handling in London. Dryden's poem was a means for taking the King's case to the nation—and to the King too, lest he should relapse.

II. THE POEM AS HISTORY PICTURE AND VARRONIAN SATIRE

In discussing *Absalom and Achitophel* as a poem, I think I may safely stipulate that it is what Roland Barthes calls a "plural" text.[7] Not only have several rather different readings of it already been produced, but there will in all likelihood be many more besides this one. In view of the historical contribution I am trying for, I should like to develop my presentation around two aesthetic structures that Dryden himself cited in discussing the poem: the history painting and the Varronian satire. Both have been used before, notably by Ian Jack in *Augustan Satire*.[8] Yet the notion of Varronian satire especially may be developed (I believe) considerably further than has been done. As Kinsley has said, Dryden moved to "a view of the satirist's function as artistic rather than corrective,"[9] which meant that he wanted to make each satire a true poem, and the merit of the Varronian subgenre is to make the text "of a piece" rather than a farrago.

The locus classicus of Varronian satire as a formal literary

---

[7] In S/Z, Paris, 1970.   [8] Oxford (1966), pp. 53–76.
[9] *The Poems of John Dryden* (1958), IV, 2013.

structure, in fact, is in Dryden's own "Discourse Concerning Satire,"[10] where he outlines a form extant neither in Varro nor in Menippus (the satires of both of them are now lost), but rather in the *Satyricon* of Petronius and in *Absalom and Achitophel*. Its most important characteristics are, in Dryden's version, the following: "those pieces . . . are sprinkled with a kind of mirth and gaiety, yet many things are there inserted, which are drawn from the very entrails of philosophy, and many things severely argued, which I have mingled with pleasantries on purpose, that they may easily go down with the common sort of unlearned readers." These remarks would refer, in *Absalom and Achitophel*, to the analyses of crowd psychology and constitutional development, or the careful study of the interest groups that made up Shaftesbury's opposition party. Yet Dryden goes on to add something more important to him as a poet: "Tully . . . addresses himself to Varro in these words: 'You yourself have composed a most elegant and complete poem.'" On this Dryden comments that "Varro was one of those writers whom they called . . . studious of laughter; and that, as learned as he was, his business was more to divert his reader than to teach him," and also that his satires were "absolute, and most elegant and various poems," far other than the travesties of Menippus, in imitating whom Varro "avoids his impudence and filthiness, and only expresses his witty pleasantry."[11] All of these terms refer to ideals of poetry and the poem dear to Dryden throughout his career. Aristotle had said that poetry was more philosophical than history, and more "serious," using the same Greek word that Dryden translates above as

[10] Watson, II, 114–115 (written in 1693). See also *Works*, IV (1974), 46–48, and the commentary and notes (by William Frost), pp. 526, 558–562.

[11] Most of Dryden's precedents come from Isaac Casaubon, *De Satyrica Graecorum Poesi et Romanorum Satira* (Paris, 1605), II, 2, 256ff. Out of these hints, and what Casaubon says about constituting a *justum poema* (e.g., p. 348), Dryden suggests the nature of a kind of writing he was really the first to identify and theorize about. There has been strangely little development of this passage by later critics.

"studious." A poet who was "studious of laughter" would compose his comic lines as carefully and as poetically as if they were epic or tragic.[12] Like Yeats, Dryden worked very hard to achieve his marvelously direct style while at the same time loading every rift with ore of sound. All the Varronian satirists he cites are masters of style: Lucian, Apuleius, Petronius, Seneca, Erasmus, Barclay, Spenser.

Besides noble verse, a work to be "absolute" or "complete" needed a forming structure, such as a narrative, in which a writer could display the fictive power that made him a poet. Dryden says of Varro that "as his subjects were various, so most of them were tales or stories of his own invention." The proof, Dryden says, is that his imitators in antiquity all invented stories, the *Satyricon* for example, Lucian's "True Tale," or *The Golden Ass* of Apuleius. This practice, of course, is like that of comedy, where the poets, as Aristotle said, "having constructed . . . through likelihoods, . . . assume whatever names they happen to assume and do not, as did the poets of the lampoons, make the plot concern particular names." Yet it was not incompatible with history, for, as Aristotle went on to say, "even if he happens to produce incidents that have arisen, he is nonetheless a poet, for nothing prevents some incidents which have arisen from being the sort of incidents that are likely or possible, and it is in respect of this aspect of incidents that he is a poet." In *Absalom and Achitophel*, names are used more or less historically by reference to the Bible, but the story has a new synthesis of the actions; and it was in this synthesis (*synthesis praxeōn*) that Aristotle centered the dramatic structure.

The stimulus to Dryden's thinking about this subgenre has

---

[12] *Poetics*, IX, 3–9. For the controversy whether the translation should be "studious of laughter" or "mingling earnest and laughter," see *Works*, IV, 560. What Dryden is getting at, however, is quite clear: his Varronian satire is comic and philosophical rather than malicious and mendacious, and it requires that the poet do his best, as in the heroic poem.

already been mentioned—it was Boileau's *Le Lutrin*, a comical satire based on a real series of events, which borrowed from the serious epic genre its machinery and much else, but especially succeeded in retaining its richness of verse. Although *Le Lutrin* concerns a mere squabble, to Dryden the Exclusion Crisis and the Popish Plot seemed vastly overblown specters too, generated from the same human pride and stubborn factionalism—except that in England, after twenty years of vacillation, the King and his government were so weak that specters could ruin them. If the King would at last hold steady, there was no real danger; in the past, however, he had always taken some easy way out. Dryden saw all this, and evidently he came to the realization that if he wished to bring the nation to its senses and stiffen the backbone of his royal master he must write a poem with more substance to it than the "loyal libels" of the previous fifteen years. He would need to put Charles in the position of feeling what a fool his enemies had been making of him, and then show him how it would feel to have the last laugh and triumph over them.

The epigraph to *Absalom and Achitophel* is taken from Horace's familiar

Ut pictura poesis: erit quae, si propius stes,
te capiat magis, et quaedam, si longius abstes.
Ars Poetica, 361–362

("Poetry is like painting: you like one picture better if you stand closer; another, if you stand farther off.") Dryden's poem, it suggests, is of the kind that repays a closer look. In this and most other characteristics it resembles the "history picture" that Dryden later discussed at some length in his "Parallel Betwixt Painting and Poetry" (1695). There he wrote that "the hero is the centre of the main action; all the lines from the circumference tend to him alone. . . . there are less groups or knots of figures disposed at proper distances, which are parts of the piece, and seem to carry on the same design. . . ."[13] The main actions were often taken from the Bible, as in a Flemish "Decollation of St. John the Baptist" cited by Hugh Trevor-Roper, which is "also an allegorical or satirical picture of the contemporary political scene, with caricatures of statesmen and personifications of states."[14] The "Instructions to a Painter" satires had such history pictures in mind.

The most famous political satire of all, the *Satyre Menippée* published in 1594 against the Duke of Guise and the Catholic League, itself a prolix Varronian satire, made use of historical pictures in the form of "pieces of tapestry with which the meeting-room of the States was hung."[15] The first picture was a figure of the Duke of Guise as a calf of gold elevated and worshipped by the people, "l'histoire . . . comme elle est descrite en Exode 32. chapitre, ou Moise et Aaron y estoient representez par le Roy deffunct Henry troisiesme, & feu Monsieur le Cardinal de Bourbon." The twelfth and last was "the portrait, very well taken off at full length, of Monsieur the Lieutenant." (Compare this with Dryden's remark, in "To the Reader," that Monmouth's portrait was only "to the waist.") The third tapestry "contained the history of Absalom, who barricaded his father and drove him from the city of Jerusalem, having won over and corrupted by unworthy caresses the most abject and rascally of the lower sort: then is shown the punishment he received for it, and how Achitophel his evil counselor ended his days unhappily. All the visages were near likenesses [*approchans*] of certain ones in the aforesaid assembly of the States, and easily recognizable were President Janin, Marteau, Ribault, & others, to whom the late Duke of Guise made so many kind greetings during the meeting at Blois. Also to be seen were . . . butchers, horse-dealers, even gravediggers, all men of honor in their professions, whom the aforesaid defunct

---

[13] Watson, II, 199.
[14] *The Age of Expansion* (London, 1968), pp. 32–33.
[15] Ed. Edouard Tricotel (Paris, 1877), I, 23–27.

martyr kissed on the mouth in pure zeal for religion." In these descriptions we see that the architectonics, or what we might call the synchronic structure of the poem, was ready to Dryden's hand. The whole process was well understood by his English readers, and the story of Absalom had been used for political allegory in English many times before.

What Dryden contributed, as many years before in the case of *The Indian Queen*, was the writing. He produced a highly original sequence of actions by combining the facts of English and scriptural history, all available to him in a repertory of almost infinite possibilities, by means of a very few, but very powerful, diachronous techniques that he had learned in the theatre. One was psychology, not of static "characters" alone (although he excelled in those), but as motivation for sustained action, which takes on the unique coloration of human will and personal interest so as to make the bare bones of a plot into a fictive work of art. Dryden also understood as well as anyone the use of the *suasio* and *dissuasio* to make a political decision into a momentous human event. Motives are largely matters of feeling, and Dryden had recently learned, at mid-career in the theatre, to strengthen and simplify his handling of "passion" and "nature." So we find that, although his name does not appear in the title, David is at the center of the history picture. Moreover, since the strength of his love for Absalom is the source of its main action and his final mastering of that excessive love is its denouement, David is the hero of the Varronian narrative as well.

III. THE CENTRAL FIGURE: KING CHARLES II

A peer pointed out that if the King did remarry he still might not have children. Whereupon Shaftesbury pointed at Charles, who was standing in his usual position by the fireplace, and said: "Can we doubt when we look at the King that he is capable of getting children? He is only

238

fifty." . . . the whole house began to laugh, and the King with the rest.

K.H.D. Haley, *The First Earl of Shaftesbury*, p. 604.

Dryden's most creative touch in *Absalom and Achitophel* was adopting the comic tone that is struck in the opening lines. Considered as a court poet's account of the personal life of a reigning monarch, that witty description of Charles's philoprogenitive behavior is unique in English literature, and perhaps in the literature of the world. It is witty in every sense of the term, but above all it is risky. Dryden's boldness is the outstanding proof of his faith in his own comic powers, in the good nature of the main part of his readers, and in their ability to respond to his new way of using old forms, all of which had been tested and proved in the theatre. He did not doubt that he would succeed by his wit and irony in placing the pretensions of Monmouth in their reasonable perspective. He trusted further that his readers would grant him his right, or more correctly the exercise of his duty as a poet, to teach the people and above all the King concerning their conduct toward each other. Finally, he trusted the King himself to accept the characterization in good part. The King had forgiven his Laureate (if he ever took offense) for some uncomfortable portrayals in the heroic plays. Moreover, certainly David was a far more acceptable cover than Mahomet Boabdelin, the last King of Granada. Let us further imagine Charles as the most important reader of Dryden's poem, studying the image there as in a portrait of himself.

David's original image is of a blessedly potent figure, a divinely favored king ruling over a divinely favored people. Yet David's time, "before one to one was cursedly confin'd," was also a time "when each had right to all," that is, an age before property rights had been settled either in wives or land—an age far distanced from the gentry and ruling class of England in 1681.[16] Nothing was more important to them

---

[16] See Locke, *Second Treatise of Government* (II. vii, 87) on the

than property, and a wife was above all a transmitter of property. The crown was King Charles's chief property. (Of all this, the then contemporary spelling, "propriety," conveyed a sense now lost.) Charles had refused to divorce Catherine of Braganza; he had accepted, like any English landowner, the right of James's collateral line to inherit. The natural children he had by mistresses, and especially their mothers, displayed a rapacious loyalty to the principle of private property, and practically all of them had their stake in the continuance of that venerable institution. Their appeals to the King that he increase those stakes were one of the severest trials to which his regime of austerity was subjected.

Dryden picks up a very peculiar phrase of the King James translation and implies that Charles like David was king "after God's own heart." He wanted to suggest that, in a very human way, Charles had been a king after God's heart, but not after God's—or, rather, any reasonable person's—mind. The present most dangerous error of King Charles was his indulgence of the feelings of the heart and neglect of the reasons of the head. The seat of prudent judgment had formerly been located by men in the breast, the heart; by Dryden's time it had been displaced.[17] Yet Dryden honored Charles especially for his good heart, his affability, his unwillingness to give pain, his forgiving nature. He makes principal use of the comparison with David, therefore, to point to a real quality of Charles, a virtue that had its corresponding fault in excess.

For Charles could indeed love. His affection for Monmouth was an exception to his practice with politicians of keeping his favor uncommitted. What we recall best from the Bible is very present in *Absalom and Achitophel*: David's unappeas-

---

people's right of association: they "unite for the mutual Preservation of their Lives, Liberties and Estates, which I call by the general name, 'Property.' "

[17] Cf. "To Mr. Lee" (1677), "We only warm the Head, but you the Heart." *Works*, I, 107, line 36.

able love for his son. It was not Monmouth's birth, or the favors heaped upon him, but Charles's immoderate love that endangered all. The mythic power of David's love for Absalom enables Dryden to do a human justice to the genuineness of the King's affection, while at the same time he can probe the causes of Charles's indulgence of Monmouth and show both their ridiculous excess and their danger. With a comic twist of the word *divine* he elevates the feeling of Gloucester for Edmond at the opening of *King Lear* and suggests it explains Charles's feeling too:

> Inspired by some diviner Lust,
> His Father got him with a greater Gust. . . .

and goes on to suggest other decidedly human motives:

> With secret Joy, indulgent David view'd
> His Youthful Image in his Son renew'd:
> To all his wishes Nothing he deny'd,
> And made the Charming Annabel his Bride.
>
> (19–20, 31–34)

The suggestion is that Charles's love of Monmouth is love of himself—and as he had never been, handsome. (The self-deceptive aspect of his love is fully exposed later in the speech of the enemy Achitophel.)

Like David, but unlike the mere politicians around him, Charles could love—and so, in the logic of the poem, he could hate. Yet what Dryden presents for his hatred is his own degraded image in the eyes of his enemies. Twenty years earlier the people of England had plucked Charles out of exile and poverty and made him their King. Dryden takes the stance of the Varronian philosopher-poet and ironically but accurately states the insecure basis of the King's reign:

> Those very *Jewes*, who, at their very best,
> Their Humour more than Loyalty exprest,
> Now, wondred why, so long, they had obey'd
> An Idoll Monarch which their hands had made:

Thought they might ruine him they could create;
Or melt him to that Golden Calf, a State.

(61–66)

Herein is a perfectly sound analysis of the political status of
the individual monarch in the English constitution; as Mait-
land comments in his authoritative *Constitutional History of
England*, it is not a Jacobite analysis, but it is close to the
historical truth of the English succession, which only began
to be hereditary in the latter fifteenth century, and which was
exempted from statutory determination only in the preten-
sions of James I (claims he could never establish and in fact
moderated in the course of his reign).[18] These lines reminded
the English of Dryden's time of what they well knew, that
some of them had chosen Oliver Cromwell as Lord Pro-
tector, as the Jews chose Saul for king, on account of his
outstanding personal qualities and achievements. They—or,
again, some of them—had decided against exercising another
choice by merit, and instead had asserted a principle of
continuity in government by elevating, first, the son of Crom-
well, and then by recalling the legal heir of Charles I. At
that time it was said that "the King enjoyed his own again."
However, the decision made in 1660 had been made differ-
ently before, and could be made differently in the future,
as proved the case in 1688. The King might lose "his own"
again. Although Dryden disliked puns, the phrase "Idoll
Monarch" above, if heard as "idle monarch," would not have
been far wrong for Charles during the whole former part of
his reign. Never idle personally, he had notoriously let the
business of the kingdom slide. Now he was threatened with
having no royal business to attend to.

Dryden wrote *Absalom and Achitophel* for no motive more
imperative than to bring home to Charles himself the depth
of contempt and powerlessness he would sink to if he should
fail to be steady. The King's great moment, and the focal

[18] F. W. Maitland, *Constitutional History of England* (Cambridge,
Eng., 1919), pp. 281–288.

point of the poem's perspective as a history picture, follows his realization that further concessions will wipe out his very being as King and the existence of government under his control. As David, his response is shame and anger; anger seethes through the lines of his final speech from the throne, culminating in his "Beware the fury of a patient man!" Yet it is the anger of a man who suddenly realizes that people have been making a fool of him, a king who sees himself as a beast of burden, "a camel, not a king."

The structure of *Absalom and Achitophel* has been described accurately by H. T. Swedenberg, Jr., as including "historical narrative, with observations by the historian and the poet; five dramatic speeches; two sections of ironical and panegyrical portraits; and an exposition of the theories of sovereignty."[19] I should restate and add to these elements as follows. On the level of sound, the writing is (to Dryden) in the noblest form of verse, the heroic couplet. The poem's central meaning is that, if every Englishman is to possess himself of his native and inheritable right, the King must assert his right to "enjoy his own again." The generic schemata Dryden invokes are allied to his audience's expectations from their knowledge of Restoration theatre, the English state poem, political and religious controversy, and the Bible; more originally, at the level of this poem itself, Dryden organizes it synchronically by reference to the conception of the history picture and diachronically in accord with the sex comedy plot of "pleasing rape" by a young wooer and cuckoldry of an old husband. At a still higher level, he infuses into the poem the nobility and the wise good humor he ascribed to the satire of Varro and makes his poem genuinely comic as a whole.[20]

[19] *Works*, II, 233.

[20] This description of the work by its strata and phases is based on Roman Ingarden, *The Literary Work of Art*, trans. George G. Grabowicz (Evanston, Ill., 1973), pp. 29–33. My idea is that the comic is a "polyphonic" quality of *Absalom and Achitophel*, arising out of the poem as a whole.

In dramatic terms, the "exposition" of *Absalom and Achitophel* is complete at the incentive moment when Achitophel decides he needs to find a "chief." We have the portrait of David, his easy government, his indulgence of the appealing illegitimate son, and the analysis of his precarious status with the people; his opposite, Achitophel, is all for troublemaking, where David is all for enjoyment. The "protatic" part ends and the action begins with an agon in which Achitophel overcomes Absalom's better nature and, in effect, seduces him. At this point the ethos becomes dynamic and dramatic in the true sense, for Absalom struggles against the tempter.

Exaggerated as it is, colored by manifest scorn for the person of King David, Achitophel's speech sounds exactly like Shaftesbury's opinion of Charles. He is made out to be King by mere luck (263–265). Daringly opportunistic though he was when young, "Old David's" sun now is setting. The English people, so happy at his Restoration, scorn him now. He has no loving friends left. Most English people, in fact, would gladly change for a man like Monmouth, of royal blood, but also a "Champion of the publique Good" (294). When Charles read this, he could only have found it plausible in the speaker, but infuriating all the same. For several years, Shaftesbury had treated him with great personal disrespect. By dishonoring his wife the Queen through the accusations of Oates, he was offering a continuous affront; in those days, many a simple gentleman who wore a sword would not have tolerated it for a moment. Finally, Shaftesbury really had seduced Charles's favorite person in the world, his son Monmouth. Reading Achitophel's words, the King's amusement, if any, should have been rather grim. There are touches in the text of the *viva voce* of "Little Sincerity," touches of Iago-like honesty such as

Betray'd by one poor Plot to Publick Scorn.

(275)

where the Earl's well-known cynicism would rub salt into the victim's wound. Notably missing in the whole passage is the least hint that defeat by Achitophel would be less than bitter, shameful humiliation.

Dryden makes it clear at this point that such evil promptings are not just bad luck or the mere personal malice of a troublemaker of genius. Sooner or later, no matter whether "David's mildness managed it so well" for a time or not, "our byast Nature," in its perpetual proneness to sin, would find the Devil present somewhere. Shaftesbury is only a typical example.[21] He had, by the "fatal mercy" of Charles, been pardoned his defection to Cromwell and then been made a leading minister of state. Not content with the prospect of praise from the King and his Laureate, he perverted his genuine talents in a grab for power. Hence the Plot, managed by Shaftesbury for all it was worth (83–84, 146–197).

Achitophel's words provoke a loyal and eloquent defense of his father by Absalom. He describes his father as

> Good, Gracious, Just, observant of the Laws
>
> (319)

and notes that he has pardoned millions of his enemies. Even Absalom, though, speaks of the impolitic nature of Charles's distinguishing trait:

> Mild, Easy, Humble, Studious of our Good;
> Enclin'd to Mercy, and averse from Blood.
> If Mildness Ill with Stubborn Israel Suite,
> His Crime is God's beloved Attribute.
>
> (325–328)

The speaker is highly conscious of Charles's propensity to forgive—a clue to Monmouth's psychology. Line 328 offers a revealing comment upon the use of the biblical expression "king after God's own heart": the "godlike" in Charles, so

---

[21] Dryden's thought here is sufficiently explained by quoting a remark of Ormond's: "Dissatisfaction, supplanting, and different opinions, are, have been, and ever will be, in all Courts betwixt Courtiers; and can no more be separated from Governments, or abolished, than passions from men. The skill is to govern them; and that may so be done, as that they shall not hurt" (Carte, III, 110).

far, has been only his mildness, generosity, and good nature, but never his authority. Here mildness is called a "crime," catachrestically, to indicate a good quality shown to excess. Absalom goes on to reject the idea that, having received all that David his father could give him except the crown, he could be so ungrateful as to attack him even if he had been a tyrant. Reading this, Charles might well reflect that his indulgence had already gone much too far, since his fate seemed to depend on his bastard son's good will.

Absalom's rebuttal, then, is based upon David's love, so unreserved that an act of aggression upon him would be villainous. Achitophel overcomes this objection with a rakish hypothesis for an action often seen in amorous comedy— the "pleasing rape." Your father, he tells Absalom, is holding out only in the way a bored wife remains faithful to a husband—half because she gave her word, half out of mere inertia. By now, Absalom is persuaded that this is actually the way his father feels. He takes the proposed course of action and, in the second phase of the dramatic "entanglement," becomes an ardent wooer of the people of England. By his hot love shown to them he will effect "a pleasing rape" of his father's crown that will gratify the desires of the People and of the King, who by now has ceased to count as an individual person. Again, if we ask how all this would seem to Charles as he read the poem, can we avoid a sense of his indignation at the effeminate passivity of the role in which he is cast?

Meanwhile Dryden had written into Achitophel's *plaidoyer* a synthesis of the strategy and tactics of Shaftesbury, much as they had been stated in the pamphlet, *His Majesties Declaration Defended*, a few months before.[22] Yet now they are rendered much more telling by an infusion of Charles's psychology as it appears to Achitophel. The latter agrees with Absalom's suggestion that his father grants too much to the people (meaning the Commons majority). However, the King's tameness, he says, calls into question not only his

[22] Probably by Dryden; *Works*, XVII, 194–225.

manhood ("manly force") but his "wit" as well—a shrewd blow at Charles, who was nothing if not witty. Charles is further described as negligent and weak—he positively invites his people to rebel. His generosity will soon enslave him to the Commons majority, and they will bleed him:

> And every Scheckle which he can receive,
> Shall cost a Limb of his Prerogative.
>
> (391–392)

The whole second speech of Achitophel is a clear, detailed, and pointed analysis related directly to the Exclusion Crisis of 1679–1681.

Again, psychology is brought skillfully to bear. Achitophel assures Absalom that he need not feel guilty over betraying his father's professed love:

> Our fond Begetters, who woud never dye,
> Love but themselves in their Posterity.
>
> (424–425)

As Charles read *Absalom and Achitophel*, these lines may have suggested to him how vain it was to attempt to conciliate Monmouth by favors short of "the last favor"—the crown. How simple-minded to fall into a trap so openly baited for him by Shaftesbury! He would indeed (in a phrase used by Ormond that keeps occurring to mind) deserve to be "rather derided than pitied" if he fell victim to such transparent deceit.

Absalom offers no rebuttal to this second speech. Like a pathetic lover, he woos the crowd, weeps and begs their pity. Their wrongs from the King are doubly his wrongs. It is given to Absalom to state the case against Charles in its grossest, most prejudiced form, yet with more than a kernel of truth:

> Now all your Liberties a spoil are made;
> *Aegypt* and *Tyrus* intercept your Trade,
> And *Jebusites* your Sacred Rites invade.

My Father, whom with reverence yet I name,
Charm'd into Ease, is careless of his Fame:
And, brib'd with petty summs of Forreign Gold,
Is grown in *Bathsheba's* embraces old:
Exalts his Enemies, his Friends destroys:
And all his pow'r against himself employs.

(704–712)

Absalom comes closest here to Monmouth, the cat's paw of
Shaftesbury. The stock issues he raises: arbitrary govern-
ment, the liberties of the subject, encroachment by France
and Holland, popish intrigues favored by Court and Church,
French bribery, the French duchess, were exactly Shaftes-
bury's mixture of insignificant truth and momentous lies.
Charles, when being most highhanded, was careful to be
scrupulously legalistic, not arbitrary; he had allowed the
papists to be barbarously persecuted; trade was flourishing
again; and almost everybody, including Monmouth (though
not Shaftesbury), took French bribes. The small truths,
however, might have been more galling than the big lies.
Not only Charles, but the Duchess of Portsmouth (Bath-
sheba) was indeed growing old; Charles now cherished her
more for old times' sake than current venery. Picture Charles
reading this passage, and it is difficult to conceive of his
taking it without some degree of resentment—not against
the Laureate, evidently, but against Monmouth. The most
unfair and reprehensible of Absalom's charges in this speech
to the crowd is that the King only could make the nation
bleed. Such depth of irony is generated by the satiric char-
acterization, however, that the statement is perceived as
true, because we see that a renewal of Charles's self-indul-
gence would lead straight to bloodshed.

This speech is rounded off by a poetic description of the
progress Shaftesbury arranged for Monmouth during mid-
1680. It had been royal in its magnificence and in the honors
and popular acclaim offered to the pretender. Dryden treats
it as the proffer, not only of royal, but again of divine honors:

"their young *Messiah*," "like the Sun," "the morning Star," "a Guardian God" (728–735). This is irony, meant as a foil to the more modest ascription of godlike kindness to Charles. The crowd's motive is actually "Common Interest," and the pious display is therefore hypocritical pageantry. For Achitophel (as for Shaftesbury) the progress is a means to organize rebels and intimidate honest men.

The vindictiveness of Absalom's attack on his father requires that an even more heartfelt rebuttal come out before the poem ends. It is given to David himself. For his anger to be plausible, a considerable change must take place in the mild and patient King David of the first phase. Dryden shows him making a choice after he weighs the probabilities for and against opposing courses of action—or opposing modes of behavior, since the course he had been following was one of inaction. David acts upon counsel too, but with a stronger sense than Absalom's of inward struggle finally overcome, and a far greater commitment of personal feeling and intention than his son exhibits. David seems changed, a virile man again, whereas Absalom had succumbed in a rather spineless way.

David's speech from the throne, which closes the final "resolving" phase of the action of *Absalom and Achitophel* as well as the poem itself (except for a few lines of prophecy), appears just after the section devoted to his counselors. His own Nine Worthies had advised Charles of the great danger from the rebel faction and its threats in Parliament, taken together with the forced exile of James and the revival of the Plot with new Irish witnesses. They warned him that half-measures would make matters worse. With Monmouth ready to head the London crowd, now, under Shaftesbury's direction, he could bring about the ruin of Church and State (cf. 917–932). Charles had accepted their counsel and seen the light. Like David,

> at last his patience tir'd
> Thus from his Royal Throne by Heav'n inspir'd
> (935–936)

the King finally was taking a stand—like David's habitual one, at last.

Even so, the throne speech is a very human performance, free of pretensions to divinity or even human reverence. It begins with what might be called a list of grievances. The first is that "Th'offenders question my Forgiving Right." Charles used his prerogative many times to grant pardons to all sorts of malefactors, from the bandit Colonel Blood to the perjured Oates and the horse-thief Bedloe. At the behest of the Commons themselves, Charles had allowed his pardoning right to be used to grant immunity to the murdering witnesses in the Popish Plot. Now, however, he was refusing to collaborate any longer with the Plot managers. His decision not to immunize but to prosecute Fitz-Harris had made the victory at Oxford possible.

His second grievance is over the treatment of his person as King as if he were a legal fiction who could do no wrong because he could personally do nothing, and whose ministers acted not for him but for the Parliament, i.e., the people. With dignity he asserts himself:

> That one was made for many, they contend:
> But 'tis to Rule, for that's a Monarch's End.
>
> (945–946)

The major theme appears: Charles recognizes that his "propriety" in himself is being denied him, and he determines to assert it. Dryden presents the King as taking the decision at the moment he makes his speech:

> 'Tis time to shew I am not Good by Force.
> Those heap'd Affronts that haughty Subjects bring,
> Are burthens for a Camel, not a King.
>
> (950–952)

Once again, this is a very human (even a physical and animal) reaction. It is not godlike anger but the fury of a man who will bear no more, for he begins to see himself as utterly ridiculous already.

The particular form taken by Charles's decision, and the denouement or resolution of the poem as a whole, is an explicit threat to Monmouth. If Charles could be firm with the person toward whom he had always been most indulgent, he would be firm all down the line. As David says in an allusion that plays with typological distance:

> If my Young *Samson* will pretend a Call
> To shake the Column, let him share the Fall.
>
> (954–955)

Let him be crushed, that is, along with those who egg him on to play for them, beneath the ruins he seeks to cause. It is significant that Dryden does not fully articulate the threat, because neither Charles nor he could wish for Monmouth's death; even its suggestion, though, was a new note so early as November, 1681. The next eighteen lines (957–974), while they express Charles's continued love for his son, also suggest that he has been convinced at long last of Monmouth's notorious weaknesses, as he was not at the beginning of the poem. The King's eyes have been opened. He applies to his son, in somewhat indirect ways, the terms already in public use concerning Monmouth: "Gull'd," "brave (in the sense of a "bravo"), "Tool," and "Fool."[23] The term most expressive of his own attitude, "poor pitied youth," seems to anticipate ruin in store for Monmouth.

The King then gives vent to his feelings toward Shaftesbury, his faction, and the "People," i.e., the majority in the Commons who claimed to represent the mass of Englishmen (here biblical allusion in the text reaches its highest transparency):

---

[23] To the more knowing, Monmouth was shallow, vain, and only capable of being a tool to someone more crafty. In a so-called novel of 1681, *Grimalkin, or the Rebel-Cat,* Monmouth is the "Perkin-Lion," employed as the "cat's-foot" of his master, the Rebel-Cat Shaftesbury. In another pamphlet of 1681 he is "Prince Prettyman Perkinoski" (Macdonald, p. 223).

Good Heav'ns, how Faction can a Patriot Paint!
My Rebel ever proves my Peoples Saint:
Would *They* impose an Heir upon the Throne?
Let Sanhedrins be taught to give their own.
A King's at least a part of Government,
And mine as requisite as their Consent:
Without my Leave a future King to choose,
Infers a Right the Present to Depose:
True, they Petition me t'approve their Choise,
But *Esau's* Hands suite ill with *Jacob's* Voice.
My Pious Subjects for my Safety pray,
Which to Secure they take my Power away.

(973–984)

These lines are restrained, dignified, and manly, but not
without a comic touch, especially the "Good Heav'ns." What
they do is to restate the tripartite political structure of Eng-
land as Dryden saw it, and which Charles was now de-
termined to set working again.

He will employ Shaftesbury's witnesses against the faction
that hired them:

By their own arts 'tis Righteously decreed,
Those dire Artificers of Death shall bleed.

(1010–1011)

Charles personally engaged in much hard day-to-day and
ward-by-ward political action, showing an unspectacular but
very real grasp of local and personal tactics. During the next
year the Crown succeeded in its drive to recapture the legal
machinery and municipal government of London. Masters of
backstairs intrigue such as Dryden's old enemy Bab May
and Mr. Chiffins, the King's procurer, proved they could be
as effective in managing the City as Shaftesbury had been.

David's speech from the throne ends rapidly and very
skillfully, with a succinct account of the course the King
had been taking since 1678, stated here, however, in the dis-
tanced form of a prophecy of things to come:

Nor doubt th' event: for Factious crowds engage
In their first Onset, all their Brutal Rage;
Then, let 'em take an unresisted Course,
Retire and Traverse, and Delude their Force:
But when they stand all Breathless, urge the fight,
And rise upon 'em with redoubled might:
For Lawfull Pow'r is still Superiour found,
When long driven back, at length it stands the ground.
(1018–1025)

The extreme decisiveness of these lines, which bring the
King's throne speech to a close, give Charles credit (which
he perhaps partly deserved) for planning his response as if
it were a hunt with a strategy foreseen from the start. The
lines have a grand élan—the rhythm of victorious resolution
sounds out in them. Hearing these lines would enable
Charles to know just how it felt to be firm, to stand one's
ground, and win.[24]

The characterization of David by itself gives the poem its
feeling structure of indulgence and indecision followed by
resolution and control. The importance of David's psychol-
ogy: his mild nature, his great love for his son, his tendency
to project upon him his own needs as he becomes old, his
forbearance under affronts, his dislike of trouble, his reluc-
tance to take a firm stand against the wishes or desires of
others, all make it dramatically effective to hinge the move-
ment of the poem upon a reversal of David's will. His ability
to control his love for Absalom is treated as proof of his
power to dominate the rebels who are on the edge of destroy-
ing the kingdom. It is surely the key to the fable that the
David of the poem corresponded most closely to David in
the Bible in this one essential trait—his love for his son.
In presenting this trait of David, the Bible story has always
made its greatest impression upon humanity; it is the most

[24] Line 1025, with the uncontracted "driven," is unusual, but it
certainly takes a stand metrically.

moving and human moment in a long and intricate history. Similarly with Charles. Dryden draws his love for Monmouth as dangerous folly, but yet as a very human failing that sprang from a generous nature. The comparison with David dignified this capacity in Charles above all. It expands the poem to a heroic dimension. Even more important, however, is Charles's self-love, toward which the poet directs his omnipresent satiric challenge. In the Bible, things happen to David, or else he performs deeds, or he feels (movingly and heroically) emotions. He has no psychology otherwise. Yet David in *Absalom and Achitophel* is given a very active inner consciousness. His *amour-propre* is subjected to shrewd attacks from several directions, and badly battered in the process. He reacts, very convincingly, with humiliation, fury, and a proud resolution, to put a stop to it all, to cease being a victim and to exert his power at last. The double effect is to make Charles at first ridiculous, then (when he resolves not to be made an object of derision) believably heroic. Shame and anger at the ridiculousness of his image as others see it, the response satirists always hoped for, makes the change in the King, and noble pride would make it permanent.

IV. PORTRAITS OF THE FRIENDS AND FOES

After Charles, the most important figure included in *Absalom and Achitophel* is (politically speaking) James Stuart, the Duke of York. However, ignoring eligible parallel figures in the Bible whose names he might have used, Dryden inserts James simply as "his Brother," and leaves him without a Jewish name. He even refers to him transparently in the terms so critical in 1681, as "the next Successour" (401). The portrait of James, therefore, appears flatly, unscripturally, and undistanced on the surface of the poem. Absalom describes him after his first defense of his father's character and reign:

His Brother, though Opprest with Vulgar Spight,
Yet Dauntless and Secure of Native Right,
Of every Royal Vertue stands possest;
Still Dear to all the Bravest, and the Best.
His Courage Foes, his Friends his Truth Proclaim,
His Loyalty the King, the World his Fame.
His Mercy even th'Offending Crowd will find,
For sure he comes of a Forgiving Kind.

(353–360)

This character, panegyric though it is, is an accurate portrait of James in his public position, set up as a kind of "frontispiece" or *entr'acte* to the drama.

James might have reestablished himself as a leader among the traditionally loyal Cavalier members of Parliament, who now realized that Clarendon and he had represented most of their attitudes (including their concern over property) better than Buckingham or Shaftesbury ever could.[25] James's loyal defense of his very Protestant father-in-law would only have raised him in their eyes.

In the past, as we have seen, Dryden saw James's firmness as a welcome offset to Charles's compliancy. By 1681, however, it had been magnified by his enemies into an implacable resentment of all opposition. In *Absalom and Achitophel*, therefore, the attitude Dryden had to combat was that James would prove vindictive, not only toward his personal enemies, but to the far greater number of loyal Englishmen who had sincerely been taken in by the Plot. This is the burden of the final couplet in Absalom's portrait of James. He would

---

[25] In his major public appearance after being recalled to London, James told the Artillery Company: "I am the first man that can command property in England, and have the greatest property of any subject in England, and therefore have the greatest reason to defend it. Any other man may have private interests, but I can have none, for I know very well that as long as this nation and this city be well, I shall be so." J. P. Kenyon, *The Popish Plot* (London, 1972), p. 184. Kenyon maintains that James was feared but not hated, and had more support than appeared (pp. 92, 150).

be no less forgiving than his brother Charles, their father Charles I, or their grandfather Henri IV of France. However, this is panegyric; and its rebuttal by Achitophel (441–445) in the image of the wakefully slumbering lion is the final touch to Dryden's whole picture of James. There was a lesson in it that James never managed to understand, despite Achitophel's calling him "wise"—a wicked flourish of Shaftesburian irony.

In his portraits of the small band of "Worthies" that precede the final action, Dryden includes two kinds of men: those who were personally committed to James by years of association in common causes, by favors done and received, by ties of marriage and family, and by common attitudes; and, on the other hand, men who had no personal reason for favoring James, except their own oath and their constitutional principles (including the principle of preserving their property). Barzillai, his son, Adriel, and Hushai represented Ormond and Ossory, Mulgrave, and Lawrence Hyde—loyal personal supporters, no less of James than of Charles. The three priests represented the official Church of England, not favorable to James personally, but devoted to him as the legitimate Successor. Jotham and Amiel represented actual personal enemies of James, who yet stood firm for his legal rights; both could stand for a very important segment of the nation—one in the Commons, ex-Speaker Seymour, the other in the Lords, the Viscount Halifax. The Nine are a very impressive group, not chosen for flattery's sake, but because they characterize what Dryden saw as the best body of sentiment in England. Further, they all had in common a willingness to endure unpopularity out of loyalty to a person or a conviction. Unlike mere politicians, they loved and they hated, and they were constant. They were fit subjects for heroic portrayal.

The Nine Worthies are grouped to cast a reflected light upon the factionalists portrayed earlier in *Absalom and Achitophel*. At first sight, the Duke of Monmouth, the Earl of Shaftesbury, Buckingham, Bethel the Sheriff, and Titus Oates seem to have nothing in common with each other.

Shaftesbury is subtle and witty, Oates brazen and dull; Buckingham is prodigal and spendthrift, Bethel a miser, Monmouth appears as a good-natured but weak *ingénu*. They threatened the typical good-humored Englishman in his secular Eden less as an organized party than as a congeries of known figures fronting for a crowd of eccentric overheated malcontents. In contrast, the Worthies knew their places and duly acted their accustomed roles. Perhaps the most noteworthy characteristic of Dryden's gallery of rebels is their ridiculous abuse of the benefits of good society. Dryden sees factions and mobs as a means for individuals to obtain release from personal responsibility by adopting a group mentality that has no proper aims nor positive common interest, but simply tries to inflict its arbitrary will upon others as a kind of collective *acte gratuit*:

> So easie still it proves in Factious Times,
> With publick Zeal to cancel private Crimes:
> How safe is Treason, and how sacred ill,
> Where none can sin against the Peoples Will:
> Where Crouds can wink; and no offence be known,
> Since in anothers guilt they find their own.
>
> (180–185)

Faction encourages the incompetent and the unsuccessful, out of their vanity and envy, to challenge the government because it has not given them places. It is the refuge (under the name of patriotism) of fallen ministers such as Achitophel—or rather Shaftesbury, for upon his disgrace Achitophel chose suicide. To hide his guilty behavior as a private man ("in friendship false"), Shaftesbury uses faction under an assumed zeal for the public. He has no decent goals, even of self-interest, and no principles. When he held power, he took no pleasure in his high position or in the respect of others. Now, old and sick, he is feverishly overactive. Instead of leaving his heir with a social position and property that would define him as a member of human society, Shaftesbury will bequeath to his son only that negative human quality of being neither fowl, fish, nor four-legged beast. This, I believe, is the correct interpretation of lines that have remained puzzling to critics. They are an instance of the recurring comparison that associates factionalism with sexual inadequacy, perversion, or excess. Thus Shaftesbury would be the opposite of Charles as David, whose sexual ardor gave faction its handsome young leader. Shaftesbury's warmth is unvigorous, lacks propagating force and germinal form, is all spent in destructive factional contention. Shaftesbury's unwillingness to enjoy a bit of leisure at the end of his long, troubled career is a proof that he had no value for the social possibilities of human association. The terrorist tactics he employed, and his contempt and cynicism toward those he destroyed and those he used, make Dryden's portrait of a ravaged, self-preying predator strike one as both imaginatively and literally true, and without drawing in the unheroic tap in his side.

On the contrary, he inserted several lines of explicit praise (180–191) for Shaftesbury's behavior in the courts, as Lord Chancellor, but especially (I suggest) when he acted as Chancellor of the Exchequer in 1667 and did Dryden the justice of authorizing the long overdue payment on his wife's claim. Here the expression of gratitude is something Dryden owed to his own self-respect, and it was particularly called for in a poem where he was attacking "ungratefull men" (149).[26]

After the men of great property, the opportunists, and the theoreticians and ideologues, a fourth group rounds out Dryden's history picture—the Dissenters of Puritan sympathies. The largest of all, this group contains several "knots" (as Dryden called them in his "Parallel"), but at its head appear the most inveterate of factionalists, "the Solymaean rout," who hated the institution of monarchy as much as they hated Charles. They formed the rabble of London ("Solyma" being another name for Jerusalem). This was no ordinary

[26] Such an afterthought is, I think, a more natural explanation than the very ingenious ones in *Works*, II, 250–251 and 411–412.

rabble. Since Dryden had spent the latter forties in London
at Westminster School, he could remember from this im-
pressionable stage of his life the grim discipline of these
Londoners and their zeal to have the blood of King Charles
I. "Hot Levites," the dissenting clergy, were their leaders—
a group that itself probably accounted for Dryden's obsessive
contempt and animosity toward all "priests." They strove
to restore the theocracy of the Covenant,

> Where Sanhedrin and Priest enslav'd the Nation
> And justifi'd their Spoils by Inspiration;
>
> (523–524)

an evil restoration-in-reverse of the parliamentarian commit-
teemen and the Puritan preachers. The rest of the passage
describes the great mass of the dissenting population. They
already, as Dryden saw them, had developed the habit of
unthinking, self-complacent certitude that they were God's
natural-born people and were bound to be right and suc-
cessful—the syndrome Arnold called Philistinism (533–540).
Their uncritical self-satisfaction is Dryden's reason for put-
ting this very large body of Englishmen next to the "dream-
ing Saints" (529)—

> 'Gainst Form and Order they their Power employ;
> Nothing to Build and all things to Destroy.
>
> (531–532)

The combination seems to anticipate Arnold's Hebraism
rather explicitly, though without showing any of Arnold's
appreciation for the merits of its "saints."

After thus listing the principal factions controlled by
Achitophel, Dryden characterizes three of their leaders at
length—Buckingham, Bethel and Oates—and only mentions
four others in passing, herding the rest into large categories:

> Wits, warriors, Common-wealthsmen, were the best:
> Kind Husbands and meer Nobles all the rest.
>
> (571–572)

By now it is clear that Dryden had extended the concept of "Dulness," which he first developed for the realm of mediocre poetry in *MacFlecknoe*, to include the stultifying and deforming pressure of vanity and unthinking self-interest that is to be found in the mass of almost any body politic. He sees this mass as being both inert and dangerously unstable at the same time. It stifles genuine creativity, but it can produce monstrous growths of its own. Clever men, worst of all, can channel it into a mob dynamism that they may control to destructive ends, but never toward building anything good.

Like Shaftesbury and Monmouth, Buckingham, Bethel, and Oates were leaders of the London mob. They have little in common personally, except for a thoroughly perverted sense of their place in society. Buckingham misbehaved in every role; but as a prince of the land (543), he fell farthest from the norm of those princes, mentioned earlier in the poem, who were so concerned for property. "In squandring Wealth was his peculiar Art:" (559)—so much for Buckingham! This portrait is the best-known passage in all of Dryden; it is repeated compulsively, I should say, in every kind of literary or historical writing about the period. It was so successful when it first appeared that Buckingham seemed plunged by it into a kind of uncomprehending despair.[27] The reason behind its effectiveness, I suggest, is that property was the most fundamental concern of those Englishmen who could still be swung, whose minds were not unalterably made up already on account of one of the other issues. When they began to think that Shaftesbury and his people were a greater danger to property than James and his people, they ceased to grumble against the succession. The object of Dryden's strategy was to suggest that the feverish, consuming instability of Shaftesbury's crowd made them bad custodians of the nation's wealth.

This generalization certainly applies to the portrait of Bethel, who accumulated gold without even a sabbatarian

[27] See Swedenberg's note, *Works*, II, 259–260.

rest, but who was too much a miser to use it decently for
his fellow citizens in his office of sheriff.[28] It applies also to
the picture of Oates, who perverted the office of witness and
the language of human intercourse with his flow of lies. The
tone of these two portraits, however, is quite different from
the tone used for Buckingham's or Shaftesbury's. Dryden
employs a very heavy irony, with profane, mock-scriptural
overtones in Bethel's, and obscene physiognomical ones, on
a real scriptural base, in Oates's.[29]

Dryden could only have loathed Oates from the start. He
was a cleric, and fake as he was, he was established in a
Whitehall apartment with a train of servants and body-
guards, granted a pension about seven times greater than
what Dryden was receiving, and encouraged to give himself
the airs of a prelate. The poet had every incentive both
personal and political to satirize Oates. A normal instinct of
self-preservation, however, dictated otherwise: Oates could
kill if he wished. This attack, therefore, was a quite coura-
geous intervention.

It begins by employing sexual images of perversion. The
sound of the name Dryden found for Oates, Corah, sug-
gests him as a sodomite. The next three lines present Oates
the masturbator:

> Yet, *Corah*, thou shalt from Oblivion pass;
> Erect thy self thou monumental Brass:
> High as the Serpent of thy metall made,
> While Nations stand secure beneath thy shade.

$$(632-635)$$

The sexual imagery is strangely, but richly, justified by a
passage in the Epistle of Saint Jude, which exhorts the true

[28] On Bethel, see Swedenberg's notes and his "Challenges to Dryden's
Editor," in *John Dryden: Papers Read at a Clark Library Seminar,*
February 25, 1967 (Los Angeles, 1967), pp. 31–37.

[29] Since Dryden, though taking great risks, has successfully preserved
a balanced tone and a sense of proportion throughout, I suggest the
term *caricature* is inappropriate for any of the portraits in this "Poem"
of the noble, "Varronian" kind; but see Swedenberg's discussion,
Works, ii, 235.

loving community of Jesus to beware of "certain men crept in unawares": "Even as Sodom and Gomorrah, and the cities about them in like manner, giving themselves over to fornication, and going after strange flesh, are set forth for an example, suffering the vengeance of eternal fire. Likewise also these filthy dreamers defile the flesh, despise dominion, and speak evil of dignities. . . . Woe unto them! for they have gone in the way of Cain, and ran greedily after the error of Balaam for reward, and perished in the gainsaying of Korah. These are spots in your feasts of charity, when they feast with you, feeding themselves without fear: clouds they are without water, carried about of winds; trees whose fruit withereth, without fruit, twice dead, plucked up by the roots; raging waves of the sea, foaming out their own shame; wandering stars, to whom is reserved the blackness of darkness for ever" (7–8, 10–13).[30] Corah is linked to the men of Sodom by Jude because they disobeyed God, though warned, and were both destroyed by fire. Dryden probably related Jude's allusions to the sexual and the fever-and-heat imagery of his poem. He suggested the community of mercy, peace, and love addressed by Jude, negatively by satiric presentation of its opposite, and positively by his faithful band of Worthies.

I began my reading of *Absalom and Achitophel* with a promise to relate the text and structure of the poem to contemporary history, showing some of what that history made available to Dryden for poetic use. I have tried to show that his use of history was poetically constitutive; that, like Jonson, "he knew, Poet never credit gain'd / By writing Truths; but things like truth, well feign'd."[31] Dryden's feigning made use of an already familiar biblical parallel, but

[30] This important New Testament passage is often overlooked by critics. Noyes went so far as to say "there is no special appropriateness in the name." *The Poetical Works of Dryden* (Boston, 1950), p. 961.
[31] See this quotation as developed by Coleridge, in *Coleridge on the Seventeenth Century*, ed. Roberta Florence Brinkley (Durham, N.C., 1955), pp. 487, and also 553, 633. Unfortunately for my argument, Coleridge remained at best ambivalent about Dryden's full poetic creativeness.

constituted it in a fresh poetic structure by developing a new psychology and a comic dynamism of feeling. He augmented the static conception of the history picture with the agon of Achitophel and Absalom and by the self-conquest of David. I have suggested that one constitutive though hitherto neglected idea in *Absalom and Achitophel* is its emphasis on property. Property transmitted by heredity makes a vast difference between David's times and Charles's. It makes the succession by heredity all-important in England, and this is probably the most important distancing factor in the perspective of Dryden's poem. He fleshed out the idea of property, or better "propriety," in his group portrait of the Nine Worthies, consistent with themselves and with their roles in an historically constituted society. Also, he used his own most characteristic (or proper) skills as a poet, satire and noble verse, in pillorying their opposites, each of whom misplayed his social role in a different way, sometimes highly dangerous but always self-destructive and ridiculous.

Dryden's David is the same as the Bible's David and England's Charles most of all because they so deeply loved a favorite son. Love in different forms runs through *Absalom and Achitophel* and affords the necessary support to its comic life. Besides primal philoprogenitive love, there is the gallant love of seduction, the friendly love of the faithful band, and finally the aroused, enlightened self-love of the King. Constituting love in these different forms is more a matter of psychology (of the creative, "fictive" type) than of linguistic skill alone; Dryden had learned it, to an important degree, in the theatre.

It has been charged against Dryden that he is the only great poet who never succeeded in creating a "world." I should argue the opposite, that the world he created with his plays, meaning the whole structure for theatrical and reading experience he furnished to audiences, thereby constituting thousands of people over the years into *his* "audience," forms the poetic matrix for *Absalom and Achitophel.* Dryden's plays, prologues, epilogues, dedications, and prefaces, not only provided characters and feelings, language and concepts; they made familiar his personal voice, a public speech, yet candid and self-revealing. The controversies they embroiled him in brought out, for the rest of the world to see, a balanced, good-humored, intensely civil and humane man. His own "propriety" was to love the liberty, peace, and ease of a community lucky enough to be sheltered by a naturally developed government, after suffering under an arbitrary one.

CHAPTER NINE

THE AUGUSTAN INTERLUDE
(1683–1684)

I. DRYDEN VERSUS THE TRIMMER

SOMETHING like a Saturnian revival germinated, at least in the English imagination, in the years just after the uproar of 1678–1683, and added "Good King Charles's Golden Days" to the legends of Merry England. Thomas Durfey's "New Market Song" for 1683 makes the claim: "The Golden Age is come; / The winter storms are gone." This imagery of calm after storm was employed by Halifax in a famous passage of *The Character of a Trimmer*, and by Dryden too, in a little-known rejoinder—as we shall see.

Charles was taking steps toward a consolidation of the universal ease Durfey celebrated. He had begun building himself a new palace on Winchester plain.[1] Winchester was once the capital city of King Arthur; its cathedral preserved the Round Table, relic of the days when a mythic Britain was the imperial nation of Christendom. The news set Dryden to work on an opera honoring the Stuarts as successors to the British imperium.[2] King James I had strengthened the rather tenuous link between his family and Arthur, because he wanted to be "king of Great Britain" rather than of England and Scotland separately.[3] His grandson Charles's motives were pragmatic, in a double sense. Winchester was on the route to Portsmouth and the Isle of Wight, where he could observe his fleet and sail his yachts; and it was also far enough from London to protect him and his Court from

[1] Evelyn, *Diary*, 23 Sept. 1683. See also 26 Sept. 1684; 15–16 Sept. 1685.

[2] Roberta Florence Brinkley, *The Arthurian Legend in the Seventeenth Century* (Baltimore, 1932), p. 16, provides some background.

[3] F. W. Maitland, *The Constitutional History of England* (Cambridge, Eng., 1919), p. 331.

the pressures of the mob, like another Versailles. Evelyn (23 September 1683) noted the King was "earnest to render Winchester the seat of his Autumnal field-diversions for the future, designing a palace there, where the ancient castle stood; infinitely indeed preferable to Newmarket for prospects, air, pleasure, and provisions. The surveyor has already begun the foundation for a palace, estimated to cost £35,000, and his Majesty is purchasing ground about it to make a park, &c." Meanwhile, everywhere Charles's subjects "followed his example, building those commodious and classical houses which in the next age were to give a park and palace to every village in England."[4]

King Arthur had been a subject that interested Milton, for a reason Dryden shared, "that historical greatness is indivisible: that literature, science and the arts flourish together with political and religious freedom."[5] Little more can be said about what Dryden made of the theme in 1684, for he himself tells us that the 1691 production had to be completely rebuilt.[6]

These golden days marked the ascendency of Halifax in Charles's affairs, when (as Dryden wrote seven years later, dedicating the altered *King Arthur*), the King "confined himself to a small number of bosom friends; amongst whom the world is much mistaken if your lordship was not first." During that time, however, Dryden was on the opposite side of the close intrigues at Court. Halifax's opponents—James Stuart, Duke of York; Hyde, Earl of Rochester; the Duke of Ormond—were Dryden's contacts and patrons. It is likely that the command to translate Maimbourg's *History of the League* came through one of them—perhaps York, for the *History* could hardly have been more favorable to his cause if he had commissioned it himself. Its editor, Alan Roper,

[4] Arthur Bryant, *King Charles II* (London, 1931), pp. 346–347.

[5] *Times Literary Supplement*, 1 June 1973, p. 602. The words are Hugh Trevor-Roper's. Arthur established a golden age by beating the Saxons and achieving equality with Rome.

[6] S-S, VIII, 135; Dedication of *King Arthur* to Halifax.

has shown that Dryden could not have begun before mid-March of 1684, before "King Arthur" and its "prologue" *Albion and Albanius* were completed.[7]

There are puzzles about the Maimbourg translation. One is whether Charles had any particular motive of his own for the command, for he could read the French well enough. His style as monarch hardly included the endorsement of history books. More likely, it was the idea of some courtier; and the interest that it best served was the Duke of York's. Another mystery is the delay between publication at Paris and the start of Dryden's translating, about five months. In April, Tonson advertised it as being pushed on with all speed; yet it seemed to hang fire before final publication late in July. Finally, there is a letter from Dryden to Tonson, after publication, in which the poet expresses his satisfaction that the book has been approved but also his relief that something in it had not been discovered.[8] Answers to these riddles can be found in a Court intrigue, in which Halifax and James Stuart were the main antagonists and the state of Charles's affection for Monmouth was the apparent deciding factor.

Monmouth had been able to remain in hiding—with the King's collusion—since the Rye House plot was unraveled in June, 1683. That fall, Halifax arranged a secret meeting at Whitehall between father and son, a very loving one, and

[7] In "Dryden's 'The History of the League' and the Early Editions of Maimbourg's 'Histoire de la Ligue,'" *Publications of the Bibliographical Society of America*, 66 (1972), 245–275, and in his edition of Dryden's translation, *Works*, xviii (1974), 466–467, Roper gives evidence to show that Dryden had barely begun his translation when Tonson's first advertisement appeared, on 16 April 1684.

[8] Ward, *Letters*, p. 22. I think it likely that Dryden and his backers at Court wanted to make their points against Monmouth, the "Moderates," and Halifax without stirring up fresh controversy or associating Halifax and Monmouth in the public mind. Dryden's anxiety that his retort to Halifax be recognized as such only in the small Court circle who knew of the "Trimmer" would explain his unique marginal note. It discreetly sharpens the very close parallel between Henri III's "moderate" adviser, John de Morvillier, and Halifax, by a distinction between the Lord Keeper of the Great Seal and the Lord Privy Seal (Halifax's "place"). See *Works*, xviii, 60 and textual notes, p. 543.

drafted a letter of submission to both the King and York, for Monmouth to sign. Late in November the King told the Privy Council of his son's happy reconciliation. Just previously, however, Jeffreys had wound up the trial of Algernon Sidney with a death verdict based on the single witness of an informer and trumped-up documentary evidence. Monmouth's friend Hampden warned him that Halifax's "submission" letter could be used as such evidence, and Monmouth totally repudiated it. However, York's people had already inserted his confession into the *Gazette*, with the hint that he was ready to add his evidence against the conspirators. The upshot was another angry breakup between father and son, and a debacle for Halifax, who lost credit with Monmouth and was ever after distrusted by the Duke of York.[9]

On the seesaw or "two buckets" principle, York's influence was at its zenith during the next few months. He or Rochester would have had no difficulty in getting Charles's assent to the Maimbourg project during March, whereas in the previous fall it would have been a questionable investment of their "credit" with the King. York soon became a full-fledged member of the Privy Council again, without taking the Test. Meanwhile, Halifax hung on. On January 10 he told Sir John Reresby of his failure to persuade Charles to call a Parliament, also insisting on his determination to remain at the King's side, using any excuse. When the Navy commission was dismissed and sole control given to York (7 May 1684), Halifax wrote to the ambassador at Versailles that "as to the public affairs, this is the most critical conjuncture that

---

[9] The standard authority on Halifax is Hilda C. Foxcroft. I shall quote the text of *The Character of a Trimmer* printed in her *Life and Letters of . . . Halifax* (2 vols., 1898). Her A *Character of the Trimmer* (1946), like the earlier *Life*, will furnish practically all of the data required to follow my discussion, except that the date she gives (with a very inadequate reason) for the composition and private circulation of Halifax's "Trimmer" is six months too late. The work was not printed, of course, until after the Revolution of 1688. For this reason I refer to it in my text within quotation marks, as still unpublished.

hath happened a great while."[10] The important thing for us is that, meanwhile, Halifax had the time as well as the compelling motive to write his "Character of a Trimmer" for circulation at Court. The main burden of that work is its attack on James's growing power, presented as divisive and vindictive, in contrast to Charles's winning clemency. This issue suddenly came alive with the capture and extradition from Holland of a rakehell boon companion of Monmouth, Sir Thomas Armstrong, then an outlaw because (like Monmouth) he had absconded instead of standing trial for complicity in the Rye House conspiracy. Jeffreys had him hung without a trial, as an outlaw, on June 20. The Trimmer blames justices who encourage people "to follow the ill example of judging without hearing when so provoked by their desire of revenge," and in a typical combination of virtuousness and expediency he warns that the laws are "a sanctuary" that the Crown, also, might have occasion to use.[11]

Dryden's preface "To the King," which must have been the last thing he wrote for the *History of the League* volume published late in July, 1684, directly engages with Halifax, sometimes using the very words later printed in *The Character of a Trimmer*. The whole preface is one paragraph about 2,000 words long. It begins with the obvious feint of begging the King's forgiveness for any errors in the translation, then quickly swings onto target by emphasizing the bad timing of any such appeal "when your Enemies have so far abus'd" royal clemency. "Frequent forgiveness is their Encouragement, they have the Sanctuary [Halifax's word] in their Eye before they attempt the Crime." Dryden also replies to Halifax's rather involved reference to "the late conspiracy" and his remonstrance against overharsh punishment, including this: "whilst our thoughts are warm, it would almost persuade us to put them out of the protection of our good nature, and to think that the Christian indulgence

[10] Foxcroft, *The Trimmer*, p. 197.
[11] Foxcroft, II, 285. There is an obvious possible reference to Monmouth's status.

which our compassion for other men's sufferings cannot easily deny seemeth not only to be forfeited by the ill-appearances that are against them, but even becometh a crime when it is misapplied." Dryden retaliates, with slightly more clarity: "If the Experiment of Clemency were new, . . . your Loyal Subjects are generous enough to pity their Countreymen, though Offenders: But when that pity has been always found to draw into example of greater Mischiefs; when they continually behold both your Majesty and themselves expos'd to Dangers, the Church, the Government, the Succession still threatened, Ingratitude, so far from being converted by gentle means, that it is turn'd at last into the nature of the damn'd, desirous of Revenge, and harden'd in Impenitence; 'Tis time at length, for self preservation to cry out for Justice, and lay by Mildness when it ceases to be a Vertue."[12] This last clause rebuts Halifax's rather sententious pronouncement: "men who act by a principle grounded upon moral virtue can never let it be extinguished by the most repeated provocations."[13] Halifax's later reference to "a healing miracle," in conjunction with his "most repeated provocations" above, leads Dryden to cry that this would be "to desire of God to work another and another, and, in Conclusion, a whole *Series* of Miracles."

The King's love, upon which Dryden had made *Absalom and Achitophel* to turn, is one of Halifax's chief topics in *The Character of a Trimmer*. His argument is that the King must be clearly superior to everyone around him, have the respect of all, and inspire their obedience through love, not terror. To this end, he says, "there must be condescensions too from the Throne," "for power without love hath a terrifying aspect."[14] Here was a case that should have been closed in 1681 (with Dryden's help). Halifax had reopened it in the fall of 1683 by playing on Charles's love for Monmouth. Now he was doing it again, after what Halifax himself admitted to be impossible behavior on the part of the young criminal.

[12] *Works*, XVIII, 4. [13] Foxcroft, II, 302. [14] *Ibid.*, p. 290–291.

Of course Halifax cared little for Monmouth, except that by bringing about his rise he could depress the Duke of York, secure a new Parliament, and draw the King from autocratic ways and too much influence from France. With a new Parliament he could also deal a crushing blow to Rochester. Something of a financial genius himself, Halifax had detected inefficiences, if not outright fraud, in Rochester's handling of the revenues, and gave warning in *The Trimmer* that he was prepared to make the most of them: "no kingdom," he wrote there, "hath money enough to satisfy the avarice of the underworkmen."[15] One of the best reasons for frequent parliaments, he more than hints, is to redress such maladministration—a threat of impeachment which Lory Hyde, as his father's son, would recognize with alarm. Halifax's most famous passage in the *Trimmer* follows this dire comment on the state of the government under Rochester: "there have been fatal instances of its sickness, and, more than that, of its mortality for some time; though by a miracle it hath been revived again."

Halifax continues with the famous weather image:

Our government is like our climate. There are winds which are sometimes loud and unquiet, and yet, with all the trouble they give us, we owe a great part of our health to them; they clear the air, which else would be like a standing pool, and, instead of a refreshment, would be a disease to us. There may be fresh gales of asserted liberty, without turning into such storms or hurricanes as that the State should run any hazard of being cast away by them. Those strugglings which are natural to all mixed governments, while they are kept from growing into convulsions, do by a mutual agitation from the several parts rather support and strengthen than weaken or maim the constitution; and the whole frame, instead of being torn or disjointed, cometh to be the better and closer knit by being thus exercised.[16]

15 *Ibid.*, p. 291.   16 *Ibid.*, p. 297.

In his preface "To the King" Dryden pointedly retorts this (of course familiar) complex metaphor: "I look not on the Storm as Overblown. 'Tis still a gusty kind of Weather: there is a kind of Sickness in the Air; it seems indeed to be clear'd up for some few hours; but the Wind still blowing from the same Corner; and when new matter is gather'd into a body, it will not fail to bring it round and pour upon us a second Tempest."[17]

The assembly of a new Parliament, Halifax thought, would be a healthy agitation in the body politic; also it would obviate "discontent in another party, those which were for the service of the Crown, but for his Majesty observing the laws at the same time, especially where they had his royal word for it."[18] Dryden, too, had urged this policy upon Charles, but never for the reason of party expediency that Halifax found to determine each case. Favoring Halifax, although officially he did not know it, was the lapse of Louis XIV's three-year subsidy, which had helped Charles to free himself from the Oxford Parliament. It brought in the annual equivalent of about £80,000;[19] not much, but Charles might regain it by resorting to an expedient of his own. To send his uncomfortable brother away, call a new Parliament, and suffer his beloved son to return, was a tested method of applying pressure to France. This reversal was exactly what Dryden had battled against all along, and he was right to feel "the Wind still blowing from the same Corner." Monmouth at the time was enjoying the hospitality of Louis XIV's great enemy, William of Orange. Another round of the vicious circle was in prospect: assembly of Parliament—redress of grievances—grant of supply for military necessities —waste of money—fears, jealousies, recriminations—chaos. For this, Dryden had been living on half-pay since 1678,

[17] *Works*, XVIII, 4–5.
[18] Foxcroft, *The Trimmer*, p. 195.
[19] Chandaman's recent and careful *English Public Revenue 1660–1688* (Oxford, 1975), p. 135, provides figures of which I have struck an average. The "established" annual grants to Portsmouth and Nell Gwyn were about £70,000; like Dryden, however, they were on half-pay.

working harder than ever, passing up opportunities to make money on the stage.

Dryden's little "fortune" was owing in great part to Rochester's father, Clarendon, as we saw, and he had never ceased to be grateful. It was to Rochester that he addressed a maladroit but painfully sincere appeal for financial support during this period.[20] We know that he lived on affectionate terms with Rochester's family.

Taken together, these circumstances meant that a great deal was at stake for Dryden when he wrote "To the King." It is an intensely personal document, despite its political ramifications. In it he is always speaking for himself, in his own voice, even when he claims to be speaking for the whole nation: "This, Sir, is the general voice of all true *Englishmen*; I might call it the Loyal Address of three Nations infinitely solicitous of Your Safety, which includes their own Prosperity."[21] We have seen that concern for basic financial security was the one thing most likely to deprive Dryden of his comic power to see the ridiculous and humane side of a vexed question. Macaulay, the great Whig historian, thought this power deserted Dryden in this "Loyal Address of three Nations," where he immediately takes up Halifax's objection to Jeffrey's handling (or mishandling) of the outlaw Armstrong, in the following highly characteristic metaphor:

> . . . Your Majesty is not upon equal Terms with them, You are still forgiving, and they still designing against Your Sacred Life; Your principle is Mercy, theirs inveterate Malice; when one onely Wards, and the other Strikes, the prospect is sad on the defensive side. *Hercules* as the Poets tell us had no advantage on *Anteus* by his often throwing him on the ground: for he laid him onely in his Mothers Lap, which in effect was but doubling his Strength

[20] Edward L. Saslow has argued that this letter belongs to the spring of 1684 rather than the early fall of 1683. See "Dryden in 1684," *Modern Philology*, 72 (1975), 248–255. Saslow's dating of *Albion and Albanius* is convincing, but the performance late in May, 1684, may have been incomplete.

[21] *Works*, XVIII, 4.

to renew the Combat. These Sons of Earth are never to be trusted in their Mother Element: They must be hoysted into the Air and Strangled.[22]

Macaulay applied this figure of speech to the Whig martyrs, Russell, Sidney, and Hampden; quite naturally, he was shocked and disgusted. Dryden's image is not nearly so obnoxious once we recognize that both Halifax and he were talking only about Armstrong. Also, behind Dryden's allusion is the *Terrae Filius* (Son of Earth) of the Oxford Act —a vice figure of the annual academic Saturnalia held in July. This son of earth had a comic license to behave outrageously; Armstrong's license—and he seems to have been a brutal killer—came from his companionship with Monmouth.

I would like to argue that Dryden lost neither his sense of humor nor his humanity in either the preface or the postscript to the *History of the League*, but lack of space forbids. I cannot, however, omit raising the issue of "fulsome flattery," for we have an opportunity of comparing Dryden's brand with Halifax's. Keep in mind that Halifax was brave, enormously wealthy, extremely well connected, and unusually independent in personality: this is how he allows himself to speak of Charles II to his fellow courtiers in 1684:

> By a blessing peculiar to himself, we may yet hope to be saved even by his autumnal fortune; he hath something about him that will draw down a healing miracle for his and our deliverance. A Prince which seemeth fitted for such an offending age, in which men's crimes have been so general, that the not forgiving his people had been destroying them, whose gentleness giveth him a natural dominion that hath no bounds, with such a noble mixture of greatness and condescension—an engaging look that disarmeth all men of their ill humours and their resentments —something in him that wanteth a name, and can no more be defined than it can be resisted—a gift of heaven

22 *Ibid.*, p. 3–4.

of its last finishing, where it will be peculiarly kind; the only Prince in the world that dares be familiar, or that hath right to triumph over those forms which were first invented to give awe to those who could not judge, and to hide defects from those that could; a Prince that hath exhausted himself by his liberality and endangered himself by his mercy; who outshineth by his own light and by his natural virtues all the varnish of studied acquisitions. His faults are like shades to a good picture, or like alloy to gold to make it more useful; he may have some, but for any man to see them through so many reconciling virtues is a sacrilegious piece of ill-nature of which no generous mind can be guilty. A Prince that deserveth to be loved for his own sake, even without the help of a comparison [so much for James]; our duty, and our danger all join to cement our obedience to him. In short, whatever he can do, it is no more possible for us to be angry with him than with the bank that secureth us from the raging sea, the kind shade that hideth us from the searching sun, the welcome hand that reacheth us a reprieve, or with the guardian angel that rescueth our soul from the devouring jaws of wretched eternity.[23]

Compare this expedient effusion, which gives the same aesthetic delight as a piece of baroque court music, with Dryden's words on the identical subject:

. . . it has pleas'd Almighty God so to prosper Your Affairs, that, without searching into the secrets of Divine Providence, 'tis evident Your Magnanimity and Resolution, next under Him, have been the immediate Cause of Your Safety and our present Happiness: By weathering of which Storm, may I presume to say it without Flattery, You have perform'd a Greater and more Glorious work than all the Conquests of Your Neighbours. For 'tis not difficult for a Great Monarchy well united, and making use of Advantages, to extend its Limits; but to be press'd

[23] Foxcroft, II, 337–338.

with wants, surrounded with danger, Your Authority undermined in Popular Assemblies, Your Sacred Life attempted by a Conspiracy, Your Royal Brother forc'd from Your Arms, in one word to Govern a Kingdom which was either possess'd, or turn'd into a *Bedlam*, and yet in the midst of ruine to stand firm, undaunted, and resolv'd, and at last to break through all these difficulties, and dispell them, this is indeed an Action which is worthy the Grandson of *Henry* the Great.[24]

Compared to Halifax's embroidery of religious terms, Dryden's Providence is both a personal conviction and a safeguard from the extreme of adulation. His praise to Charles for their survival is nicely adjusted to the contrast with Louis XIV that he often used before, and it is one that we can sympathize with today. The last sentence is both a reminder of the thrill of resolution projected in *Absalom and Achitophel* and a summary of the tale of troubles and victory sung and danced in *Albion and Albanius*.

II. ALBION AND ALBANIUS

This short opera was called a "prologue" to *King Arthur* by Dryden. It is reasonable to think that its composition followed that of *King Arthur*, and since it incorporated an elaborate scenic version of an atmospheric phenomenon seen on March 18, 1684, it probably was not begun much before April, at a time when Dryden must have been working hard on Maimbourg. If, as Saslow argues, it was the "singing opera" referred to in the letter to Tonson of August, and "King Arthur" was the opera that lacked an act on which Dryden was relutcant to "drudge," we are faced with the interesting likelihood that when Dryden added Acts II and III to his prologue he was acquainted with some bad news. For in August, Rochester was "kicked upstairs" as Halifax put it, coining a phrase. He lost his ministry and was rele-

[24] *Works*, XVIII, 6.

gated to be President of the Council, a post originally cre-
ated to insulate Shaftesbury from real power. Most of the
unhappy events of *Albion and Albanius* are in Act II; this
fact would explain why Charles ordered Acts I and III "es-
pecially" to be performed before him two or three times.

The Duke's Company spent £4000 on the production,[25]
which is perhaps one reason *King Arthur* was not performed.
Dryden hopefully mentions a royal subsidy as the usual basis
of support for an opera[26]—but none was forthcoming for
either of his, any more than it had been for *The State of
Innocence*. However, payment was granted to a company of
French comedians who entertained the King at Windsor,
Winchester, and London during August, September, and
October of 1684.[27]

For the design of *Albion and Albanius*, Dryden again em-
ploys the analogy of sex to present what he saw as the two-
fold restoration of Charles II. The beloved woman is called
Augusta, a name destined for the city of London. She and
Charles are brought together at the start through a lavishly
painted "frontispiece" that surrounded the stage scenes, re-
calling the universal joy of 1660 and applying it to 1684.
According to the descriptions—by Betterton, not Dryden—
the frontispiece represented Peace and Plenty. Above and
between were the King, offering Augusta her new charter
"restoring her to her ancient Honour and Glory,"[28] and the
Queen, ordering the Graces to unbind the River, who was
shown shackled. The setting for the first act is very local and
urban—it shows "a Street of Palaces," and a view through
the Royal Exchange to the Arch and the street beyond; that
is, it shows the newly built London of Charles, an Augustus
to this extent at least.

Hermes enters and calls to Augusta to rise. He reproaches
her, however, with her broken "Nuptial Vow" and in turn
she blames Faction (also called "Commonwealth" or "De-

---

[25] *LS*, I, 334.   [26] *S-S*, VII, 230.   [27] *LS*, I, 333.
[28] See *Works*, XV, 1–55 for the text. My citations of stage directions
may easily be located without page references, since I follow the un-
folding of the opera.

mocracy") and Zeal. Her rescue by Archon (General Monck) is then shown: he brings to her "Peace, and freedom and a King." Then Democracy and Zeal are charmed into sleep by Hermes (he is called "Mercury" in the stage directions, although Dryden uses the Greek form in his text). A dance presents watermen in the liveries of the King and the Duke of York. After much on faithful nuptial love, Hermes, Iris, and Juno (as the power who unites souls) leave for heaven, to send Astraea down. Albion (Charles) and Albanius (James the Duke of Albany or York) then enter, proceeding through the four triumphal arches built for the coronation in 1661, and the act concludes in a ballet of the Four Corners of the World. The main political point of this act seems to be that London was saved from total ruin by Heaven and General Monck, who manage the restoration of Charles without other assistance. More important is London's destiny, to gather the wealth of the whole earth via her River Thames.

The second act requires a "total" change to a "Poetical Hell," where its master, Pluto, laments that his realm is being depopulated, after its great increase during the Civil War period. Democracy, quite at home in hell, sings:

> Were Common-Wealth restor'd again,
> Thou should'st have Millions of the slain
> To fill thy dark abode.
>
> (II. i. 59–61)

Pluto then orders Democracy (whom he calls "Common-Wealth") to appear like a Patriot, and Zeal to burn like True Religion, in order "to gain the giddy crowd's esteem." They suggest that James can be tricked into seeming disloyalty, and thus arouse the jealousy of Charles. Yet this is vain, says Pluto, even to imagine. Instead,

> The Peoples fear will serve as well,
> Make him suspected, them Rebel.
>
> (II. i. 82–83)

At which Zeal puts in,

278

Y'have all forgot
To forge a Plot
In seeming Care of *Albion's* Life;
Inspire the Crowd
With Clamors loud
T'involve his Brother and his Wife.

(II. i. 84–89)

Here Alecto presents Titus Oates, as the reincarnation of Cain and successive evildoers. (Oates, who had been living well though in prison, was not indicted for perjury until November 12, 1684 and then was held for trial for several months more.)[29] The invective is worth quoting in full:

Take of a Thousand Souls at thy Command,
The basest, blackest of the *Stygian* band:
One that will Swear to all they can invent,
So throughly Damn'd that he can n'er repent:
One often sent to Earth,
And still at every Birth
He took a deeper stain:
One that in *Adam's* time was *Cain*:
One that was burnt in *Sodom's* flame,
For Crimes ev'n here too black to name:
One, who through every form of ill has run:
One who in *Naboth's* days was *Belial's* son:
One who has gain'd a Body fit for Sin;
Where all his Crimes
Of former Times
Lie Crowded in a Skin.

(II. i. 90–105)

Pluto, crying "The Wretch that is damn'd has nothing to lose," calls for a dance of twelve devils to celebrate the "Jubilee here when the World is in trouble."

The scene then changes to another familiar London prospect, of both banks "taken from the middle of the *Thames*."

---

[29] Jane Lane, *Titus Oates* (London, 1949), pp. 302–317.

Augusta appears with a poisonous snake dangling from her bosom, to figure these temptations insinuated by Democracy:

> With Crowds of Warlike People thou art stor'd,
> And heaps of Gold;
> Reject thy old,
> And to thy Bed receive another Lord.
>
> (II. ii. 25–29)

Augusta both loves and hates Albion, but she feels now that "Hate is the nobler passion far." Zeal continues to use the metaphor of fidelity to a marriage vow:

> And when 'tis for the Nations peace
> A King is but a King on Tryal;
> When Love is lost, let Marriage end,
> And leave a Husband for a Friend.
>
> (II. ii. 31–34)

Actually, it is Albanius who must take his leave, although Albion, saddened at his people's ingratitude, laments: "I thought their love by mildness might be gain'd" (II. ii. 67). The leave-taking of the two heroes is tender and very reminiscent of Dryden's plays, especially when Albion cries out, "My Brother, and what's more, my Friend!" (II. ii. 110). Mercury earlier comments on their parting as but a means to "Delude the fury of the Foe" (II. ii. 81).

This scene would have been singularly moving if the current plan of Charles and Halifax had gone through. That plan called for James to depart, all over again, early in 1685. Ostensibly, he was to preside over the Scottish Parliament; in fact, James's removal would enable Monmouth to reoccupy his old favored place at his father's side among his London admirers. This plan became known to the French, even before the period between November 10 and December 10, 1684, when Monmouth actually paid another secret visit to his father in London. The French informed James;[30] through his contacts with James's people Dryden no doubt

---

[30] Foxcroft, *The Trimmer*, p. 202.

learned something of the affair. It would not be surprising, considering the French interest that the Duchess of Portsmouth served, if this second act was once performed for Charles, at "the repetition . . . made before His Majesty at the Duchess of Portsmouth's" that pleased mightily.[31] From what Dryden says about Charles's preference for Acts I and III, Act II failed to please His Majesty so mightily.

As usual, everyone among the Duke of York's adherents accepted the necessity of his banishment to Holyrood, which Charles communicated to James late in November. Dryden was trying to put the best possible face upon it, proclaiming a heroic degree of affection and respect between the two royal brothers, which, perhaps, was more ideal than actual on the part of Charles.

Nevertheless, Dryden still managed to couple a sharp psychological observation with a rather ironic "Augustan" comment on the politics of the whole maneuver. He suggests James's Catholic attitude toward expiatory suffering as a means of gaining merit in the eyes of Heaven:

> *Albanius.* Oh *Albion!* hear the Gods and me!
> Well am I lost in saving Thee.
> Not exile or danger can fright a brave Spirit
> With Innocence guarded,
> With Vertue rewarded;
> I make of my sufferings a Merit.

Charles, the Augustan politician, then is made to reply:

> *Albion.* Since then the Gods, and Thou
> wilt have it so;
> Go: (can I live once more to bid Thee?) go,
> Where thy Misfortunes call Thee and thy Fate;
> Go, guiltless Victim of a guilty State!
>   (II. ii. 98–107)

The expression "guilty state" is a strong one to put in the mouth of the King.

[31] *LS,* I, 334.

The second act concludes in dances exploiting to the limit the mythology of the weather image and the Age of Gold. Albion and Albanius declare the omen:

> The Sun, returning, Mortals chears,
> And drives the Rising Mists away,
> In promise of a glorious Day.
>
> (II. ii. 125–127)

Apollo appears in his chariot, "holding the reins in his hand," with a great glory about him, and reassures them:

> The Tempest shall not long indure;
> But when the Nations Crimes are purg'd away,
> Then shall you both in glory shine;
> Propitious both, and both Divine:
> In Lustre equal to the God of Day.
>
> (II. ii. 137–141)

The poet writes here for the whole nation. Whig, Tory, Trimmer, all are guilty, all have been punished, but all of them as a nation may count on the continued protection of Providence through the providentially preserved government of Charles and James.

The source of their glory is then presented: not the land but the ocean. For Neptune, with his train of Rivers, Tritons, and Sea-Nymphs, now rises out of the water, and James is called to sea in a lovely barcarole sung by Thames:

> Old Father *Ocean* calls my Tyde:
> Come away, come away;
> The Barks upon the Billows ride,
> The Master will not stay;
> The merry Boson from his side,
> His Whistle takes to check and chide
> The lingring Lads delay,
> And all the Crew alowd has Cri'd,
> *Come away, come away.*
>
> (II. ii. 142–150)

Two nymphs and Triton open a "chacon":

> When earth is grown disloyal,
> Show there's honour in the sea.
>
> (II. ii. 161–162)

And they conclude Act II with the promise of a second restoration:

> See at your blest returning
>   Rage disappears;
> The Widow'd Isle in Mourning
>   Dries up her Tears,
> With Flowers the Meads adorning,
>   Pleasure appears,
> And Love dispels the Nations causeless fears.
>
> (II. ii. 175–181)

Following out the pattern of Act II, Dryden wrote Act III to present Charles's second restoration as, above all, a final reunion with his brother and Successor, for the King could never be at liberty in his own realm while separated from his friends and overruled by his enemies. Act III must have offered brilliant entertainment with its dancing and spectacular stage effects. It also offers us an imposing probability: that the figure of Proteus in Dryden's allegory is meant for Halifax. Not that Proteus has much to say, or is very explicit, simply that it was a bold move by the poet to suggest him at all, and even more to have him forced into this prediction:

> Albion, lov'd of Gods and Men,
> Prince of Peace too mildly Reigning,
> Cease thy sorrow and complaining;
> Thou shalt be restor'd agen.
>
> (III. i. 142–145)

The effect is that Proteus-Halifax is made to say the opposite of what he urged when, in "The Character of a Trimmer," he said that mildness was Charles's best policy; nevertheless, it is pretty much what he said soon after in his *Character of King Charles II*: "That yieldingness, whatever foundations it might lay to the disadvantage of posterity, was a specific to preserve us in peace for his own time."[32] Proteus also predicts that Charles shall be miraculously preserved by fire, in keeping with the presumption of royal miracles implied in "The Character of a Trimmer."[33]

The allegorical allusion to the fire at Newmarket, which prevented the assassination or capture of the King at the Rye House, involves significant alteration in the actual chronology. In fact, James was at home a year before the Rye House plot. Yet Dryden delays the return of Albanius until after Albion has been saved from the arrows of the One-Eyed Archer. He thereby makes the happy ending of the piece to be the return of Albanius and his reunion with Albion. This ending would have suited the renewed exile of James, had it duly taken place. One can look on the whole performance, then, as a sort of conjuring act by the poet, who wanted to create a theatrical counterpart of the structure of affairs as they had to be, if Charles was to remain a peaceful prince and England was to remain happy. Charles must cease to rule *too* mildly; he and the Successor must again be reunited.

The political allegory Dryden offers so entertainingly in Act III arrays the "Property Boys" (or "White Boys" who escorted Monmouth at the Oxford Parliament) against "Six Sectaries," i.e. the Whig Council of Six. Their quarrel has been instigated by two male figures, themselves opposites, Tyranny and Democracy, assisted by opposite female figures,

[32] Foxcroft, II, 359.

[33] Mulgrave is ironic over Halifax's faith in "miracles" from Monmouth, and his skeptical refusal to take the Duke of York at his word. He wonders "if ever there was a conduct more disinterested, more humble, or more submissively obedient" than that of James to Charles; "which I confess is so extraordinary a thing, that I cannot blame the *Trimmer* for so prudent a precaution, it not being a politician's business to depend on miracles." *Works of John Sheffield, . . . Duke of Buckinghamshire* (1726), II, 28–51: "The Character of a Tory. In answer to that of a Trimmer. Written at the same time but never printed" (see p. 31).

Ungodliness (called "Asebia") and Zelota, or Zealotry. Their conspiratorial dialogue is a brilliant network of contradictions:

> *Tyranny.* Ha, ha, 'tis what so long I wish'd
> and vow'd,
> Our Plots and delusions,
> Have wrought such confusions,
> That the Monarch's a Slave to the Crowd.
> *Democracy.* A Design we fomented—
> *Tyranny.* By Hell it was new!
> *Democracy.* A false Plot invented,—
> *Tyranny.* To cover a true.
> *Democracy.* First with promis'd faith we
> flatter'd,—
> *Tyranny.* Then jealousies and fears we scatter'd.
> *Asebia.* We never valu'd right and wrong,
> But as they serv'd our cause;—
> *Zelota.* Our Business was to please the throng,
> And Court their wild applause;—
> *Asebia.* For this we brib'd the Lawyers Tongue,
> And then destroy'd the Law's.
> *Chorus.* For this, &c.
> *Tyranny.* To make him safe, we made his Friends
> our Prey;—
> *Democracy.* To make him great we scorn'd his
> Royal sway,—
> *Tyranny.* And to confirm his Crown, we took his
> Heir away.
> *Democracy.* To encrease his store,
> We kept him poor.
> *Tyranny.* And when to wants we had betray'd him,
> To keep him low,
> Pronounc'd a Foe,
> Who e're presum'd to aid him.
> *Asebia.* But you forget the noblest part,
> And Masterpiece of all your Art,
> You told him he was sick at Heart.

Zelota. And when you could not work belief
In *Albion* of th'imagined grief,
Your perjur'd vouchers in a Breath,
Made Oath that he was sick to Death;
And then five hundred Quacks of skill
Resolv'd 'twas fit he should be ill.
   Asebia. Now heigh for a Common-wealth,
We merrily Drink and Sing,
'Tis to the Nations Health,
For every Man's a King.

(III. i. 43–81)

This succession of contradictions could be explicated line by line, if I had not told the story already. However, it should be pointed out how discordant the aims of the two pairs are in this quartet-with-chorus. Tyranny is presented as arbitrary, autocratic rule with the inevitable outcome, observed by the Greek tragic poets long before Hegel analyzed the master / slave dialectic, that the tyrant owes his existence to his ability to play up to the worst instincts of the crowd. Tyranny's marks are godlessness, expediency, corruption, destruction of law, terrorism, cruelty: adding up to an atmosphere of helpless distrust. The role of Democracy, or rather of the sainted republicans, was to flatter the crowd with the belief that each one of them was as good as the ruler, personally, and that collectively they were everything and the ruler was nothing.

The master stroke is Asebia's pregnant assertion: "You told him he was sick at heart." The meaning must be that Charles was encouraged to believe that his wife, his brother, and a number of his closest associates and most intimate friends were unfaithful and actually plotting against him. The phrase "sick at heart" puts us in mind of the opening of *Hamlet* in a country rotten with plots of usurpation. History, in fact, is full of instances of reasonably decent princes like Charles who became bloody tyrants (something that bothered Hamlet too) when they succumbed to the paranoia that lies in wait for every monarch in his court. Of course, the whole nature of this entertainment prevents any moment of it from achieving tragic heights. Yet, modest as it is, the comic adroitness and point of what Dryden put before his audience (whether at the Duchess of Portsmouth's or at Dorset Garden or in their taverns or closets throughout Britain) still comes through as something inherently difficult, done finally though lightly. The point made by Zelota is more obvious; the comparison of Parliament to five hundred kings was banal. However, it was witty to turn them here into political diagnosticians—"quacks of skill"—who pronounced Charles Stuart dead and nominated themselves to rule England, declaring the King's members, his ministers and officers, to be morbid and untrustworthy.

There is a degree of the grotesque in this dialogue that matches well the dance that follows. First the White Boys, all harmless, do their "Fantastick Dance," and the Six Sectaries mime the plot of the Council of Six: "the two gravest whisper the other Four, and draw 'em into the Plot: they pull out and deliver Libels to them, which they receive."

The allegorical mime and dance relate directly to the pairs of onlookers, Tyranny and Asebia, Democracy and Zelota. When the Sectaries drive the White Boys off the stage "with Protestant Flails," Democracy and Zelota exit with them and soon return to the stage; but Tyranny and Asebia are seen no more. Monmouth's protectors, who refused Shaftesbury's Association because they had some sympathy for monarchy (and even more for property), have lost out to the "brave republic souls" such as the assassins Rumbold and Ferguson. In their turn the fanatics are destroyed by encircling fire. The whole scene agrees with Dryden's analysis in *Vindication*, where he argued that the shamelessly godless, or else naively profligate behavior of conspirators such as Shaftesbury and Monmouth would jar with the sober hypocrisy of the sectarian zealots. An amusing aspect of the eccentric dancing done here is that it probably imitated the dance of the cardinals Dryden mentions, about this time,[34]

---

[34] *Works*, XVII, 285.

as taking place in *The Rehearsal*—one of the many "updatings," no doubt, of that protean farce.

There follows the return of Albanius in a machine where with Venus he rises out of the sea. He is restored to his brother, after dances by the Graces and Loves, to the accompaniment of a dance of heroes. At this point comes the "apotheosis of Albion," to which Dryden says he needed only to add "twenty or thirty lines" after Charles's death. Albion is to be raised to the skies (like the Caesars) but not, as Neptune suggests, next to Orion. Phoebus sings:

> No, Not by that tempestuous sign:
> Betwixt the *Balance* and the *Maid,*
> The Just,
> August,
> And peaceful shade,
> Shall shine in Heav'n with Beams display'd,
> While great *Albanius* is on Earth obey'd.
>
> (III. i. 212–218)

The glory of this Augustus is ease and peace.

After another very exact local representation, this time of Windsor and the ceremonies of the Garter, the opera ends with an appearance of Fame on her globe singing an intricate, repetitive stanza with "A full Chorus of all the Voices and Instruments." Then "Trumpets and Ho-Boys make Returnello's of all *Fame* sings; and Twenty four Dancers joyn all the time in a Chorus," to affirm in this way the renewed community of all and "Dance to the end of the *Opera.*" In Betterton's scene description, we are made aware of a scurrilous design for Fame's pedestal, on which "is drawn a Man with a long, lean, pale Face, with Fiends Wings, and Snakes twisted round his Body: He is incompast by several Phanatical Rebellious Heads, who suck poyson from him, which runs out of a Tap in his Side." Since there is no reference to Shaftesbury anywhere in the text, it is probably just as well to absolve Dryden of responsibility for this picturesque touch,[35] appropriate as it may be to some theories of the comic *pharmakos.*

III. THE DEATH OF CHARLES

Threnodia Augustalis was the last work Dryden composed as the Poet Laureate and Historiographer Royal of Charles II. Almost uniquely among obituary panegyrics, it possesses considerable historical value. It faithfully narrates the course of the King's illness and the alternations of dismay and hope felt by his subjects, who (not wisely, perhaps) had made Charles their best-loved ruler. The poem reflects their judgment in a highly personal way, for Dryden (who knew several sides of Charles) manages to do justice both to himself and to the King. His poem is ironic and fair, witty and truthful, all at once. This "funeral-pindaric poem sacred to the happy memory of King Charles II" deserves an important place in a study of Dryden's political writing. It not only reasserts several political points of view that we found in the plays, but in a generic sense, it takes its whole argument from the conception of hero-friends that Dryden had been working out dramatically from the first.

Early in February, 1685, King Charles had an attack of a kidney disorder that seemed immediately fatal. The news came, Dryden says, like the Last Day; it was as if

> . . . with a mighty flaw, the flaming wall
> (As once it shall)
> Should gape immense, and rushing down o'erwhelm
> > this nether ball.
> > (31–33)

The shock felt by all is presented first in the figure of the Successor, James. He is represented at his morning prayers, where "guiltless of greatness," he is asking long life for

[35] After Shaftesbury's death, Dryden declined to "quarrel with his memory," *Vindication,* S-S, VII, 201.

Charles. Hearing the news, James rushes off "half-unarrayed."
On his way, he has a fancied encounter, like one of Dryden's
heroes tempted by a Lyndaraxa or a Nourmahal:

> Approaching greatness met him with her charms
>   Of pow'r and future state,
> But looked so ghastly in a brother's fate
>   He shook her from his arms.
>
>   (56–59)

He finds Charles apparently dead. The lines that follow
show that Dryden's appreciation of the brittleness of glory
was strong and sincere, and incidentally they show his total
rejection of arbitrary rule and the divinization of mortal
kings. As he enters, James sees, in the bedchamber

> A wild distraction, void of awe,
> And arbitrary grief, unbounded by a law.
>   God's image, God's anointed, lay
> Without motion, pulse, or breath,
>   A senseless lump of sacred clay,
>   An image now of death.
>
>   (61–66)

One could not ask for a better proof of Dryden's willingness
to make a political comment, even at considerable risk to
his diction. Just as grief on the part of his attendants, if law-
less, is unbecoming to majesty, so arbitrary power (he wants
to remind us) would be unworthy of the true notion of a
king. "A senseless lump of sacred clay" might be thought,
perhaps, the worst line Dryden ever wrote; it betrays to an
extreme degree his characteristic fault of overliteralness in
the use of metaphor. Yet it leaves no question in our minds
of the King's mere mortality.

The Duke, as he stared at "that adored forgiving face,"
was overcome by the deepest sorrow:

> No wife, no brother, such a grief could know,
>   Nor any name but friend.
>
>   (76–77)

All of Dryden's critical theorizing during the seventies on the heroic theme, and on love and friendship, now goes toward shaping this scene of more-than-brotherly grief. Friendship, he had said, is both a virtue and a passion. By thus incorporating the two Kings into his heroic scheme, it would appear that he sought to cast a spell over their behavior, weaving an ideal version of it into the web of his poetry.

This first attack passed, however, and Charles seemed to recover. Dryden describes the happy relief felt by all London. The passage, though not unique in his verse by any means, is rarely striking in the sense of actuality it conveys:

> The drooping town in smiles again was dressed,
> Gladness in every face expressed,
> Their eyes before their tongues confessed.
> Men met each other with an erected look,
> The steps were higher that they took,
> Friends to congratulate their friends made haste,
> And long-inveterate foes saluted as they passed.
>
> (121–127)

(The pindaric loosening of the heroic couplet accounts for a great deal here.) However, King Charles sank again after the brief rally. Dryden describes the "intolerable pain" that the royal physicians made their "Caesar" undergo,

> More, infinitely more, than he,
> Against the worst of Rebels, cou'd decree,
> A Traytor or twice pardon'd Enemy.
>
> (181–183)

Finally, with death at hand, nothing (Dryden says) could describe the "tenderness" of the King's parting from his brother. Charles asked James's pardon for exiling him. James is overcome with pity:

> His dauntless heart would fain have held
> From weeping, but his eyes rebelled.
> Perhaps the godlike hero in his breast

> Disdained or was ashamed to show
> So weak, so womanish a woe,
> Which yet the brother and the friend so plenteously
> confessed.
>
> (274–279)

All the elements of heroic passion are present: tenderness, pity, tears, forgiveness, and the quartered breast of godlike hero, successor, brother, and (most of all) friend.

These preconceived heroic and dramatic notions undoubtedly helped Dryden to compose *Threnodia Augustalis* (a poem of over five hundred lines) within a month of Charles's death. They unfortunately did not make it an entirely good poem. Yet it is rich and interesting, perhaps most of all for its picture of Charles II, which does great credit to Dryden the Historiographer. He is judiciously grateful for the solid achievements of Charles's reign; for

> . . . property with plenty crowned;
> For freedom, still maintained alive,
> Freedom, which in no other land will thrive,
> Freedom, an English subject's sole prerogative,
> Without whose charms ev'n peace would be
> But a dull quiet slavery.
>
> (298–303)

Yet he insists, once again, that the great achievement of Charles as a politician was the preservation of the succession. Through many twists and turns he had kept the throne for James, and saved the principle of monarchy:

> Not faction, when it shook thy regal seat,
> Not senates, insolently loud
> (Those echoes of a thoughtless crowd)
> Not foreign or domestic treachery,
> Could warp thy soul to their unjust decree.
> So much thy foes thy manly mind mistook,
> Who judged it by the mildness of thy look;

> Like a well-tempered sword, it bent at will,
> But kept the native toughness of the steel.
>
> (318–326)

The judgment so pithily stated here has become the judgment of history on Charles II.[36]

After closing the account of Charles's death with a summary of his personal character (as was customary in the classical forms of the *vita*), Dryden proceeds to a lament:

> O frail estate of human things,
>   And slippery hopes below!
>   Now to our cost your emptiness we know,
>   (For 'tis a lesson dearly bought)
>   Assurance here is never to be sought.
>
> (399–403)

These are terribly flat and conventional lines, but it is important to our understanding of Dryden to recognize that they express the poet's deepest conviction, and the only one he succeeded in handling (in *All For Love*, though not here) with full tragic power.

This straightforward account of *Threnodia Augustalis* as a political piece could be enlarged by attention to other dimensions, such as the typological, that have been the object of excellent recent criticism. Instead, I have tried to show that, even when we remain within the mythos Dryden created in the course of his own writing, the poem is full of significance. The primal element of water, for example, sustains a thoroughly practical interpretation when prodigious phenomena of river and tide are conveyed within Dryden's decorum of heroic excess in friendship and passion:

> Above the rest Heroick *James* appear'd
> Exalted more, because he more had fear'd:

---

[36] Recent historians such as Kenyon and Haley, who reject Bryant's very favorable estimate (which in fact he qualified later), concede credit to Charles for his determination in maintaining the succession.

His manly heart, whose Noble pride
      Was still above
Dissembled hate or varnisht Love,
Its more then common transport cou'd not hide;
But like an Eagre rode in triumph o're the tide.
    Thus, in alternate Course,
    The Tyrant passions, hope and fear,
      Did in extreams appear,
And flasht upon the Soul with equal force.

(128–138)

This passage refers explicitly to James alone, by contrast to the whole group of watchers at Charles's deathbed. The genuineness, even more the excess, of James's grief, first, and then his joy when the King seemed to recover, are what call forth Dryden's comment. These transports were in keeping with the "manly heart" of James, too proud to conceal his feelings or to feign what he did not feel. An open, frank, plain-dealing, un-Machiavellian man, like all of Dryden's heroes.

We must also bear in mind the immediate circumstances, and the likelihood that James would be accused of foul play when Charles's seeming recovery (he had been in good health and riding in Newmarket races a few months earlier) took a suddenly fatal turn. Dryden wanted to show the inveteracy of the illness, and compares it implicitly to the normal ebb tide, while he likens the joy of James to the opposing but transient and local eagre. The other half of the heroic pair, Charles, is shown as no longer concerned, regretting his too-brief glimpse of a heavenly sphere, and "soon weary of the painful strife" (154). Dryden had already represented James as leading all the rest in prayers for Charles's life, attempting (in the Gospel metaphor) to take the kingdom of heaven by violence, heroically if rather literally. One is left with a vivid impression that James's love fought against the ebbing away of Charles's life. The impression is also strong that the strenuous efforts of the physicians to save his

294

life were barbarously cruel, and once his rally failed, uselessly
so. One feels, perhaps, that the poet wants to show Charles
expiating his personal sins here on earth. Still, Dryden seems
quietly to suggest, death is nothing to fight against so grimly,
even the death of a king.

The poet makes Charles's heavenly destination as likely
as possible by stressing his forgiving nature and remorseful
self-accusation. The best quality of the dead King remains
his mercy:

> That all forgiving King,
> The type of him above,
> That inexhausted spring
> Of clemency and Love.

A few months before, Dryden had warned against the excess
of this virtue. Now, in his role of history painter, he has rea-
son selectively to highlight Charles's mercy, while, as he says,
"I cast into a shade" the fact that the dying King had noth-
ing at all to say of Monmouth—whose name Dryden does
not mention either, using the evasive plural, "Those, for
whom love cou'd no excuses frame, / He graciously forgot
to name" (244–245). In his forgiveness, he had been a type
of the Heavenly King; but not, perhaps, of a prudent earthly
one. Also, Charles is penitent toward his brother; he is con-
trite as he dies, asking to be forgiven as he has forgiven oth-
ers. This, exactly, is the Christian death that carries with it
the hope of a peaceful eternal life, and for this reward the
poet prays, not to Charles, but to "th'Almighty" whose "still
Voice," as the prophet found, needs peace and quiet to be
heard.

There follows a magnificent panegyric (292–326). It is
"pious praise," not offered to a god, but earthly respect due
from the members of a family to its founder or reviver. His-
torically, Charles's greatest achievement was that, despite
weakness and failure in many other directions (naturally
not referred to here), he had maintained the one essential

point of the succession. After first restoring in his person the royal line, he had founded it anew. Just as property, plenty, peace depended upon freedom for their worth, so the freedom of the subject depended upon maintaining the constitutional integrity of the Crown in relation to Parliament. It had been lost for twelve years with the death of Charles's father, then regained and maintained for just twice twelve years by Charles, who had passed it on intact to James. Furthermore, Dryden couples this "pious praise" with the "Subsidy" that it is now too late for a Parliament to grant to Charles. He thus foreshadows the concluding stanza, including the prayer in lines 491–503, where the poet prays to heaven to grant Parliament, "for once," a measure of foresight. He pictures James's new Parliament, repudiating the "Malignant penury" that had kept Charles at a disadvantage against "Gaul and Batavia" (478), and showing their trust of James by a generous subsidy. Thereby they will assure:

> The long Retinue of a Prosperous Reign,
> A Series of Successful years,
> In orderly Array, a Martial, manly Train.
> Behold ev'n to remoter Shores
> A Conquering Navy proudly spread;
> The British Cannon formidably roars,
> While starting from his Oozy Bed,
> Th'asserted Ocean rears his reverend Head.
>
> (507–514)

Writing in 1685, Dryden is stating the Tory policy of the next thirty years, as Swift was to uphold it against Marlborough: disentanglement from land warfare on the Continent, prosperity based on unanimity at home and a powerful Navy around the globe. The nation had failed to support Charles in this policy; now he was dead, it could only offer him posthumous praise for maintaining the succession entailed on James. Yet the new Parliament could be more far-seeing than its predecessors. In the final stanza Dryden suggests

(with prudent indefiniteness) that as Englishmen express
their religious faith by taking the Test, so they should give
evidence of their faith in the Successor:

> Faith is a Christian's, and a Subject's Test,
> O give them to believe, and they are surely blest!
> They do; and with a distant view, I see
> Th'amended Vows of English Loyalty.
>
> (502–505)

The point here is that James had shown his high regard for
an oath by refusing to take the Test in violation of his con-
science. Therefore he would be true to his Coronation Oath
and to the assurances he had given of a strictly constitutional
government. In return, his subjects should pass the test of
loyally supporting him with money when "*James* the drowsy
Genius wakes / Of *Britain* long entranc'd in Charms" (470–
471). Eventually the Test Act itself may be "amended."

All this is important context to Stanza X, where seem-
ingly general praise of Charles is a highly selective panegyric
upon his preservation of the Stuart dynasty:

> Succession, of a long Descent,
> Which Chastly in the Channels ran,
> And from our Demi-gods began,
> Equal almost to Time in its extent,
> Through Hazzards numberless and great,
> Thou hast deriv'd this mighty Blessing down,
> And fixt the fairest Gemm that decks
> th'Imperial Crown.
>
> (311–317)

"Our Demi-Gods," of course, would be Brutus, founder of
Britain, himself derived from Aeneas, Anchises and Venus,
as well as King Arthur, from whom, also, the Stuarts de-
rived. This is the sense in which Dryden praises Charles for
deriving "this mighty Blessing down" ("deriving" might be

mistaken to mean "obtaining" a direct benefit from Heaven).
By preserving the succession of the heirs of Arthur and Bru-
tus, Charles "fixt the fairest Gemm that decks th'Imperial
Crown." This fanciful claim is made, I suggest, not com-
pletely in bad faith. If an English king were to rule im-
perially over any other nation, he could do so only as an
invader and oppressor. The Stuarts, as successors to Arthur's
imperium, ruled the three nations of Britain by native right,
and their conquests by sea would oppress no Christian na-
tion, but rather would enlarge the domain of Christendom.
Of course this sounds flimsy today, and in fairness to Dryden
one must say that he merely hints at such a train of thought.
Everything fits in, nevertheless, with the view of a very in-
nocuous Augustan regime that would be expansive yet lawful
and peaceful.

Charles, then, is godlike in his mercifulness, though cer-
tainly not divine. He is to be praised, not prayed to, espe-
cially for deriving down to James the imperial succession. So
Dryden concludes the first ten stanzas of *Threnodia Augu-
talis*, devoted to an account of the manner of Charles's death.
In Stanzas XI–XIV, he draws a portrait of the late King's
"mind," claiming to leave a factual record rather than a
panegyric. In Stanza XI he presents Charles as Descartes's
homme de bon sens, opposed to the *homme de livres*. Yet
Stanza XII shows the King at the genuinely Augustan task
of husbanding the growth of Arts, Sciences, and Humanity,
bringing a double harvest of cultivation to a land that before
had been but a rich wilderness, and making it by comparison
an Eden.

Stanza XIII is one of the most artful things in Dryden,
and among the most candid expressions of his mixed feelings
as both the premier poet of Charles's reign, and one "between
two ages cast:"

> Th'officious Muses came along,
> A gay Harmonious Quire like Angels ever Young:

(The Muse that mourns him now his happy
                      . Triumph sung)
Even *they* cou'd thrive in his Auspicious reign;
  And such a plenteous Crop they bore
  Of purest and well winow'd Grain,
  As *Britain* never knew before.
Tho little was their Hire, and light their Gain,
  Yet somewhat to their share he threw;
  Fed from his Hand, they sung and flew,
Like Birds of Paradise, that liv'd on Morning dew.
Oh never let their Lays his Name forget!
The Pension of a Prince's Praise is great.

                            (370–382)

The picture of King Charles negligently scattering "some-what" of largess to his poets, as if feeding his ducks, is not only infinitely witty but downright magnanimous on Dryden's part. It shows that he too could be good-natured in the midst of frustration and disappointment. Such humor is the highest expression of maturity. What Freud says of Colonel Butler's laugh in *Wallensteins Tod* is true of Dryden here, except that his laugh is not bitter.[37] He did value Charles's good judgment, and had won Charles's praise; he was willing to let the King's praise be the makeweight for his seven years on half-pay. Dryden's candor clears the air for the perfectly sincere lines that follow (383–387), offering the poem as the poet's pious vow to his former patron and, now, his present "Guardian Angel," whom he prays may "Live Blest Above, almost invok'd Below." Clearly, he does not pray to Charles; even as a guardian angel of the English nation, according to Dryden's proposed (but never subsidized) epic machinery, Charles is not quite, but only "almost invok'd."

Instead, Charles's "Art" is praised, the helmsman's art that

[37] *Jokes and Their Relation to the Unconscious* (New York, 1963), p. 221.

brought the ship of state through the tempest of faction. This praise, then, is the climax of the three stanzas that deal with Charles's Augustan, or Golden, Age of science and the arts. Charles the artful politican, steady under the severest trial and when it counted most, is the man Dryden finally praises.

INDEX

LIBRARY OF CONGRESS CATALOGING IN PUBLICATION DATA

McFadden, George, 1916-
    Dryden, the public writer, 1660-1685.

    Bibliography: p.
    1. Dryden, John, 1631-1700—Political and
social views.   2. Dryden, John, 1631-1700—Friends
and associates.   I. Title.
PR3427.P6M3   821'.4   77-85551
ISBN 0-691-06350-8